AVATARS
OF THE
PHOENIX LIGHTS
UFO

Avatars of the Phoenix Lights UFO

Ishuwa and the Yahyel

Material channeled from
Ishuwa of the Yahyel
by **Shaun Swanson**

Questions developed and asked
by **Jefferson Viscardi**

SOUNDS
OF
LIGHT

Copyright © 2010 by Shaun Swanson and Jefferson Viscardi

Book Design by Shaun Swanson and Jefferson Viscardi

All rights reserved. No part of this book may be reproduced, or stored in a retrieval system, or transmitted in any form or by any means, electronic, mechanical, photocopying, recording, or otherwise, without prior written permission from the publisher.

The authors of this book do not dispense medical advice or prescribe the use of any technique as a form of treatment for physical, emotional, or medical problems without the advice of a physician, either directly or indirectly. The intent of the authors is only to offer information of a general nature to help you in your quest for emotional and spiritual well-being. In the event you use any of the information in this book for yourself, which is your constitutional right, the authors and the publisher assume no responsibility for your action.

Published by:
Sounds of Light
www.ishuwa.com

ISBN 978-0-9844108-0-4

First Edition, November 2010

Printed in the United States of America

Acknowledgments

We express brilliant rainbows of gratitude to Ishuwa and the Yahyel for their sharing and support in the inspired co-creation of this fascinating book! It is the first book in our "Galactic Family Series."

Warm waves of love and appreciation to everyone around the world and throughout the Youniverse!

Shaun also sends a warm hug of gratitude to Group of Friends and:
Alex Cross, Clare Patterson, Daniel Bronk, David Bartholomew, David Thomas, Drunvalo, Frank Viauso, Florence Riggs, Gilgamesh, Glen Tobias, Ione Linker, Kam Yuen, Ken Klingbeil, Kevin Ryerson, Krista Kirkwood, Lee Carroll, Liah Howard, Linda Tesar,
Margaret Rogers, Phil Angemaier, Sharon Marvel, Shawn Randall, Sheridan Hailley, Sonya Fairbanks, Uri Geller, Violet Schindler, and Gene and Barbara Swanson.

Jefferson extends a lovely word of appreciation to young master Jesus and Giordano Bruno for their inspirational and most enlightening life teachings and examples of unconditional love and perseverance.

Preface

Ishuwa is an Extra-Terrestrial human being and Jefferson Viscardi is a Terrestrial human being. The wealth of information in this book is the result of their ET & T conversations together.

The conversations that were recorded for this book took place between July 14th, 2009, and November 5th, 2009. During each conversation, Jefferson Viscardi was in San Francisco, California, and Shaun Swanson, who channeled Ishuwa, was in Maui, Hawaii.

Although some editing was done to account for the language differences, the majority of the material in this book was transcribed verbatim from the audio recordings.

This book is the first in our "Galactic Family Series." The second book is "Feline Humans: A Timeless Exchange of Love and Light."

For more information about Ishuwa and the Yahyel, visit the websites at, ishuwa.com and yahyel.com.

Contents

Preface vii
Introduction 1

Chapter 1: Invitation to Share Galactic Family Knowledge 5

- The invitation to create this book.
- Our "sphere of consciousness" spacecraft.
- This book can expand your inner library of understanding.
- Ishuwa - The Explorer and Translator.

Chapter 2: Our Genetic Connection with Human ETs 11

- Our vacation resort in Space.
- Our home-planet and home-satellite.
- The genetic connection of Earth humans and Yahyel humans.
- Contact with you heart to heart.
- Why we are here with you.
- We live in the "now" of your future.
- The joys we realize from interacting with Earth humans.
- Moving out of "haunted houses" and into "houses of the Sun."
- Binoculars of biology and belief.
- The Universe is fundamentally neutral so there's no good or bad.
- The motivation behind every choice you make.
- Pleasure and pain exist only in the ways you define them.
- What pleasure and pain let you know about who you really are.
- The ideas of "fault" and "blame" don't exist in our world.
- We are responsible for all we create and experience.
- The physics of our physical contact with you.
- Mechanisms that can lift you out of darkness.
- Do all extraterrestrials have good intentions?
- Our planet as a vacation resort for galactic growth and sharing.
- There is no more need to hide your true joy and who you really are.
- The idea that your Creator is outside of you is brilliant but illusory.
- Living through challenges simply and joyfully with heart guidance.

Chapter 3: Your Value and Worth is Infinite.............................35

- Our heights and weights.
- Yahyel children are cared for by our whole society.
- Organic classrooms occur in the family.
- Parent-child pre-birth agreements.
- Graduation ceremonies through sensorial sensations.
- We retain what is of value so we don't need banks.
- We all understand who we are and where we come from.
- Contact with people on "the other side."
- Our heart's internal guidance mechanism.
- Remembering who knows all there is to know.
- The supreme-Creator god-intelligence that is in All That Is.
- You all have your own unique way to self-realization.
- Reincarnating on more than one planet.
- More physical characteristics of the Yahyel body.
- ET races that are closest to Earth humans.
- Powerful programs in DNA, and time travel.
- Bursting the "bubbles of fear" related to contact with human ETs.
- The meeting we had with you 2,000 years ago.

Chapter 4: Sensual Telepathic Communications......................59

- The Yahyel experience great playfulness in all of their interactions.
- Clothing is optional on our world.
- Our body's "thermostat" provides year round weather comfort.
- Beyond our skin, nose, and lips, comes feelings telepathically.
- Earth's animal kingdom is a link to ETs and your actual nature.
- Musical instruments that are alive, and living sculptures of light.
- The 5-kilometer sized pet-like friends on our planet.
- Male and female dating.
- Early stages of maturity that a Yahyelian can go through.
- Pleasurable and meaningful bonding without marriage.
- Description of the planet where Ishuwa is transmitting from today.
- Our connections with the Alliance of Worlds.

Chapter 5: Dismantling the Towers of Babble..........................77

- Is your hair like ours or like cats?
- The various colors of our skin.
- Iridescent coloration of our eyes.
- Eyes resonate with the frequency of the world you tune in to.
- Sunglasses that cover our entire eye.
- Micro-sleeps.
- Why we sleep.
- Head shapes.
- We don't have teeth like yours, and the forms of food we do eat.
- Living off the energy that "Is."
- Ingesting food to commune with nature.
- Traveling from A to Z faster than the blink of an eye.
- Translating over 2,000 languages.
- Unifying languages that dismantle the "towers of babble."
- "Yah oohm = Be in Joy." The Yahyel's Yahbwah language.
- Exchanging the gift of our presence with each other.

Chapter 6: The ETs of First Open Contact.................................103

- Riding on horses, giraffes, and flying birds.
- Rich laughter on the planet of the Yahyel.
- How Yahyelians experience aging, dying, death, and rebirth.
- Reversing the aging process reveals Creatorship abilities.
- Your society has a way of having a say on what is revealed.
- Proof is ever-changing.
- Growing beyond the astrological imprints of your birth date.
- Share your visions with people that enjoy them.
- Always do the most enjoyable thing that you are able to do.
- Your "meaning and purpose" in life.
- The planet I am on today is good for floatational walking.
- The clouds here acknowledge our presence with them.
- Color variations of a human's energetic body language.
- Planets in your solar system have a lot to share with you.
- Mathematical formulas exist for all experiences, including Contact.
- Which ETs will be the first to openly contact humans in public?
- Power centers, power places, and windows into other realities.
- Our participation in the "Phoenix Lights" UFO sighting of 1997.

Chapter 7: Earth, 2012, and the end of the ET Quarantine....129

- Beliefs based in lack and invalidation are becoming extinct.
- The end of fear.
- We have no governments telling us what we can or can't do.
- Inside the Phoenix Lights spacecraft.
- Interplanetary travel within relationships of spiritual maturity.
- Your collective consciousness attracts the type of ETs that visit.
- Are there ETs on Earth that are negatively oriented?
- A warring mentality restricts how far off-planet you can travel.
- Go within yourself to determine what is or is not real for you.
- Become very aware of the "fight-or-flight" system in your brains.
- What is real and what is not real...inner self, media, education, TV.
- December 2012, ET no-contact laws, and the end of ET Quarantine.
- The Association of Worlds is a very nurturing community of ETs.
- The ETs that are excused from having to follow the ET Quarantine.
- Ishuwa translating for the Association of Worlds.
- The name of Ishuwa's mother.
- Go out tonight and explore the North Pole region of your starry sky.

Chapter 8: Keys That Can Open You to Peaceful ET Contact..151

- "What you put out is what you get back," 3rd Law of Creation.
- The creation instruments of thought, feeling, action, and belief.
- The Youniverse is listening and responding to your every send.
- Realizing you are the powerful Creators of your reality.
- Motivation = choosing what is most pleasurable and least painful.
- Being a victim is simply a choice to experience that illusion.
- Shooting stars of the North Pole for you.
- NASA astronauts and the living life forms in their Space.
- Past-life memories and the Chinatown catalyst.
- Heart centered ETs and symbols of a Chinese dragon.
- Imagination as a key to open peaceful contact with us.
- Creating physical reality with imagination and "make believe."
- The triangular rendezvous-spacecraft of purple and blue.
- Phoenix Lights UFO, spaceships, and relationships.
- Details of the planet that I am transmitting from today.

Chapter 9: The Ego, the Heart, & Masters of Creationships......179

- Orbiting patterns of interstellar planetary energies.
- The difference between "feeling" and "concepts in the mind."
- The ego-mind and the heart-mind of your Creator-Self.
- The ego's false sense of power and control.
- It's time for the ego to let its "costumes" drop to the floor.
- The ego's false fear of mortality, pain, and purgatory.
- How the ego can sit back, let go, and enjoy life's lovely ride.
- You are masters of creationships in your relationships.
- Our first contact with the people of planet Rorkin.
- Receiving gifts can uplift a lifetime of relationships.
- The museum of interstellar and extraterrestrial objects.
- The Yahyel and Rorkin gift exchanges.
- Transforming foods with our hands and thoughts.
- When the student is ready, this book will appear.
- Schools of wizardry and magic in the Yahyel world.
- Our Yahyel houses are in tune with the ground they rest on.
- The house Ishuwa grew up in with his biological family.
- Roads, energetic passageways, and non-physical spacecrafts.

Chapter 10: Existence is Actually Amazingly Magical...........207

- ET spotlight on Northern Californians' newspapers and TVs.
- Merlin and the world of magic.
- Existence is not ordinary; it is extraordinary, amazing, and magical!
- Where would you like to go with Jesus?
- You all can walk on water but collectively you choose not to.
- Living in the movies of your brain's powerful image-projector.
- Value your imagination, then manifest your greatest imaginings.
- Mind over matter, imagination over mind.
- How you have hidden the "buffet of infinite life-choices."
- Money and why people can have an abundance of lack.
- Your society has been taught to fear the universal teachings that reveal your true Creatorship.
- When you consume the fruit of knowledge on your tree of life, you will experience your Garden of Eden's heavenly nature.
- There are an infinite number of ways to create time and space.
- Being aware of your omniscient self.
- Following your heart lets you live your most meaningful purpose.

- Two major differences between your society and ours.
- Why humans created the illusion that your Creator is outside of you.
- Your true state of being is a real Garden of Eden.
- Locating the Creator of All That Is.
- There is an infinite supply of fascinating and joyful life experiences.
- Your actual nature is of infinite worth.
- Visiting Chinatown and the beautiful idea within the dragon.

Chapter 11: The First Time Ishuwa Heard About Earth........237

- We enjoy all our experiences equally in ever deepening ways.
- Transitioning into higher dimensions of consciousness.
- Following our greatest joys provides us with all we need to know.
- Your Heart knows the way.
- Dimensions of physical reality and dimensions of consciousness.
- Greatest accomplishments.
- Experience anything in your life with great comfort and joy.
- We have opportunities rather than problems or conflicts.
- The first time Ishuwa realized he could interact with Shaun on Earth.
- Ishuwa learned much about Earth by visiting it on many timelines.
- How Ishuwa's civilization has grown from visiting Earth.
- Fascinating relationships within the Association of Worlds.
- A second book and opportunities to learn from your ET children.
- Over 312,000 people tune in to the channeling sessions for this book.
- TV screens and telepathic images for ET viewing.
- Life on a planet in the Helios realm near Sirius.

Chapter 12: Making Contact with Your Inner Aliens............261

- Will your spacecraft appear again like it did in the Phoenix Lights?
- How open and peaceful ET contact can occur in public places.
- Understand who you are and thus fear your true self no more.
- Make "contact" with your beliefs about life that are "alien" to reality.
- When you are at peace with who you are, you can be at peace with us as well.

About Ishuwa & The Yahyel..................................267

About the Authors..................................271

Introduction

Jefferson: What are the initial words you would like to offer for the beginning of this book?

Ishuwa: As an introduction, in that sense?

Jefferson: Yes, it could be.

Ishuwa: Very well. There has become in your world a very large, very powerful, very magnetic and electric consciousness that is lifting up your world now, lifting up the collective consciousness, lifting up that which is available for individuals to tune in to and thus become more aware of their truer nature and become more in tune with the joys that are most in alignment with what they will find to be of greatest pleasure and be free from having any sense that there is something in life that they are missing! As people tune in to this powerful consciousness, they will feel as though they are in touch with, in contact with, living their life on the perfect path of greatest and most fulfilling potential.

As people choose to read the type of information that's contained in this book and in related books that others have written and will continue to write well into the future, this information becomes a catalyst in the most subtle of ways and at times in very evident ways for the readers. It becomes a wonderful catalyst for those who are reading the material word by word, page by page, chapter by chapter.

ISHUWA AND THE YAHYEL - INTRODUCTION

And so it is with great delight that we have this opportunity to bring forth information, to bring forth suggestions, and also energies that will be contained in this book's format! In the moments that a person is reading through the spaces, between the words, and also reading the words, they may not recognize what is happening, but they will grow as a result of having this information, as a result of having read it. It will be something that will engage their innermost heartfelt frequencies, the codes within their genetic structure. It will be like a door knocking and inviting them to find their new home, a very delicious, a very deeply fun, playful, and abundantly nurturing world, simply by reading, simply by going over page by page, chapter by chapter, the information that is shared in this book that is brought from many sources, not just Ishuwa, but brought forth from many beings that have been sharing and have had the desire to share with humans for some time.

The process of personal growth and expansion and becoming more in tune with the heart can flourish more fluidly, more easily, with less effort, with more joy, and in the ways that each reader will find to be unique for them, a joy for them, a delight for them. They will look forward to every moment of their life with a sense of delight from the information contained herein that comes from many realms and many conscious beings that are all of great heartfelt joy and intention to uplift and expand human consciousness, human cooperation, and the ability to experience more whole cooperation and peace on this planet!

Thank you for taking the time to read through the introduction to this book! We look forward to joining you on the pages that follow, in the chapters that follow. In many instances as you read through it, if you so choose to, you will find at times a tingling taking place in your energetic body that will delight you, and those moments will be indications that catalysts are awaking you to more expansive states in your etheric being, your subtle bodies, your angelic bodies, your physiological bodies, and your genetic structure, your codons, the DNA within your biology as well!

We thank you for having read through the introduction to this point. Know that even if you don't feel any tingling at some point while reading this book, you will still grow from having read through page by page, chapter by chapter, and have great stories to share with others from the experience gained from this adventure of reading a script written for your eyes to take part in visually, encompass, and play with note by note, letter by letter, word by word. It is with great joy that we engage with you in this adventure literally in literature!

Jefferson: Wonderful! I thank you for sharing with us today and being willing to bring forth more ideas and opportunities in the future for people to get in touch with new knowledge and be able to see life and understand how it works from a different perspective offered from outside our boundaries, outside our planet, from a perspective that comes from beyond that can be so deeply enriching for us. So thank you very much!

Ishuwa: Thank you as well dear one! It's a great joy we have to participate with you in this adventure, in this collaboration, in this creation! We and many others appreciate your efforts greatly and are very delighted in your choice to move forward in this way at this timing as well!

Chapter 1

Invitation To Share Galactic Family Knowledge

"This book can open more doors within your intelligence and your heart, which can allow information to more instantaneously be available for you."
— Ishuwa

July 14th, 2009

Ishuwa: Fantastic! Always a joy to know that there are those as you who have the desire, the interest, and take the time and energy to have this form of communication with someone that is so close and supportive in their life process. Always wonderful and rich to be able to interact and share and experience life in the ways that we are able to. Thank you for being willing and having this courage to step out into that space and explore!

Jefferson: Indeed!

Ishuwa: What then in this timing is on your mind that you would like to ask or share with us?

Jefferson: Okay! Is that you Ishuwa...or Gilgamesh? Ishuwa, right?

Ishuwa: Yes, Ishuwa!

ISHUWA AND THE YAHYEL - CHAPTER 1

Jefferson: Ishuwa, I had an idea this week that I shared with Shaun. The idea is to work with you and Shaun and through this channeling venue we could write a book for people on Earth that would be about life and the nature of reality as it's experienced by the people on your planet. What do you think about that?

Ishuwa: We would very much enjoy having the opportunity to share our perspectives and our experiences in such a manner with you and the channel, Shaun.

Jefferson: Okay. So it would be something you could do. Great! How would it work for you? How hard is it for you to come here because right now you have a physical body right?

Ishuwa: I have a physical body of a frequency that will provide me with more flexibility, in a sense, than what you are currently used to experiencing in your biological form. I and those on my planet also have a light body which we spend time in frequently as well. It's a little less physical than you would experience your form to be in.

Jefferson: Okay. So right now you are on a ship above our planet, right?

Ishuwa: There is a sphere of consciousness that we embody and share together with others that could be likened to a craft. It is not of metallic quality, but it nevertheless does provide us with many ways to interact and communicate together with others in a very close space location. It serves the purpose like a ship or a craft, as you are familiar with.

Jefferson: Does your physical body stay on your planet while your consciousness goes to this craft?

Ishuwa: I am, in that sense, not on planet at this time.

Jefferson: Oh, okay. So you are not on Yahyel. Is that the name of the planet?

Ishuwa: That is the name we call our selves, Yahyel. The planet is in a very distant location at this timing, and those are ideas we will be happy to share with you on another day of your time. This certainly would bring us joy!

Jefferson: Okay! We are going to organize ourselves, Shaun and I, to have ongoing channeling communications with you and put the channeled information into a book. Then we will deliver it to people here so they can understand there is life outside our Earth and that intelligent and loving humans that live beyond Earth, like you, are out there and willing to help us grow and become more whole, more at-one with "All That Is."

Ishuwa: In that way then, we will help by providing ideas and perspectives, other points of view, that we know have been most supportive in our growth and experience, that we have come into knowledge of by interacting with other forms, other races of extra-terrestrials as you might call them, and other forms of life that you aren't familiar with. And so, to have that opportunity for others on your planet to read about and to take from it what serves them is a way we can be of help. Yes!

We look forward to anyone here on your planet that is interested in sharing such information in an open way, in that sense, not restricted, not hidden, but something that people can read and do with as they choose in terms of choosing to accept it or not.

Jefferson: Okay.

Ishuwa: They don't have to believe. They don't have to buy into it. They don't have to create a religion around it.

Jefferson: Yeah, and I don't mind that, just whoever resonates with the book's information will learn from it and enjoy it.

If the circumstances were reversed Ishuwa, if you were to ask me, "Please tell us Jefferson about life on your planet because we are going to write a book about it and distribute it on our planet," then I couldn't really talk as a representative of Earth because I am just one human being and we are not that unified in that sense. How does it work for you? In this book that the three of us are now talking about putting together, I would be asking you to tell us about life on your planet. So would you be speaking on behalf of your planet or just for yourself?

Ishuwa: There is certainly a perspective of a personal quality that I would bring, in that sense, but we are a group that is more in our mind-heart together, more whole in that way and able to share the experiences of many on my world through one voice more readily than you experience in your world. So what I have to share takes in more of the overall experiences that we have had on our planet, and it wouldn't be, in that sense, as limited in its nature, in its description, in the sharing. However, it would not encompass all ideas and all experiences that are and have taken place on our world, for there are many ideas and experiences. It would take more than one book worth of information before you would have the ability to take them all in.

The ideas that I with you would bring through into a book would focus more on the ways of how you and your society could begin expanding your world and also be in a position to take in more of our world, understand more of our world and then not need to read as much in order to gain that insight, that feeling, that experience, that understanding, that knowledge, that wisdom. In that sense, you would gain access to more of the expansive database of understanding already within you.

This book can open more doors within your intelligence and your heart, which can allow information to more instantaneously be available for you. It would be as if your inner "database of computer knowledge" would suddenly be multiplied instantaneously through reading information that we share! It wouldn't work that way for everyone who read the book, but for many people it would be like a catalyst or a download that would expand their "library" of understanding and realization.

Jefferson: Yes, okay! Have Shaun and I met with you before in our dream times or on spiritual levels to discuss this book?

Ishuwa: There has been some meeting in this capacity, yes.

Jefferson: What do you do? For example, I am a Teacher and a Counselor in Metaphysical Sciences. What do you do?

Ishuwa: I am an Explorer, and I am a Discoverer, and I work often to translate so that one form of life may communicate with a different form. For example, if there is someone who speaks Swedish and someone else who speaks Italian and if neither of them speaks a similar language, then I could sit with those two and be like a translator for them so they would be able to communicate with one another. This is something I do with other forms of life. I am a Translator, in that sense.

Also, as I said, I am an Explorer. Other realms of life are fascinating to me. I take note of what I learn, and I share it then with the Library. I provide information to those who are most capable of, in a sense, taking notes, documenting the information. I download it, and they receive it. They have ways of amplifying it to others in our society and in other societies so the information can then be accessible for others. That is a simple description of my function at this timing. I am an Explorer, a Discoverer, and a Translator!

Jefferson: Okay. I am really excited with this project and excited to meet you in this capacity! I thank you for making yourself available for that!

Ishuwa: We thank you! And we look forward to more of these communications and the growth that we can have together. We also look forward to developing formats of information that your society there with you will enjoy reading, or watching, or listening to, or all of those above, and grow from, and be enriched by! It is a wonderful endeavor you chose. That you feel excited about it, we are most excited about that as well!

Jefferson: Yes!

Ishuwa: We share the excitement with you and we all, for there are many of us here, we look forward to these channeling sessions. So great day with you and for you. Until we have this opportunity to communicate and blend in this way again, good day to you dear one! Much love!

Jefferson: Thank you. Much love! Bye!

Chapter 2

Our Genetic Connection with Human ETs

"The sky is not the limit for you." – Ishuwa

July 20th, 2009

Ishuwa: All right! I say how are you this afternoon of your time as you create your experience of time to exist?

Jefferson: Fantastic! It is lovely to speak to you again!

Ishuwa: And to you as well!

Jefferson: How have you been?

Ishuwa: I have been in the worlds of perfection and experiencing great joys and great wonders! It is delightful that you have chosen to put together a format to record our interactions together in this third new reality that we are now creating so that others may read and experience and have the opportunity to learn and live this information in a form that your society is capable of taking in, ingesting, digesting, understanding through reading and perhaps by listening to it on audio tape, or by viewing it, or who knows, the sky is not the limit for you!

Jefferson: Lovely! Ishuwa, I would love to start this adventure by learning more about who you are and where you come from?

Ishuwa: We will share with you a little bit about where we come from at this time. In the pages that follow, we will share more info if that question arises from you again for we sense that it would be more beneficial in that way. We will unveil more about our society as these interactions progress through our sharing and growth together. In this way, when we sense it is appropriate, we will share more about who we are, where we come from, and how we enjoy being a part of this world with you, with human beings, with humanity on Earth at this timing of your growth and acceleration.

We have the experience in our realm of growth and acceleration that can be realized to be taking place in all forms of conscious physical expression and non-physical expression.

So back to the idea of who we are. We are a society that is very similar to human beings on Earth. Physiologically we have some differences, and you would notice it. You would recognize it. You would know that we weren't necessarily from your planet when you saw us, and yet we would be similar enough in form and appearance so that we would be "easy on the eyes." It would be easy for you to make the adjustment and feel comfortable in the presence of us physiologically in terms of our body, our shape, our dimensions, our sizes, our colorations, the energy vibrations that we give off. So, in that sense, there are several similarities but enough differences so you would know we are not of your Earth.

We have within our society several hundreds of thousands of Yahyel. That is what we call ourself. We live on a ship that is non-structured relative to the types of ships and crafts on your world. Our craft is very much in a more ethereal non-physical format. It can change its shape and form rather easily and it does so from time to time in accordance with that which would be greatest good for all those who are on-ship, who are on-board. There are other societies, other extraterrestrial races who share and co-exist on our craft at any given moment in time for the purpose of sharing and learning more about one another. It can, in that sense, be like a vacation resort that you are familiar with on your world.

Our craft is like a vacation resort in space. There are departments, in a sense, that operate what you might consider administrative duties and maintain many components that could be considered mechanical functions of the spacecraft, but not quite like what you would see in engines of the crafts on your world. Our craft isn't so physical, isn't so metallic, isn't of such a heavy vibration. This allows us to move, and to fluctuate, and to change the craft's shape at a very rapid pace, as you perceive time and space. So that's a little bit about the ship.

We do have a planet, and there is also another satellite, another planetary like world that is within our solar system that we also inhabit and co-exist on. Not as many of us live on that place, but it's very much like a planet. There are more of us living on our home planet, which is a very wonderful place and it is living very happy with us, very cooperative relationship between planet and humans. We are a type of human too so we will refer to ourselves in that way.

We have been here observing and interacting with your world and people for some time, and we have within our world some of your offspring in a sense. There are those here who have a genetic lineage from humans on Earth and that then makes us very connected genetically. There is a very close genetic connection between our humans and your Earth human beings. That is one of the deepest connections then that we have. It is in our genetic structure together, Earth and Yahyel, very similar genetic components in some respects.

There are many other genetic components, codes, that are very different, and that then allows us to have experiences that are quite different from those that you have. It allows us to be in a different solar system and to travel and to experience differently. Thus then, we have rich experiences to share, and we will have the opportunity to share many in this book as it grows and develops in this form of channeling collaboration.

We know there will be in the future, shortly, a time when we have contact and interact with Earth humans who are there in physical form. Contact face to face, eye to eye, in that sense, where we can actually have contact physically. For now that isn't something that will occur right away, but the timing is soon. Perhaps within a few of your light years as divided by the fractional interest in your Earth's orbit around your Sun. That is a formula that won't be solved at this time because we didn't give you quite enough information. But soon it will make sense, and we will expand on that formula, that idea, in the appropriate timing as it relates to our physical contact with Earth humans in what will be a great celebration for all, a great upliftment for Earth humans and for humans in our world as well. We are looking forward to that meeting with you and until then we maintain joy with our presence in this moment of experiential exchange and play together too!

Jefferson: I see. Ishuwa, what brings you and the family of Yahyel, the Yahyel family, what brings you to our shores?

Ishuwa: It is something that together our societies have chosen to do. There are many reasons. Simply put, we find it to be a very exciting homecoming of sorts, a very lovely gathering of family, a very joyous interaction, a rekindling of those you could consider to be brothers and sisters, mothers and fathers, daughters, sons, and children who enjoy the opportunity to come back into the company of family after having been away for some time exploring other realms, having other experiences. So it is as though it is a Thanksgiving weekend, a re-grouping when we are all in great joy, feeling, understanding how beautiful the embrace is and how expansive it will become and how it will grow and amplify for Earth humans and for our society as well in ways that we all will find very enriching and uplifting!

Jefferson: Do you exist in a space and time that we would consider our future?

Ishuwa: There is that, yes, the future. We do have the ability to time travel as you understand the past, present, and future, as you create the concept of linear time: past, present and future. We still operate in that function of time and space, a little bit differently, but there is enough overlap for us to be able to communicate with you, to understand the idea, and to engage with you in a way that you perceive with your awareness as taking place in a past, present, and future timeline course.

More and more, we perceive everything as being here and now, and we simply are able to come into your reality, which you would call our past, and we engage with you in your present now which is also for us the present now. The now in both realities always exists in the now and we simply remove our focus of awareness out of the linear timeline of past, present and future awareness. We focus into the now and we are then able to connect with you and those people there when they are choosing to engage in the now as well. Thus then, we are all here in the now. We are all able to resonate together communicatively in this format. Do you have any questions around this answer?

Jefferson: Yes. I understand that the place where we can meet is in the present, the now.

Ishuwa: Yes.

Jefferson: But how far in the future would it represent for us, the place where your society happens?

Ishuwa: Approximately 125 years in general terms. That is the most prominent focus of frequency, and it will be around that time that there will be more ability for your world to look back on this time in your world's history, herstory, and see how the adjustment between different timelines, your 2009 and our 125 years in the future, how it can come together so simply in the now.

Your society, approximately 125 of your years from now, will be very well versed and understand very completely the idea of time travel, and it will be able to go back in time and re-live even a moment such as this one and hear this communication as though it was taking place for the first time, even though you would be experiencing it from 125 years in your own future.

Jefferson: A question that I would like to ask now is, does time for you count the same way it counts here on Earth?

Ishuwa: We have a more amplified time, in this sense, perhaps a year in our world would be about one seventh of a year in your world. So for every seven of our years it is one year for you.

Jefferson: Okay! How long can you maintain the physical body? How many years on average do you live or is it a choice?

Ishuwa: About three-hundred years.

Jefferson: Three-hundred. So do you think the idea of longevity, is it more related to the level of consciousness of a society rather than outer circumstances?

Ishuwa: It can be.

Jefferson: I see.

Ishuwa: But it doesn't always need to be. Life forms have the ability to have a varied length of time in any given physiological form they may choose to incarnate in. They may have a very brief physical incarnation and be very highly expansive in their understanding of the nature of Existence and their "oneness" connection with it.

Jefferson: I see! So I've asked who you are and where you come from, now let me ask you this so we can have a perception of your point of view about us, who are Earth humans for you?

Ishuwa: You have been for many of us a Teacher, teaching us a great deal, providing us with perspectives that have enriched our world and also given us the opportunity to share with other societies what we see your world going through so that these other societies may then learn from your world and more easily move through what they previously had been perceiving as obstacles in their world of co-created experiences.

We find Earth humans to be somewhat like a fathering-mothering component for us. For as we mentioned, there is the genetic lineage connection. In a sense, many of us are like your children, biologically, genetically, not one-hundred percent for we do have some genetic make up from other, what you would consider, extraterrestrial life forms.

We also consider Earth humans to have a vast and powerful imagination that allows them to "turn out the light," so to speak, and to play around in a "haunted house" of their own creation, so to speak, and to bounce off of "scary little creatures" in what for some is a "hall of horrors." We appreciate, and understand, and realize these ideas are simply experiences that many of you choose to create on your world to see how "dark" you can be, to see how far you can go away from your true nature simply in terms of how you experience yourself. Of course you never are actually "dark," never actually disconnected from your actual expansive knowledge and understanding. We simply find great joy in realizing how "that which is" can explore and create itself in ways that are so distant and so removed from the "light of day," and still have the determination, and the motivation, and the endurance to propel your selves to keep moving from one life to the next, from one generation to the next, and play over and over again with this very deep and detached darkness that Earth humans have been involved with for so long. And we do not refer to darkness in any sense as being less than or non-holy, simply darkness in the sense of humans not being aware of their true, expansive, beautiful, joyous nature.

Jefferson: Oh.

Ishuwa: We do not perceive any life in any judgmental, less than or greater than, holier or more evil than, right or wrong, way.

Earthlings, humans on Earth, have simply chosen to create a very vast array of experiences that can be labeled as "dark" in the sense that humans don't know while they are having such experiences how beautiful and how powerful as Creators of their reality they actually are. They feel often times as though they are helpless or that they are at the beck-and-call of some force outside of them that determines their future, that determines their fate, and in that way they often seem to give up their power to forces that they perceive in darkness to be outside of them.

We do take great joy in not only experiencing how powerfully imaginative and creative Earth humans are to come up with such a "haunted house of horrors" but also in seeing how you move through the haunted house and come out the exit into the "light of day" and then laugh and play and carry on throughout the rest of your day. We are able to take those mechanisms of how you do this transformation and share it, as we have said, with other societies that are in a similar place of consciousness as Earth that have been playing with their own forms of "haunted houses" for some time as well.

We also enjoy providing perspectives that we feel will allow humans to become aware of their truer nature, their great joys, of their true Creatorship, their real empowerment as Creators of this reality. Thus then they will soon find it unnecessary to continue building haunted houses to get lost in. They will more frequently have a "house of the Sun." A theater, a theatrical production house filled with light, playful uplifting energy, cooperative energies, nurturing energies, and they will feel nurtured by others and they will feel like nurturing others and their selves as well.

So these are some of the great joys that we find from interacting with our kinship, our kindred souls, our family, our fathers, our brothers, our sisters, our mothers, our dear heartfelt companions.

Jefferson: Okay, I see. If I were to define "light" as information and "darkness" as lack of information, would it then be appropriate to say for example that the human family on Earth is made up of brave souls that wanted to explore the idea of living in a state of darkness or not knowing who they really are in order to then find their way back into the light?

Ishuwa: There is that as one of the ideas, certainly, yes. Another idea then is when you choose to embody or incarnate into a physical body, as an analogy, your body and your belief systems are, in a sense, like a pair of binoculars. Binoculars allow you to focus on a very specific part of a mountainside or a landscape and in that way you don't see the whole mountain or the entire landscape around you. You are only experiencing those portions of life's infinite landscape that you are visually focused on through the binoculars. You only experience that which you believe and thus focus on and in doing so you can lose your awareness of all the expansiveness of the countryside that is outside of the eyes, outside the vision of the binoculars of your body's biological being. In that sense, this can be using focus and limitation in a positive way so that you're not aware of "everything" while you're a human on this world. You can then have experiences that are new, and fresh, and exciting, and you can live in a world of the unknown with the mystery coming into every moment of your experience here in ways that can excite you, in ways that can move you forward, in ways that engage you and others with new life in fascinating ever-unveiling and revealing ways that you enjoy!

At some point you might start feeling the un-comfort or discomfort that can result from playing around in a world where your beliefs or "binoculars" have been focused for to long on "dark" definitions about reality that limit your ability to see your true joyful nature. You might even find it within your creative genius to create the idea that pain is just a part of life and if some experiences are painful to you, you just accept them in your life and define them as being better than other experiences that you could have had that would be more painful in terms of how you create the perception of pleasure and pain in this "haunted house," in this realm of "darkness" where the "light" seems to be absent, where you don't have a view of the whole "countryside" because you have been focused for so long with the "binocular of beliefs and bodily biology" on only one component of the countryside of life potential where there hasn't been much "light," hasn't been much information of who you all really are, hasn't been a full awareness of your inner-nature's true landscape.

Jefferson: So there's no reason actually to say that "darkness" is evil and "light" is good.

Ishuwa: Yes! In terms of the Youniverse's actual nature of existence, the you, y, o, u, Youniverse, in terms of how and what energy actually is, there is no good or bad. Light and dark are neither good nor bad in this context that we are referring to in your asking about. The actual nature of the Youniverse is fundamentally neutral. It is neither good nor bad. Within this neutral energy, you have the ability to create the concept and the misperception that there is good, light, dark, bad, right, wrong, evil, holy. However, all of the energy that you use to create these ideas, all of the experiences in which you perceive such ideas, for example if you were to choose the idea of good and bad, right and wrong, holy and evil, the energy itself which makes it possible for you to have that experience is actually neutral and accepts and supports All That Is. You are able to utilize and work with the energy of Existence in a way that allows you to experience the Youniverse in whatever way you choose to!

Jefferson: I see. So basically these are definitions we create for the sake of the experience.

Ishuwa: Yes.

Jefferson: Because obviously everything we do, we do out of the reasoning, out of the idea, out of the understanding that there will be a desirable benefit on the other side of the stick, so to speak, that we will be better off after the living of the experience.

Ishuwa: You always make the choice that you perceive, based on your current belief system, that you perceive will be most pleasurable, most in line with your true nature of infinite support and acceptance of All That Is, and farthest away from the idea of the misperceived experience of pain, of discomfort, of displeasure, of depression.

You always make choices based on your belief system, based on the particular "binoculars of belief" that you are currently viewing the "countryside" of your life's potential from. You always make the choice you perceive will bring you greatest pleasure and the least pain. Pleasure and pain are also things that you have a belief system about. So the mind of your physical body, your physical mind, can create belief systems of what pleasure and pain are that are in alignment with your actual heartfelt nature of pleasure. There is no pain in the actual nature of Existence. However, your mind, your physical mind, can also create experiences of what pleasure and pain are that are out of alignment with your actual pleasurable nature of being.

So here is one way to discern whether your definitions of pleasure and pain are in tune with your actual nature or out of tune with your actual nature. If you feel any pain, then your definitions are out of alignment with your actual nature. If you feel pleasurable, then your definitions are more in alignment with your actual nature.

Whenever you are experiencing any pain, you can acknowledge that your definitions and beliefs about life and yourself are too limited. They aren't in alignment with who you really are. They are too focused on a "darker" region of the "countryside of life potentials" where there isn't enough information about who you really are. And you can then expand the range of your vision through the "binoculars" until you see more "light" in the countryside. That is, you can expand your beliefs about who you really are and allow new ideas about who you really are to come into your awareness, into your "field of view." You will then see more clearly how to re-define yourself and make new choices and establish new beliefs that involve less pain and are of greater joy in terms of how you feel, how you feel in each moment.

You can enhance your ability to discern pleasure and pain in a way in which you use your "heart" rather than your "head." Learn to recognize what feels good to you rather than what you think feels good. We are saying you in general terms here, not necessarily talking about you, Jefferson.

Jefferson: Thank you! If we get a handle on this idea, maybe it's going to assist and support us to apply self-forgiveness because we are going to look back and say that was the best I could have done with the information I had in that particular moment.

Ishuwa: Yes! Very good! We feel that is in alignment with the whole idea now. Humans expand in their awareness as they come to understand more of who they actually are, and it becomes even easier for them to forgive because their awareness of who they actually are expands. They realize there is no need to hold any grudges against other people for they also more clearly see that other people are actually expressions of their self.

Jefferson: I see. So the danger in clinging to such a belief system that says, "Who I am is determined by what I have accomplished," is that we then tend to identify ourselves mostly with results.

Ishuwa: There are many people who feel that who they are is what they have accomplished.

Jefferson: You were talking about pain and pleasure. Do you think that as we evolve, our ability to work out our definitions with more flexibility will also increase?

Ishuwa: Yes. There will be fewer definitions as well.

Jefferson: How does it work in your world? How does it work in your society? For example, do you attribute the fault of something adverse that happens to you as being caused by someone that you perceive is outside of you?

Ishuwa: That would not occur in our awareness. No. We would not have that experience. We do not place fault on another or blame someone or something else for anything. We operate from the realization that the Creator exists in all things and in every moment and very simply then that is who we are. The Creator is what all things are, exists in all things, and so we don't in any way, shape, or form, experience the sense of separation or experience something as being "outside," thus then, to blame another would only amount to blaming our self. We don't blame or place fault on another, instead we take complete responsibility for all that we are experiencing and all that we are!

We are very in tune with the idea that all that we are experiencing is of ourself, and all that is of ourself is what we are experiencing. There are an infinite number of potential experiences in life, forms of expression in life, and we are always in great joy and excitement for life however it is that we are choosing to create and experience all that we are in any given moment. We know what we are experiencing in each moment is in alignment with our greatest joy. We know that it is most appropriate. It is the result that is of our infinite self. It is a result that we need not work to accomplish. We only need to allow our selves to acknowledge that we are always accomplished in the most accomplished way we possibly can be when we simply recognize the beauty that we are in all expressions that are being expressed by all that we are.

Jefferson: I think it was Einstein that said something like, "a mind that evolves can never go back to the state it had been at previously." My question based on this would be, is it possible for beings like yourself that are experiencing life through "binoculars" of a higher or wider level of consciousness, is it possible for you to also experience a higher degree of darkness or forgetfulness?

Ishuwa: It is possible to focus on other lifetimes using the idea of timelines and tap into other experiences that could be considered of a deeper pain, of a less aware state of being of the nature of their actual existence, but that wouldn't be something that would occur very often. It could occur, but it would occur through a choice. A conscious choice would be made to make that type of adventure. The idea isn't that we can't go back and experience what you might consider a lower frequency. The idea is that it isn't something that would be any need for us to do. It's something that wouldn't really excite us.

Jefferson: Oh.

Ishuwa: Every possibility is a possibility in that sense. There are an infinite number of possibilities. So we wouldn't count out the possibility, but we know it generally wouldn't be in our greatest joy.

Jefferson: I see. Is that the reason why you aren't already interacting in physical form with us down here on Earth? Is it because you are of a different vibrational frequency than us and you have to wait for us to catch up in order for our frequencies to match so that kind of interaction can happen?

Ishuwa: The idea of catching up isn't so much a requirement. It's simply more in terms of physics. The idea is that when two conscious energies are at a similar vibratory frequency then they are able to come together resonantly and interact in whatever way, shape, and form they may choose. Your current frequency is such that we can't really come together fully and be in contact physically.

Jefferson: Oh, is that right?

Ishuwa: The physics of it won't really allow for that to happen at this timing as you create your timing to exist. So there is, in a sense, a natural component that repels, that provides a sense of distancing that then is built into the equation, so to speak. And if you as a society simply make the choice through your own efforts, desires, and collective agreements to attain a particular collective frequency that is more in resonance with ours, as we move more into a direction of frequency that is more in resonance with where you might choose to go, then we can meet at a similar frequency of rapport.

You need not catch up. If you want to dialogue with us more as a collective society, then your society would simply have to choose to make the choice to do that. More of you are making that choice now, but you're usually not aware of making such choices because you do so on realms of your consciousness that can at times be considered sleep states, when you are asleep at night or daydreaming in the day. There are other ways in which this can occur during your waking hours but always through your own choice.

Jefferson: I see. So it would be almost as if you would go half way and we would go half way?

Ishuwa: Yes!

Jefferson: And then we would meet physically at the point where our frequencies would be resonating together, right?

Ishuwa: Basically, yes.

Jefferson: Okay. If there was an extraterrestrial on Earth today, would they have to lower their consciousness to ours and "plunge into darkness" and possibly forget the great being that they are and start behaving the same way we do?

Ishuwa: There is that possibility if one of us was to just take that plunge. But you see, perhaps you have heard this analogy before from other channels, the idea is we don't really take the plunge into the big deep blue of your oceanic consciousness of collective human beings by our self as just one individual.

Jefferson: Ah, I see.

Ishuwa: We have a strong hearted group-mind, and we wouldn't get lost in the way that you are suggesting which could occur if one person went there all alone. We understand that going there all alone wouldn't serve us. We realize that we could in that way get lost.

We recognize that humanity on your planet did choose, in a sense, for a long period of Earth years to make that choice. As a collective of human beings on Earth, you did, in a sense, plunge into the big deep blue by embarking into the oceans of planetary Earth consciousness. It may seem as though you got lost in this deep dark realm of "haunted houses." However, before you took the plunge, you set up a homing device, in a sense.

There are mechanisms that you did place outside of Earth and onto the surface of the sea of consciousness so that you wouldn't get lost forever in this dark realm with its spaciousness and physical universe of stars, solar systems, comets, suns, and so on and so forth. You made arrangements to have a tether, to have access to an oxygen hose, so to speak. You have a communication line that is connected to you.

Earth and humans are now, in a sense, choosing to pull themselves back up to the surface of greater awareness and reconnect to the communication line to get more "oxygen from the air hose," to "strengthen the tether," to remember more of who you actually are.

Our communication with you now is one of the ways that you have chosen to rekindle awareness of who you really are and to resurface once again. It is no accident that we are here. Together with us and others, you are all coming together and choosing to rise to the surface once again and recognize how lofty you are as spacious, beautiful, creative beings within the realms of the infinite one Youniverse that we all are together!

Jefferson: Okay! So we are re-emerging now and stepping up into a greater community of intelligent life that can include interactions with the inter-stellar Alliance of Worlds.

Ishuwa: Wonderful. You're doing it, and you're acknowledging that you're doing it! You are recognizing it! This helps to support the choices that you have been making to do so. Simply recognizing it and acknowledging it helps the seed to grow into a plant, helps the plant to grow into a tree, helps the tree to grow blossoms and flowers and to even bring fruit that can then create a new cycle of nourishing foods for thought and joyful consumption in ways that are delicious!

Jefferson: Yeah, that's great! Thank you! As we are re-emerging into this greater community of intelligent life, wouldn't it be naive to think that all extraterrestrials have good intentions?

Ishuwa: There are a few in your realm that have their own agendas that aren't necessarily in your highest good as we perceive the choices humanity would like to take now, the directions humanity would like to take now in reconnecting more to the heart, more to their feeling nature, more to who they actually are, re-awakening, coming out of the haunted house with greater ease and with more frequency to experience the light of play.

There are a few who aren't interested in seeing that type of growth process for human beings. But they are fewer and farther than you may think. And the more and more you stay focused on uplifting expressions and directions, and as more humans realize it is in choosing what is truly uplifting for them and embellishing their day in that way, talking about it, appreciating it, acknowledging it, writing about it, and dreaming about it, and creating art, and music, and plays, and films that support that direction, then the stronger their frequency moves in that direction and thus the farther away they move from the few extraterrestrials that are still choosing to bounce around in the darker places of what could be considered control and misinformation, misdirection, and lack of true guidance.

Jefferson: I see. I would like to ask you something that I find right now in this moment of our conversation intriguing. On two other occasions I have asked you the name of your planet and you have chosen to say the planet of the Yahyel rather than saying something like, "the name of my planet is Saturn," or "Venus." Are you by any chance endangering yourself by giving us a helping hand that could raise our level of consciousness and —

Ishuwa: No. We simply find it more adventurous to allow for that label, that name, that title, to come through at a particular timing. Our planet, as we mentioned briefly before, is in a very supportive place, and it has a good long future. It is very nurturing, not only to our society, but also to others who come and visit it just as they come and visit our craft from time to time.

Our world is very much like some of the vacation resorts you have on your world in many respects, but there are many differences as well. It is a place where people come for play and to experience more playful adventure, be at ease, and play from the perspective of how they perceive their present reality as they currently are creating their perception of what is most joyful and what feels like a resort location for them to play within. So our world is very happy, not only the people, but the planet itself!

Jefferson: Okay. We may talk about it at a later time. The reason I was intrigued and I brought this up is because you are sharing with us these ideas that certainly will help many to step up in consciousness from wherever they are. It's going to add value to our lives in general and help us evolve.

So my previous question was more about getting to understand if your choice to share this information with us puts you and your society in danger in any way from some other race that may not want us to have access to information that reveals who we really are?

Ishuwa: There is no ability at this time for that to occur, but we understand the idea, and we realize in Earth's experience for many generations there has been the need to hide information that some of you perceived would be to revealing for everyone to learn about. We understand there have been many secret societies, and we realize that creating secret societies has been useful in some instances and at other times it has only prolonged the belief in "needing to hide" information that can reveal your actual nature.

As more people let go of the belief that they need to cover up their joy, hide their actual nature, and hide understandings they perceive would enlighten others, then great growth can occur. As more people let go and are more open to be expressive in each moment from their heart, letting their eternal heart and their physical throat form a communion of expressiveness that is very uplifting and in alignment with their actual nature, as more people do that, then more people will realize they have no need to hide understandings of their actual nature, no need to hide this frequency of being. It is an eternal frequency of support and mutual nourishment. As people let go and open up, they begin realizing the value of being open. In time, concepts such as copyrights and legal contracts within your society will also fall by the wayside. This will occur in appropriate timing.

So we are not holding back specific information about us to protect our self. We realize our frequency is of such a nature that it will not be penetrated, as you would perceive the idea, from some other consciousness that would like to perhaps "pull the curtains" over this form of communication that we are having with you.

Jefferson: Understood. Ishuwa, there are people here who research and try to understand to the best of their abilities the communications and interactions that take place with beings that are not from Earth. They have the idea that some off-planet beings view Earth as a rare jewel-like planet that has evolved naturally without aid or assistance of any technology and it has a rich diversity that cannot be found anywhere else. From your perspective, are there any other "game boards" in Space like our planet that is such a rare jewel?

Ishuwa: We believe, because of the infinite nature of Existence, that there are. Perhaps some are quite similar to Earth as well. We have had some communication directly with a few that are quite similar. There are other worlds that we haven't had direct interaction with, but we have heard from others who have shared with us their experiences and we then are able to identify those worlds as being similar to Earth. Earth is unique, as all worlds are, and yet all worlds are containing of the one Creator, the one whole infinite being that is Love, that is Is-ness, that is the Youniverse, that is the Infinite, that is All That Is, that is All Life, whichever label you want to use.

However, we find our selves greatly attracted to your world. More so than to the other worlds that we have come into contact with. We understand the reasons for the attraction in many instances, and in other instances we don't. We just recognize that the joy, the pleasure is greater in our interaction together. So we, in a sense, focus more of our time with Earth beings for that reason.

There are many wonderful qualities that are unique to Earth at this time, and we are very, very appreciative to be able to co-create our experiences with you in this way at this time.

Jefferson: Can you share with us just a couple of these qualities, because I know you have the experience of being around and visiting and interacting with other beings of different solar systems. What are the top two most interesting things that Earth does have that other planets don't necessarily express?

Ishuwa: One is the idea on Earth that humans in such a great collective have come about with this ability to create the belief that they are disconnected from themselves and they then worship the idea that there is something outside of their self that is greater than them that is responsible for their world and their experiences and choices. This is very unique for the most part in our experience. It is possible that there are other worlds that have done this. In our experience, we find this to be one of the top two unique qualities of Earth and humans on Earth.

You have found ways to create and to design "binocular of belief systems" that allow you to focus on your infinite nature in such a focused pinpointed fashion. You've lost vision with the rest of the infinite horizon of your potential nature, and you have not only focused in such a pinpointed aspect of your existence, you are looking at a very "dark" point that allows you to feel lost, to create conflict, to cry in sadness, to feel hopeless, to have depression and perceptions of illness, and dis-ease, and cancers, and wars, and fights, and lack, and arguments, and anger and fear.

All of these things can only occur through a "binocular of belief" that focuses itself so deeply on the idea that your Creator is outside of you somewhere in the heavens watching over you and judging every moment of your day everyday to see if you've been good or bad and is evaluating whether you are going to receive any gifts under the tree on Christmas morning, so to speak. There is a belief in some external being that supposedly knows if you've been good or bad, knows if you've been naughty or nice.

This perception of a conscious external Creator is very rare in our experience. Earthlings have so ingeniously created the perception of disconnection and separation from their Creator and thus from the very nature of their own true existence.

Perhaps the second component that we find so endearing is the ability to create that separation perception. You have found the mask, the filtration system to cloak yourselves so deeply, so darkly, so fully, that you have been able for so long to create such a vast variety of experiences of separation, of disconnection, of darkness. We place no judgment on that for we experience and observe it from a very neutral state of mind, as does the Infinite, All That Is. It simply is a choice you are making in the realms of what you experience to be reality. We recognize that it isn't the real nature of your existence. We appreciate your willingness to share with us and to engage with us, and to be willing to awaken from this dark place, and to expand and make it easier for yourselves to let go of these "old binoculars," these old belief systems, and to let go of the belief in separation so that you may then more easily experience not only the joy you are but the joy that all other forms of life are that don't presently reside on your planet at this time.

Jefferson: I see.

Ishuwa: Does that answer your question?

Jefferson: Yes! Yes it does! Thank you! So it's a choice to incarnate on this planet, isn't it?

Ishuwa: From our perception, it is the only way you could have come into this perception of your existence. You chose to create the idea of incarnating into a physical body, yes.

Jefferson: So we were excited to incarnate here no matter what "the weather" would be like because of what we could accomplish while, in a sense, cloaking our real identity from ourselves.

Ishuwa: Yes. The pleasure outweighed the pain. So you made the choice to incarnate.

Jefferson: There is a saying that if it was easy to be a human then everybody would want to be one. What are some of the difficulties or challenges that you go through on your planet, not necessarily in the sense of forgetting or experiencing darkness or anything, but could you share one or two challenges that you encounter?

Ishuwa: Would you for us express your definition of challenge in that context of the question?

Jefferson: Yes. When I want to accomplish something, but I have not yet figured out a way to do it, or there are obstacles that make it difficult to do.

Ishuwa: Thank you for that definition in terms of how you are defining the idea of challenge in your question. We have a different definition.

Jefferson: Yes?

Ishuwa: Given the context in which you have asked this question, challenge for us involves some activity that we have an interest in moving into and experiencing but we aren't aware of how to do it yet. When we aren't initially aware of what we need to do to "get there," we know the challenge will be an enjoyable experience.

We are very comfortable and confident knowing that if we just follow our heart we will effortlessly move into that place of experiencing what interests us. There isn't any sense of an obstacle in the challenge. It's more of a joy for us to discover how we will get there. Going from point A to B can really be like going from A to C and point B is the experience, the "boat ride" as it were. We know we will know what we need to know when we need to know it so we can arrive at that experience, at that frequency. We also know that by knowing this we are able to relax more and experience each moment more fully with more acceptance and appreciation of ourselves and of what we are experiencing. This state of being is then given off in the consciousness pattern or conscious frequency to others and they are able to pick up on this vibration in a positive way.

They then are able to learn and share in the experience with us if they want to, share a sense of the journey, of the boat ride. And they may join us and know with us that it's going to be an enjoyable ride and realize they will know what they need to know when they need to know it to get there and there's no reason to fret, to fear, to feel that we are without the necessary mechanisms that would support us along the way, along the boat ride.

We know it works this way because we have for so long chosen to know that it works this way, thus then we get back experiences again and again, and again, and again of it working this way. We do not doubt that it works this way. We have experienced it working this way for a very long time.

You and humanity on Earth have the ability and the opportunity to begin making the choice of wanting to recognize your internal guidance mechanism and wanting to remember how to make choices that will be more fruitful for you and most meaningful and give you the greatest sense of purpose in life.

Human beings on Earth now have the ability to start defining the mechanism, their guidance system, as being that which is from the heart and is of a sensorial or sensational feeling, a mechanism of what feels good, not what they think feels good, but what feels good. As more people on Earth make choices based on what feels good and define "feeling good" as their true internal guidance mechanism, as their compass that guides them to their heart's true north, in that sense, then more people will begin getting back experiences that support the value of doing this, which makes it easier then to follow their heart more fully in making choices the next time around, which then brings back to them more experiences that will be of them living a very meaningful, purposeful, joyful, accomplished life, which will then give them even greater internal support for believing in this mechanism of following their heart.

The internal support will give people more energy and more willingness to be confident in defining their heart as the guiding mechanism in their life, and thus then they will get back more experiences of greater joy and of always knowing that whatever may be a challenge will simply be a joy to live through effortlessly, joyfully, easily and they will be able to invite others along in ways that others will be able to recognize and enjoy and appreciate as well.

That is one idea of how we define and work with challenge and attaining the goal of experiencing and accomplishing our life purpose. In each moment, we are accomplishing our life's purpose and it brings us great joy to experience it, acknowledge it, appreciate it and share it with others as well.

Jefferson: If you want to be in constant realization of your life purpose, all you have to do is listen to and follow your heart?

Ishuwa: Yes!

Jefferson: Some people on Earth may ask how can they just believe that by following their heart something is going to happen without them first making a lot of plans for it happen. Also, our society is very good at focusing on getting a challenge accomplished rather than focusing on enjoying the process of accomplishing a challenge. It seems to me that the actions we take and the experiences we have along the way are what we would be better off focusing on.

Ishuwa: There is great joy in accomplishing a goal. Experiencing the joy of each step, each segment coming into fruition, each component being created and fitting in place with the whole. There's great joy in that. The more that a person allows their self to enjoy each step, that act in and of itself invites others of like mind and joy to move and share, and cooperate, and co-create and offer even more colors to the final completed project!

Jefferson: That's so good! Wonderful Ishuwa! I think today we are approaching the end of this most knowledgeable experience and joyful interaction together. I want to take advantage of this last minute to thank you for being present and for being excited as much as I am. Thank you for sharing with such great willingness and enthusiasm and with the joy of living in self-honesty that you so eloquently express and present as an option, as a way to be. You share knowledge that is not only from yourself but is representative of others on your world too, as you mentioned before. The charisma and empathy that we find abundant in your words and discourses is very much appreciated, and I know it is allowed to sink in and have a positive effect in people's heart and mind in ways they enjoy. Thank you very much!

Ishuwa: Yes! Thank you! We are honored to have the opportunity to share with you, to engage with you and your society in this way, to create this third reality, to move into an enlightened space together that is enriching for us and for you in ways we agree are fascinating and very adventurous and pleasurable to have. And there certainly is great delight in your presence and in your willingness, and in your desire to share, and to be curious, and to discover, and to explore, and to offer insights in this collaboration as you have on this afternoon.

We thank you! And we look forward to the next session together with you and the channel in this format so that you can bring forth more material to publish into a printed form that others may someday share and grow from in ways you perhaps haven't even imagined yet, but uplifting ways we assure you! So thank you and we will meet again. Any parting thoughts or sharings you have before we go?

Jefferson: Due to the level of consciousness where you are, you can see the future, right? Because I remember the first time we interacted together on my radio show back in February when you said, "We are going to have further interactions," and you already knew it, right?

Ishuwa: You could say that there was some "writing on the wall" and we opened the door to see that script of potential as it was written at the time.

Jefferson: Every word you say I am really attentive to because here and there during our interaction you let escape some clues that can already describe the future.

Ishuwa: Thank you! Yes. We like to leave some "popcorn on the trail" for you to adventure along as you choose. Yes!

Jefferson: Popcorn, that's good! (Laughing upliftingly). Okay Ishuwa, thank you very much. I look forward to the next time, and I am sure Shaun also looks forward to the next time when we can have interactions with you in this format again.

Ishuwa: And us as well dear one. Thank you and great joys in your adventures! Until then, much love! Good day!

Jefferson: Much love! Good day to you, bye!

Chapter 3

Your Value and Worth is Infinite

"There are no individuals in our society that don't "get it," that are repressed, that are hiding in fear, that are without the ability to recognize they create their own reality. We are all able to take responsibility and we do so for all that we are experiencing. There is great joy in all that we are experiencing at all moments." – Ishuwa

August 3rd, 2009

Ishuwa: Always enjoying these moments of blending together in these ways! Bringing forth information and sharing to co-create a third new reality together! Bringing in light, ideas, truths, and information by interacting together into realms previously unseen! How are you this afternoon of your time?

Jefferson: Lovely! It's great to have the opportunity to interact with you in these ways again!

Ishuwa: Yes, for us as well! How would you like to move forward this afternoon of your time?

Jefferson: I am going to start with questions to find out more about you. The first thing I would like to cover relates to a statement you made previously that it is no accident that your civilization is here communicating with us now. You said these communications from you are one of the many ways that our Earth civilization has chosen to experience re-membering more of who we are. In other words, human beings on Earth arranged to have an adventure into the unknown realms of limitation and separation, and now we have chosen these sort of communications with you and your society as one of the many ways of re-emerging back into the awareness of who we truly are. So from your perspective, can this book serve as a trigger or a catalyst that will allow more of a person's light, more of their inner knowledge, to become available so they can deal in physical reality with greater malleability and thus be freer to play in life's field of infinite potentiality?

Ishuwa: Yes, that is our understanding. It is what we experience.

Jefferson: I would like to ask you about the physical features of people in your society so we on Earth can have a better idea what you look like, what colors, shapes, and forms a "human space brother" can have. Is that okay with you?

Ishuwa: Yes. We have some information that we can bring through related to those ideas at this timing.

Jefferson: Okay. Very good! You said in a previous interaction that we have some differences. You said you inherited Earth human DNA but also enough DNA of other races to the point where you would be noticed and recognized as being a space brother and not an Earth human.

Ishuwa: Yes.

Jefferson: According to my research from many different sources, I've come to the conclusion that the average height for females on Earth is 5-feet 4-inches or 1.625 meters tall, and weighs 125 lbs. or 56.70 kg. The average height for males is 5-feet 9-inches or 1.75 meters tall, and weighs 175 lbs. or 79.38 kg.
 How tall are you Ishuwa, and what's your weight, and what's the average size of humans in your race?

Ishuwa: There are variations, but an average would be approximately 5-feet 6-inches for the male, as you measure feet, and approximately 5-feet 6-inches for the female as well. The weight of females is usually somewhat lighter, on average, but the heights are quite similar. Again, there are variations, some shorter, some taller, some lighter, and some heavier. As you experience the variations in your society, we as well do. So those are merely averages.

Jefferson: How about yourself? How tall are you?

Ishuwa: I am approximately 5-feet 4-inches.

Jefferson: And how much do you weigh in pounds or kilograms?

Ishuwa: Approximately 120 of your pounds.

Jefferson: Are people on your planet born in a way that is similar to how we are here on Earth?

Ishuwa: This is very similar to you. Our genetics are very similar to yours. We have the period of development in the embryo of the female that can take anywhere from seven to eight months before the birth occurs.

Jefferson: So is your family structured the same way as it is on Earth?

Ishuwa: Our children are of the whole society. The biological parents will often tend to the early years of raising, caring for, and providing some of the primary needs for the young child. Then the child moves out into society and is considered a child of all of us and can find a home with any of us.

Often a child will stay between four to five years with their birth parents before they, in a sense, move out into the world. They don't move out on their own, but with other members of our global family. The chosen family will recognize such a child as being someone that is appropriate to bring into their home for a given period of time to assist that child in its next stage of growth, life education, and further development as well as receiving new information from that child.

In this way, the adults and the children are able to share with one another that which they have, that which is most in tune with their path at that given time in their journey in their life.

A child might live with four or five families before the age of ten or twelve. At times a child will live their entire life with the biological parents. Sometimes they will move out into Space, as it were in your experience, move out into other worlds and realms and may be gone for a span of anywhere from 50 to 75 years before they return back to our world. At that time they are able to provide us with experiences not otherwise available to us. They share from the adventures, from the learnings, from the travels that they have encountered over the 50 to 75 year span.

Jefferson: Do you go to school or do you learn from the others?

Ishuwa: The schooling isn't necessary in the way your society sets up classrooms, not that there is anything about that that we would consider unworthy, not in that sense. It is simply that we have only so much that a young one must learn before they are able to fully operate and function to their fullest capability. The biological parents will usually provide them with that necessary education in the first few years of their development. Thus then, a child moving out from their biological family will, in a sense, understand intuitively when it is time to step out to another family to learn from it and to also share information with that family that the child is guided to become a part of. The adults in the new family will recognize the child as having information for them that can, in a sense, teach them too, school them, instruct them. In a sense, this way of mutually sharing information while living together can be our form of classroom. So at various times in a family's life together our families bring in children who are of other biological parents. This allows and affords for the children to be, in a sense, teachers teaching information that the child was born with, in a sense, already able to share and to talk about freely and instructionally in ways that others can understand and learn from. And yes, the adults are able to share valuable information in the appropriate timing with these children as well, information that will enlighten the children, enliven them, and do so in ways that they all find fascinating and enjoyable.

In that way the family becomes more like a classroom for our world, our society. Do you understand? Do you see a difference there?

Jefferson: Yes, thank you. So another question on this same idea is, when a being wants to incarnate into your society, do the receiving parents acknowledge on a conscious level that he or she is wanting to incarnate through them into society?

Ishuwa: Before the birth occurs?

Jefferson: Yes.

Ishuwa: Frequently this can occur but choosing to be aware of this on a conscious level isn't always a choice that the biological parents will make. There is always an understanding that whatever child they do bring forth there have been agreements made before that conception, before that physical birthing takes place. For some biological parents that recognition is enough. They do not need to make any communications ahead of time, although there are several parents who will choose to do that.

Jefferson: I see. Do you know the child's past lives?

Ishuwa: There may be some past lives that are helpful to be aware of even before the choice is made for an incarnation, for a conception, for a birthing agreement to be made, but sometimes the parents will have no awareness of their biological child's previous incarnations, will not be aware of other lifetimes their child has had or other planetary systems they may have experienced living in. This information is generally more readily available for us then you would often find in your Earth's society simply because we are at a place of choosing to be more aware of the nature of our existence.

As a society, you are still working to become more aware of your backgrounds and the lineages and the connections with prior lifetimes. As your society chooses to become more aware of these kinds of relationships, there will be opportunity for more parents and children to have these forms of communication before conception is made, before a birth takes place. We sense that is a choice that your society is moving into and is making.

Jefferson: I see. So do you have graduation ceremonies that are to acknowledge when a person moves from one stage of life to another, like celebrations to say "now you are an adult," or "now you are on your own," or anything like that?

Ishuwa: There is a recognition within all of us that something that was, in a sense, being studied by a person has now been recognized fully and acknowledged within that being. In a sense, they have learned that module of information, realized it. We all acknowledge that realization in a very deep heartfelt connection of understanding and awareness. It is a very rich moment for us, and it is embraced very deeply and related to by those who have been a part of the learning process. There is a very deep acknowledgement, embrace, and awareness.

We have a sensorial sensation, a feeling as well as an understanding from a cognitive sense, that this person has learned, or reached, or attained a particular point of beingness in that moment of their life. In a sense, you could call it a graduation ceremony, but it isn't just a going through the motions of throwing their hats in the air in that sense. Their consciousness in that moment rises very high into the air, so to speak, and then the others who are present will recognize this rising energy. Others will see the higher vibrational sphere rising up in the air, and they are able to connect with it consciously in a way that affords everyone that connects to it to have, in a sense, an appreciation, a ceremony, a celebration for the growth in realization or "graduation" of that person.

Jefferson: Do you have commerce on your planet like here where we have money and a monetary system? How does it work on your planet?

Ishuwa: We have no banking system, in that sense. We do not have a bank account. We do not have to save anything. We simply do not lose anything. We retain our understandings. We are aware of our value and the unique talents and abilities that we each have, and we can easily recognize the talents that others have. It becomes very easy to discern who has some abilities that would benefit a given person in a given moment, and if they choose to they can exchange the talents and gifts one for the other or one to another. In that sense, there is an exchange of individual understanding of value; individual heart value is able to be exchanged. And that, in a sense, cannot be lost. It need not be saved. It is infinite and available to be shared in each moment by those who are drawn to take part in that sharing, to receive that understanding or that experience.

There is no structure of money management. There is no interest being charged. There are no robberies taking place. There are no vaults that need to be secured, that need to be guarded. There are no police institutions that need to be brought in to see what happened to personal items that had been held in a vault that suddenly were stolen, as you perhaps might experience in your society.

Jefferson: Here on Earth we have different levels of consciousness. Some people are aware of who they are and who other people are so they don't harm others since they know that others are a part of their Self. And there are people here that have no idea who they really are because of their limited belief systems, limited concepts, and limited definitions. Some of these people do things like stealing or mistreating others. Is this the same on your planet as it is on ours in this regard? Do you have some people who are not aware of their true nature and other people that are highly aware of who they really are or does everybody on your world have the same level of consciousness?

Ishuwa: We all understand where we are from and who we are in that sense. We understand the nature of our existence and that Existence exists infinitely. We recognize in all of us, in All That Is, the value of all. We have grown up in this understanding for so many generations that we do not have the perception that one of us is more learned, more wise than another. We recognize that each has a very valuable contribution that is unique and different from all the others and will be valued, will be shared by those others in any given moment that they are attracted to a particular experience with them.

There are no individuals in our society that don't "get it," that are repressed, that are hiding in fear, that are without the ability to recognize they create their own reality. We are all able to take responsibility and we do so for all that we are experiencing. There is great joy in all that we are experiencing at all moments.

There is no "great master." There are those who have been chosen at given times to share particular forms of understandings that can allow our society to step up a bit in a way that you might consider a higher frequency of consciousness, but it is not better than the one we had been on before. It is simply a higher frequency that affords us greater flexibility to connect more effortlessly to the worlds that we enjoy creating and experiencing in our interaction with life together.

You may say that there are people in your world who are quite dark, or dull, or dim witted and that there are others who are very aware and expansive. From our perspective you are all equally capable of being wise and knowledgeable. Some of you are simply choosing to create the perception that you aren't really that bright or "with it" in any given lifetime or any given moment. It takes a lot of "light" to dim your consciousness so that you aren't aware of how bright you all actually are. We appreciate that form of "make-up" and "costuming" that so many of you enjoy "putting on" in your theatrical plays.

Jefferson: Was your world, the planet of the Yahyel, was it created all ready for your civilization to function at a level of consciousness that was from the beginning already higher than the one expressed on Earth?

Ishuwa: Higher only in the sense that we all understand who we are. We take responsibility for what we are experiencing. We don't have any capacity to place blame on others. We have no need to take from others. We share with all that interact in our society in ways that are beneficial for all those who are in the sharing interaction.

Jefferson: What about on a spiritual level? Here on Earth we have an idea that the soul of people who have passed away is on "the other side" and can be contacted by Mediums. Do you have guidance from the other side or a spiritual counterpart that would inspire you to follow the life theme you chose before you incarnated?

Ishuwa: We have a feeling or a sensation that is very uplifting, that is very positive and very strong. It's very obvious. It's very evident. It's something we can't miss. It is something that is always in our present state of awareness, and we understand that it is there to guide us into those locations, and experiences, and passions, and moments, and interactions, and relationships that are most representative of who we are best capable of being in that lifetime, in that given moment. It is a very obvious guide in that sense.

We don't need to have dialogues in the form of talking with spirits from the other side like you have spoken about. We don't need to have letters that we write. We do not have to sit and send questions out into "space and time" and wait for some form of interaction or communication to come back to us from either the trees or the animals or other people who may be in some other plane of reality.

We simply have a very powerful, strong, uplifting, enjoyable sensing that guides us. It's something that you all are capable of tapping into. As more of you become aware of that and are willing to define your guide as such an energy, as such and intelligence, then the more you will be guided in that way, the more you will sense that mechanism within your own being and the more you then follow that sensing, that sense of joy of the stronger guidance mechanism that grows within. As you choose to do this more, the internal guidance mechanism becomes very obvious. It becomes a very bright light. It is something you will not miss in any given moment.

Jefferson: Good!

Ishuwa: Also, we would like to say that all of you on Earth are fully tapped into all of the knowledge that there is that can be capable of being aware. However, you are choosing to wear "make-up" and "masks" over this level of conscious awareness, in a sense, to limit your awareness of all that you actually are so you can play on this stage of Earth and have particular experiences. The experiences are vast and some explore illusions such as having to face obstacles, and difficulties, and being limited, and feeling hopeless, but they are all simply experiences that you have because of the "make-up" and the "costumes" that you are dressing yourself into with your belief systems. These belief systems are in that way then filtering through your conscious awareness and giving you the perception that perhaps you don't know very much, or that this person knows more than some other person. In terms of your actual nature, you all know an equal amount. You all know all there is to know. On Earth, you are simply choosing to create the perception that you don't know that you all know it all, and that choice is simply part of your "world play."

Jefferson: From your perspective, would you define God or the prime Creator as a supreme intelligence and primary cause of everything that is, was, and will ever be?

Ishuwa: You can create the idea that there is a god that has that ability, but it all simply "is." When you start reaching out into one simple idea, it all simply exists in its infinite, expansive, oneness. This oneness finds an infinite number of ways to express itself, to play, to create All That Is.

You can label this oneness as a god, as a supreme intelligence, and yet this god that we're suggesting, this supreme intelligence, is an understanding of Isness as All That Is. Even in the experiences of "theatrical productions" where the "actors" seem to think that they are very disconnected from God or a supreme being, "Isness" is what is making it possible for them to have that experience. That which "is" is the supreme Creator intelligence, and it is contained in All That Is.

There is no place you can be in which there is no Isness, no supreme-Creator god-intelligence. There are many places you can go in your mind and create labels, and names, and concepts and have a number of different "theatrical productions" centering around what the Creator is like, or what it can or can't do, or why it does this and doesn't do that, or why it helps these people and doesn't help those people, or why it seems to be present one day and off on vacation the next day while things are going bad for someone. Those are all simply "productions" that people are choosing to create. Those are simply perceptions that they're choosing to play with on the "stage of life."

All That Is, the one supreme Isness, is actually in all places at all moments at all times, but people can create the perception that there is no Isness, no supreme being, or that it exists in some particular fashion or way that suits their "screenplay," or their "playwright," or their circumstantial interaction in any given moment in their day and time of life.

Jefferson: I have noticed that for some of us here on Earth it's not that easy to relate to the idea that we are extensions of a supreme Creator intelligence. How can you help us understand this? Can you coach us on how to relate to the idea that we are like self-aware energy that is already endowed with the Creator's attributes and we all can co-create from that informed perspective?

Ishuwa: That realization will occur in a timing that will be most appropriate for each of you. The way in which it will occur will be unique and appropriate for each of you. It will occur in a way that you each have chosen.

Usually people will make this choice from a deeper level of their consciousness, such that they aren't aware of making the choice. This allows there to be a sense of mystery and newness to their life. It also affords there to be a number of potential adventures that people can have in their life and it is the living of those adventures that becomes the mechanism, the journey, the path, the steps they take that will awaken them back to remembering this understanding that they and the Creator are one.

People on your world enjoy, perhaps you could say as an analogy, going on a hike through a forest along a trail of their own making, a trail of their own discovery. At some point they like to venture off the heavily traveled trail and craft their own trail, find their own way to remember or reconnect to this realization.

In general terms, doing things that feel good, that are of a heartfelt nature, that are uplifting, that are easy, joyful, pleasant, pleasurable, exciting, in that sense, those experiences will expedite a person's reconnecting and remembering to the idea, the recognition, the awareness that they contain and they are the infinite Creator, the omniscient One. They will understand that they only need to know and remember those aspects of All That Is that are most enjoyable for them in a given moment. So the idea isn't to suddenly be aware of all knowledge, of All That Is. That isn't what we are suggesting. The idea is simply to follow your heart's guidance. Then you will know what you need to know to have experiences in your physical life at the given moment that is most exciting to have them in that journey, in that travel, in that adventure.

There are many ways and many mechanisms that people will use to come back to this remembrance, to this understanding, to self-realization. Doing activities that are heartfelt will quickly expedite this coming back into remembering.

Jefferson: In regards to the evolution of the soul, would it be safe to say that a natural method of remembering who we are is the process of reincarnation in which a person undergoes numerous different situations, challenges, and obstacles to learn how to deal with the Self and to master the ability to work with their god energy responsibly?

Ishuwa: There are those that have reincarnated in several lifetimes on your planet who have gained greater awareness of their actual nature and that of Existence from building upon their prior life experiences. It isn't the only way a person can expand and become more aware of their nature, but it is one that you have as a society, as a global race on Earth, chosen. It is a form of, if you will, a play with many different chapters, with many different scenes, with many different levels, and locations, and backgrounds, and families, and costumes. There are thus then many who are having the ability to create the perception of evolving their soul from one lifetime to the next, but again, it isn't the only way to become incarnated on this planet in a physical body and be very aware on an expansive level of their actual nature and have experiences that they enjoy creating and interacting within.

Jefferson: I see. So I think the next question is, does a person become fully self realized through the process of reincarnating on just one planet or does the person's spirit inherit different physical bodies that allow it to incarnate on several planets before it attains complete self realization?

Ishuwa: In a sense, from a broader perspective, it's all here now. If you were talking to a person on Earth and they could talk to you about 30 previous lifetimes that they have had, the idea that those were past lives could make it seem as though they happened in the past, but it all exists here and now. All of those ideas of past lifetimes are occurring now. A person simply chooses to create the perception of having lived them in the past and then chooses to create the perception of talking about them as though it's the past. But it's all now. It's all here. People will simply choose to create this idea of a past, a present, and a future so they can have a particular kind of experience, a particular flavor of their infinite nature.

How does that sit with your question? Would you like to explore some more of that idea?

Jefferson: I missed some of your answer.

Ishuwa: Could you ask the question again?

Jefferson: Yes. Does a being of creation have to stay on a particular planet and reincarnate on the same planet over and over again until the planet reaches its completion or can this being reincarnate on many different planets?

Ishuwa: They can create one connection throughout the entire lifespan of a planet. This doesn't occur in your physiological form on Earth because the Earth has gone through many changes that would have required the physiology to have made great changes that wouldn't be considered a body as you know it. So there are those whose consciousness could perhaps be considered to have lived as long as Earth has been in existence and have been here residing with the Earth plane. They wouldn't at all times be in a body like your present form though.

Some people come from and go to other planets and live one lifetime here and then live another lifetime on another planet. There are some who are, in a sense, bi-locating. They are present on this planet in what you would consider a biological life form and they are simultaneously on another planet. Some of these, a few, very few, are aware of being on both planets and being in the world of both realities. It is possible for them to see both worlds and experience both worlds, but this is very rare at this time in our perception of life on Earth.

Jefferson: And how about beings from your planet. Can they do that more frequently?

Ishuwa: There are more who could do that.

Jefferson: But they don't necessarily choose to?

Ishuwa: There are some who do.

Jefferson: Does the human DNA play an important factor in having this happen or is it more about the evolution of the soul?

Ishuwa: Yes, the biological DNA is a factor for the biology to be able to function at that level of conscious awareness.

Jefferson: The human DNA is a blending of how many different extraterrestrial races?

Ishuwa: There are at least seven in our understanding.

Jefferson: What are they?

Ishuwa: There are the Annunaki.

Jefferson: Yes.

Ishuwa: And there are those who have been referred to as the Zeta, but not understood. They are basically humans from a parallel reality gone a bit eschew, a bit disconnected due to some experiments they made in time frequency adjustments such that they would not appear to be quite like you, but they are actually quite similar, very much on a parallel frequency of reality.

Jefferson: Okay.

Ishuwa: There are five others that we are aware of.

Jefferson: Yes?

Ishuwa: The names, perhaps you are aware of more than the two we have given, the names of the other five are...as of this timing we will wait for another moment.

Jefferson: Okay. Is the Yahyel society the one that's closest to us in terms of appearance?

Ishuwa: We are quite similar in appearance to those on your planet. Not necessarily closest, but very similar. There are some who might seem to be identical. We tend to be a little bit different, thus that most of you would notice the variations, but it would be so subtle that it wouldn't be at all disconcerting.

Jefferson: So you have five fingers, two eyes, and in that sense there's nothing about your body shape that would be unusual to us?

Ishuwa: We have four fingers and one thumb.

Jefferson: Well, that makes five. (Laughter).

Ishuwa: We have two arms, two hands, two legs, and two feet. On each foot, we have one large toe and three other toes.

Jefferson: Four! I see. So what is the color of your eyes?

Ishuwa: There is some coloration that would be similar to what you would find on Earth but even in those similarities the colors are quite eye-catching from your perspective.

Jefferson: And do you guys have hair?

Ishuwa: There are those present who have hair of varied length and those with only a very tiny follicle on the integument, on the skin of the body. So they don't have the need for hairspray or shampoo.

Jefferson: Oh, I see. So you do have hair, but it's not as long as humans?

Ishuwa: Yes, for me.

Jefferson: That means you are not bald?

Ishuwa: From a distance, I might appear to be bald, but there is a very slight and short follicle of hair. There are many, many hundreds of thousands of these that are on the physiological structure of the skin.

Jefferson: Do you have pointy ears or no ears at all?

Ishuwa: We have ears.

Jefferson: Okay.

Ishuwa: They're not usually pointed. There are some of us who have pointy ears, but it isn't something that generally takes form. The ears are somewhat smaller on average, about half the size of those you would find on your world.

Jefferson: I see. So I would like to ask, are the Pleadians the society that is closest biologically to Earth humans?

Ishuwa: Well, we are not Pleaidian. We are perhaps not the closest, but we might be the closest. This is an idea that begins to take into consideration the idea of time travel, thus then, which reality you're tuning in to in your interaction with us. There are those frequencies in which we are the closest, but there are a couple others in which we are not the closest, but very close.

Jefferson: Can you explain more about that idea because you spoke about it before and I got a little bit...I wasn't sure how to relate to that? So what about this idea that in one frequency you are the closest society and in another you may not be. Can you expand on that?

Ishuwa: It could be like, as an analogy, you're on a path and it forks into three different directions. Any one of these three paths will be connected to your steps only if you take that path. So the path that you focus on and thus walk upon then becomes the one you are closest to in that moment of your interaction with it. Whichever path you choose to connect with through your focus will be the closest one. Either of the other two could have been the closest one if you had chosen to walk their path. If you choose to walk the path to the left, then the one in the center will appear to be not as close, and the one to the right will appear to be even farther away. The genetic structure of one race can, in a sense, appear in research or analysis as being closer of further away from your race depending on which one you are placing the greatest focus on.

As you focus more on the path of interaction with us, then you are most closely connected with our society. That doesn't mean you're always going to be focused closest to us, and when your strongest focus is elsewhere we will not be as close to you genetically.

Jefferson: I see. What society would be in that case?

Ishuwa: Those societies, both of them, we will not refer to at this time. There will be a time to share this with you. There might even be some co-blended channelings allowing one or both of them to interact with you but that time is not present. They are very uplifting races. They are very much a part of the upliftment that interacts with your world in various ways.

Jefferson: Okay. I look forward to the day when that blending is going to happen and maybe we can talk to them.

Ishuwa: Yes, thank you!

Jefferson: I have another thought about the body structure. We used to think the characteristics of our body were controlled by our genes. Today we are aware that the genes are like templates that we can make some changes to. Do you have command over your physical structure to the point of being able to change it at will?

Ishuwa: It could perhaps appear that we do from your vantage point if you were observing us. The idea being that we can appear and then disappear. Time can be altered and that can make it appear as though we are changing our form and this has something to do with DNA.

There are very powerful programs, if you will, within the genetic structure that are sending and receiving information that will usually be most keyed into accepting the sending of the person they are connecting to in the biological format. We are at a frequency that allows for a more aware conscious connection with this sending and receiving mechanism within our DNA, so we can have more of an aware and immediate communication link with the DNA that will then begin sending out to the body instructions of information that will put the body into a different state of physical expression that it can then appear to be changing form from your perspective.

More of this ability, in our perception, will be available for you and your society as you choose to be more aware of who is making the choices and who is creating the experiences that you are all having. As more of you recognize who is creating the physical expressions, there then comes more awareness of how you are doing it, which increases your ability to do it in the ways you find enjoyable.

So we can change our body in the ways that suit us, in the ways that are fashionable for us to wear at any given moment, but we wouldn't say that we are like chameleons that could show up on your planet and turn into a tree or into some other expression of life like a bear or an Earth human. That isn't something we would be doing. It would be far easier for us to appear before you and then quickly move to a location out of your view to make it look like we vanished, as though we could time travel.

Jefferson: I want to speak more about that tomorrow by all means. We are getting to the final moments of our most enjoyable encounter today, and I have some parting thoughts before we depart.

Ishuwa: Yes, share them!

Jefferson: You said before that there are beings from your civilization that have already interacted with beings of our civilization and that you have already walked among us unnoticed, right?

Ishuwa: We have some encounters of that sort from time to time.

Jefferson: What would be the effects on a person from our civilization encountering you personally? Would there be any side effects at all?

Ishuwa: A side effect being what in your definition?

Jefferson: A side effect being something bad that can happen as a result of the encounter because of the lack of harmony in frequencies.

Ishuwa: There are those who have had what could be considered side effects, but the effects aren't detrimental when understood properly. When the effects are understood, the valuable information that they gained during the interaction can be remembered. Because there is a tendency for many in your world to hold onto patterns or frequencies of fear, people will at times awaken on Earth with a memory in which they are holding a fear pattern from an encounter they have had with one of us or with other extraterrestrials. So that fear pattern will temporarily become their only way of relating to their interaction with extraterrestrials. However, if they work through that fear, understand it and let it go, it will allow for the valuable experiences that they had, the more uplifting ones that they did have, to begin to find their way into their awareness. Then they will remember that the encounter they had with us was actually very enriching.

How each person might interact with us isn't always that clear ahead of time. There are factors we look for in determining if an encounter is appropriate before any kind of contact physically would be made. The general idea of any encounter is that it will be uplifting overall for us and for that individual. They will, after having had the contact, have the choice from day to day on Earth...they will have the choice as to how they come back into remembering that experience. At first the fear is often the one pattern that comes through, because as we said, it is such a common channel for humans to hold onto, as though it were a blanket that they feel is comforting them for some reason based on their current belief systems. Again, there's something familiar about that fear that is comforting to them, so they hold onto it as though it were a blanket that brings them a sense of comfort. When they realize that this fear is simply without content and cannot really harm them, then they choose to step through it and the "bubble of fear" bursts, in a sense, and then they become free to start tapping into the treasures of that experience, that contact, that encounter.

We would like to add that there are many on Earth who have had contact and have had no real fear. They are generally the people for whom the memory isn't something that comes into their awareness in a way that makes them think the encounter was just a bad dream. Rather it is something that to them seems like it really happened. In a sense, it's as though they were having lunch one moment and then the next thing they knew they were talking to an ET. They weren't frightened by the initial contact so they were able to remember that encounter the following day within the construct of their psyche.

We do have some ability to measure ahead of time how a person will handle a contact and how much they will remember of any encounter. However, this measure doesn't always provide a one-hundred percent accurate forecast when compared to how they actually end up choosing to remember the contact they had.

Any side effects, as we said, are truly just a "bubble" in which the effects are the idea that they would have a frightening memory. Such fear is simply like a bubble that will not truly harm them. From a higher level, it was their choice to have had the encounter and to then come back and to feel fear. There was something about having the experience of feeling fear that was more the choice they wanted to have, the memory they wanted to come back to first for their own reasons, for their own experiencing. They could have just as easily chosen not to be frightened. They could have moved through the bubble before they came back into the memory of having had an encounter so then it would be, like we said, something in their experience that just happened to them yesterday while they were having lunch and there was no fear at all for them.

So those who do have fear choose to have that experience of fear. They choose to remember the contact idea as having been frightening. This is simply a choice they are making. It is a side effect that they are choosing to create. Side effects from contact are something we aren't always able to fully predict in advance. We always understand that it is their choice whether they come back into the memory of the encounter as being one that frightens them or one that is enjoyable for them. Do you follow that idea?

Jefferson: Yes. So it's not like the exposure to your energy would cause a human being to go into psychotic shock?

Ishuwa: Those encounters wouldn't take place from our world. We would be able to see that type of response ahead of time and thus then we wouldn't choose to have the encounter with them.

Jefferson: I see.

Ishuwa: That isn't to say there aren't some extraterrestrial societies that might not stop at that. They might decide they still want to move forward with the encounter, but it can then only occur if that human chooses on their higher level of consciousness to move forward with that society.

Jefferson: In a previous conversation with you, I asked you if myself and Shaun, the channeler, had ever met you in a previous life and made plans to write a book together in this life. You said, yes there was a meeting of some sort. Can you talk about where we met you before?

Ishuwa: There was the lifetime you previously referred to as James. This was in the physical form. There was some interaction, not as biological brothers, but a brotherhood and a mutual respect for the differing teachings that were taking place at the time and the different cultures that were engaging in a form of combat as well as cultures that were nurturing to one another. It was a very diverse mixture, some support and some combative conflict. But the two of you were by all means in a mutual support of interaction in that life. Does that provide you with more information related to the question?

Jefferson: Yes. So I was James, and Shaun was an Essene?

Ishuwa: There was some overlapping in that lifetime with the Essene teaching, brotherhood, sisterhood, some engagements over several moons of living together with that community, sharing with that community, in that sense. But not born in the Essene community.

Jefferson: So it was back some two-thousand years ago that Shaun and I had an encounter of some sort with you?

Ishuwa: There was a very distant communication. A very light subtle frequency of communication that took place. The stronger connection then for this idea is multi-layered. The question you have recently asked has opened a door and so now we can add more in our answer that relates to the multi-layered nature of this question. Within this lifetime presently, the frequency has been rekindled now, reconnected to a much stronger energy that has enabled you to get my attention adequately so as to support the co-existence of all of our frequencies simultaneously in this rapport, in this form of communication. So what was then said 2,000 years ago could be seen as having paved the way somewhat for this encounter now, this communication now. But that again is only a portion of the answer to the multi-layered question.

Jefferson: That's lovely, fantastic. It's great, thank you! And how do we go about meeting you physically here on Earth if that's even possible?

Ishuwa: The timing will be soon in your terms of your reference of time and space that you have labeled as a decade. It could be as short as one or two decades, which might seem longer than you would like, but maybe it will be sooner than you expect it. There are a number of factors involved. There are many "steps yet to walk upon" before that would become a reality. The idea isn't so much to focus on that as an objective. It is in following your heart, being in the spaces of greatest joy for you as best as you can in each moment, that will allow for that experience of an encounter to occur in a timing of one or two decades.

Jefferson: So I was referring to you meeting Shaun and me, not open contact with all of humanity. Is that what you are saying as well?

Ishuwa: Yes.

Jefferson: Okay. Ishuwa, it's been delicious to interact with you today. In a sense, we are all becoming these interactions that we are having. I thank you immensely!

Ishuwa: Thank you! It is a great joy! It is a wondrous occasion to interact, to share, to communicate with you in this way today! Our society and yours have many wonderful occasions available to share together. Just as two individuals can come together and create new experiences, new partnerships, new bonds, and create ideas, and discover new realms of experience never before imagined, so to can our society and your society come together in this way to create new experiences and have new sharings together.

We thank you for being willing to share in this way with us. It is with great joy and we acknowledge your willingness and your energy and we thank you for this! We look forward to the next occasion when we walk together in this way. A co-creation in this relationship. Good Day!

Jefferson: Thank you, and Good Day!

Chapter 4

Sensual Telepathic Communications

"We also communicate telepathically, and there is a great deal of feeling that can be transferred sensorially in telepathic communication that can make contact with the biological skin, in that sense, and create a tingling sensation. It can create an erotic sensation for us physiologically." – Ishuwa

August 4th and September 15th, 2009

Ishuwa: Always with you in these blending moments is a wonderful opportunity to share, and to interact, and to experience new realms of Existence, new worlds, new places that are of joy for you and for all who are present in this interaction! How are you this day of your time?

Jefferson: Very good! Thank you so much! It's lovely to speak to you again!

Ishuwa: Yes, and with you as well! How would you like to move forward in direction this day of your time with this interaction?

Jefferson: I would like to start by asking you Ishuwa, are adults as playful as children on your planet or do they have to be concerned with "matters of importance?"

Ishuwa: There is a great sense of playfulness in our interaction! Even when we are encountering and taking part in activities that may be most crucial in terms of their function and the need for them to be done properly. There is a great sense of play, of freedom, of flexibility, of cooperation, of ease and of acceptance for all forms of participation and contribution. We really don't have a sense of heaviness, a sense of seriousness, even in moments where it might be that we are all very focused in accomplishing a specific task with utmost care and delicacy.

Jefferson: I see. Do you resemble your parents?

Ishuwa: There is a resemblance as there are in your world, yes!

Jefferson: I see. Do you wear clothes?

Ishuwa: We do at times wear something, for certain types of travel, that will shield us from the idea of higher more powerful frequencies that we may not be fully adjusted to in the time that we arrive at those specific locations that could be a bit challenging for our structure, for our exterior skin elements. But generally in our day to day interaction we don't have any need for that form of clothing as your society does. If we were to interact with some group of beings that were in a given state of their daily life to have clothing, we could accommodate them and then wear clothing for such occasions as that.

Jefferson: So you walk naked on your planet?

Ishuwa: To some degree there is that sense, yes. Although, we don't experience it quite the way as those in your society generally do. You have the idea of having to go to specific areas where then there is only allowed to be in that way, or only in their private locations of home. We are born with and have an understanding that it is our natural state of being and it is a very familiar experience and expression to us that is accepted in all planes of our home both publicly and privately as well.

Jefferson: We wear clothes not only because some of us may feel uncomfortable to be seen naked but it is also a way that we can keep ourselves warm and clean.

Ishuwa: Very well. If you enjoy it, continue as a society and as an individual. You have some very enjoyable costumes and clothing designs and colorations that we enjoy observing in our interactions.

Jefferson: But don't you feel cold since you don't have fur covering the entire body? We don't have fur like bears do. Our skin is just skin.

Ishuwa: We are able to emit a particular frequency around the body that is like a thermostat that allows for us to maintain a particular environmental and sensorial experience that keeps us at a state of temperature and environmental that is comfortable for us. Even in moments where the ambient temperature as you experience in your world might get hotter or colder, this sphere of energy around our biology is able to maintain a particular temperature rate. That keeps us more removed from the changes of the environment wherever we are at in any given moment.

Jefferson: That's interesting! Let's look at another idea Ishuwa. Lips on Earth humans are seen by many as a symbol of sensuality and sexuality because of their erogenous and very sensitive nature. It would be very cumbersome not to have lips, especially for those of us that love kissing. How does it work in your biology? Do you have lips, as we understand the idea?

Ishuwa: We have a mouth. We are able to talk and have physical communication. We also communicate telepathically, and there is a great deal of feeling that can be transferred sensorially in telepathic communication that can make contact with the biological skin, in that sense, and create a tingling sensation. It can create an erotic sensation for us physiologically.

So there are ways in our world of having erotic experiences from one being to another that don't require the actual physical contact, the actual lip to lip contact that is so prevalent in your society.

Jefferson: I see. So do you have lips or just the mouth?

Ishuwa: We do have a membrane that is somewhat more sensitive around the opening of the mouth, but we don't generally have a large bulbaceous protrusion around this mouth area that many of you do that you refer to as a lip.

Jefferson: Oh.

Ishuwa: But you could see on our physiology an area that you could identify as a lip but just not as round, not as full, not as protrusional from the facial area. We don't generally utilize it in that form of contact that you do in your world. There are other ways of interaction, as we have suggested, and telepathy is one of those ways. Physical embrace is something that we will do at times. There are other forms of intimate sharing and experiencing that we are more in resonance with that are not any better than those that you have in your society and your world. Our forms are simply how we have grown and how our biology supports that form of embrace and erotic sharing from one being to another.

Jefferson: Okay. Do you have a nose like ours or is yours more like the dolphins or other highly intelligent mammals on our planet that are adapted for aquatic life?

Ishuwa: Our breathing apparatus or nasal olfactory region, is somewhat similar to that in your society, to your human nose. It isn't quite as large though. We also have less intake of volumes of oxygen than that of your world and your human biology. So there isn't quite as much need for as large an opening. There are other factors involved that have over time been responsible for the smaller nose size that we have. But there are those in your world who have noses that are somewhat similar in size to ours.

Jefferson: Do the animals on Earth serve as a link to the extraterrestrials or to whoever engineered them?

Ishuwa: There was a choice that people within your world made to explore the idea of separation and limitation and to have the illusory experience that there is no intelligent life except for what is on your planet. So while there may be lights up in the night sky, there may be stars, there may be a Sun, there may be a Moon and other planets, one of the ideas here on Earth has been to experience the sense of being all alone, of being all that there is in terms of intelligent life forms in the Youniverse.

Jefferson: Okay.

Ishuwa: One of the more interesting components of that choice to explore separation and limitation was then to bring into this world on Earth a vast array of life forms that would co-exist with you to, in a sense, provide you with an unseen anchor that keeps you connected to some degree to your actual nature. The various life forms on Earth carry and convey consciousnesses of many kinds and some can be considered extraterrestrial. There are so many life forms on your planet and so many provide you with a connection to your actual nature just by interacting with them. The interaction can be like a catalyst that reconnects you to more of an inner realization that you aren't alone in the Youniverse.

When you communicate or interact with your animals and plants and other organisms and substances of life on this planet, although many of you may not be aware of this occurring, when you interact with nature and animals, there is taking place within you in that moment a rekindling of your more expansive nature simply because so many of those life forms carry a more expansive frequency of being. A sense of this can be felt by you as a feeling of being more at peace. That's one reason why many people feel more at peace in nature while walking in the woods or swimming out in a lake, or in a river, or in an ocean. There are many conscious beings in these places that are in such moments rekindling a person's connection and re-awakening them, although the person may not be aware of this occurring. They may only be aware that they are feeling more at peace, more comforted, more at ease. It is in these interactions that they are communicating with other forms of life, many of which are not living on Earth. Some are extraterrestrial. This allows people to have experiences, frequency wise, that are more in tune with their actual nature.

The idea to have these life forms here with you was accepted collectively, and it was then incorporated into this world, onto this "stage," so these life forms could provide a way for humans to reconnect with ETs and the other conscious life forms while at the same time not being aware that the reconnection was taking place. You could remain in the "dark," in a sense, but still not become completely lost in a state of despair, or desperation, or hopelessness without any ability to carry forth from day to day.

There is then within the ability to go and visit nature and connect with these animals and life forms, a hidden but very strong energy source that revitalizes the will of the human being that is still choosing to live with the idea and experience that they are all alone in the Youniverse.

Jefferson: Okay! Thank you for sharing that! Now I would like to ask a question of a very different flavor. Do you have sports on your planet?

Ishuwa: We don't have sports in the form of competition in the sense of one side victors over the other. We do see value in that in your world for it is a very common practice of interaction.

We have other activities that can be considered games, but they generally aren't about seeing who can get ahead and who can victor, who can win. They are more about finding ways to elicit within each individual more expansive states of their own joy, their own playful nature. That is more the way we play games, games to create more expansive states of playful awareness in one another.

Jefferson: What particular game do you like the most?

Ishuwa: I like to play hide and seek!

Jefferson: (Amused laughter). Share with me more about the ways that art is expressed on the planet of the Yahyel? Do you play musical instruments? Can you name one you prefer?

Ishuwa: We have music, yes. We have those who sing notes. We have sounds that come through instruments and also telepathically. We have some life forms that emit particular sounds, and we have discovered that when we put them with certain other life forms on our planet they will begin changing the notes and sounds they emit. It can be very harmonious. It can be very much a melody as though they are playing instruments, but it is only a sound emitting from them. Somewhat like a cat on your planet that purrs. There are sounds of musical quality emitting from these life forms.

There are musical arrangers who can arrange these various life forms together and they will then emit different songs that aren't with words. They are more like soundscapes. This creates an "orchestra of life form players" in that way. That is one of my favorite forms of sound concerts to attend. At times I also play musically with these life forms in that way as a sound arranger myself.

We have a variety of art forms. There are art forms similar to canvas paintings where people place colors into images on a canvas to create a picture. There are some images of sculpture that we work with and images of light in a form that you don't readily incorporate yet on your world that bring out sculptured images made entirely of light. Not of clay, but of light. They can take on a holographic quality and begin, at times, to even interact with the environment and change in ways that perhaps the sculptor wasn't aware would occur. So the sculptor allows the light creation to playfully change its form through the organic interactions of the environment it has been created in. This can be quite enjoyable to simply sit down and watch this type of sculpture and see how it changes shape as the light on any given day might change over time. So these are a couple of ideas of our art and music.

Jefferson: You spoke of a cat. Do you have pets?

Ishuwa: We don't have pets. We do have some living organisms and physiological life forms that could be like a pet, but they take care of themselves entirely.

Jefferson: Ah, I see.

Ishuwa: They are able to come and go as they please, find food as they need, and interact with other families. They aren't kept at one home, one house, or one abode on a regular basis. Some of them are able to communicate with us very clearly and concisely while some others are a bit more unusual and with these we haven't really come into a clear communication with them like I am communicating with you now.

Jefferson: How lovely.

Ishuwa: With these life forms, we communicate in a way that might be more similar to how we sense most you communicate with your pets. There is affection. There are many ways in which we are able to have a relationship and communicate, but with some of these life forms communication isn't in the way you and I are communicating now in this simple, clear, concise, and spoken way.

Jefferson: Which one do you like the most?

Ishuwa: I don't have a favorite myself, in that sense, but a couple of them I enjoy include the one that rolls around most frequently. It is a very large animal that is about five kilometers in size.

Jefferson: (Surprised laughter). What?

Ishuwa: It is rather round and very light. It is able to float off of the ground to a height of approximately fifteen feet, and it will generally come back down onto the ground after floating for approximately one minute. When it does this, it is possible to get underneath it and to tickle it. It has a very soft texture that actually changes colors when in contact with our fingers, and it seems to enjoy the contact. We don't have real clear communication with it the way I am communicating with you, a language in that sense that we both are able to share, but it is a life-form that we have had on our planet for as long as our history records, and the relationship has always been mutually nurturing. That is one that I enjoy.

There is another life form on our planet that will follow us while we are traveling alongside our waterways on any given day. It's like a fish, but it doesn't have any scales like the fish on your planet have. It is capable of moving in the water very quickly, and it is nearly the size of your kittens. It is rather disk shaped with a few fin-like protrusions on the top and the sides, and the bottom, and the back. It has a couple of eyes at the front and it has a gill-like mouth at the front that it feeds through. It is capable of flying through water, but it doesn't ever express the ability to move up into the air above the water surface. It doesn't jump out of the water the way dolphins in your world do. It can at times float along the surface but generally when it follows us it is one-and-a-half to two feet below surface. It emits a very large current of water that rises to the surface and bubbles, a very large bubbly trail that it leaves. That is one of the ways we recognize that it is present and following us. A very bubbly friend they are.

Jefferson: You said it follows you. If it's a water being, does that mean you walk on water?

Ishuwa: No. We at times walk alongside a waterway, and it is in the water beside our foot-trail. At times we can walk through the water with our feet submerged below the surface and then along the bottom of the waterway our feet walk upon.

Jefferson: How do you engage a person on your planet for dating? For example, do you send them flowers or text messages? Do you invite them for dinner? Do you invite them for an interplanetary ride in your spaceship? How do you do this?

Ishuwa: We can all move about freely in terms of the idea of spaceship. We can all ship around in the space that we interact within freely. Giving flowers is something we enjoy observing in your world. It's something we don't do.

If there is a desire to share more intimately with someone we meet, then we will have an innate understanding and recognition of that desire when we meet them. The desire to share more intimately with, there is simply a recognition of it. It just occurs. There is no, "I wonder if that person likes me because I have an attraction for them." This type of wondering, questioning, doesn't occur. We know that the feeling is there within us because it is mutual. So it is very easy then when this type of encounter occurs for both parties to understand that this is a moment, an opportunity to come together in a more intimate way for some reason that each one of the two isn't necessarily aware of in the moment of the meeting initially. But they know that there must be some reason for the meeting and for this deep heightened sense they feel from coming together or they wouldn't have the sensation to begin with. So they openly interact and know that whatever the reason is for meeting, it will through the journeying together become revealed to them in ways they will both enjoy that can be educational and very long lasting, enriching in that sense.

Jefferson: I wonder if you have ever dated any one?

Ishuwa: I have had interactions with what you would consider the female expression, but it isn't like a preset date. It happens spontaneously and organically, usually. There are times were I have known in advance that there would be a meeting occurring before that meeting actually occurs. This is like having an intuition of the future meeting. I may be aware that I will meet someone that relates to a union, the male female union, but usually becoming aware of a meeting before it happens doesn't come to us. Usually with an encounter that occurred synchronistically and organically, and spontaneously, we just go with the flow. The energy that brought us together will continue for as long as it is of great value for us both to remain together. In that sense, it isn't likely to be a lifelong bonding, a lifelong pairing. That does occur still at times, but it isn't as frequent as it occurs on your world.

Jefferson: Is there any separation between childhood, teenagehood, and adulthood as far as age?

Ishuwa: There is essentially a stage of infant and then a Yahyelian that is fully capable and fully prepared to be, and to express, and to support one's own life as necessary. The infant will generally require parents to look after them in ways you can understand such as providing shelter, food, guidance and connecting to their path. The infant generally becomes what you might consider an adult at an age of two-and-one-half to three years old in our experience. There is not an age of teenage rebellion or awkward development taking place. The transition occurs rather quickly, and it is something as you had spoken of before, the idea of a graduation.

Jefferson: Yes, what about that?

Ishuwa: The energy of the infant at about two-and-one-half to three years old will exhibit a particular light, a particular consciousness that will extend out of their biology to quite some height that many of us who are present will recognize and also appreciate. We understand that it is a graduation from the idea of infant to adult Yahyelian. After that we will begin to experience that one, that being, as being capable of self-sufficiency in all modes necessary for them to continue their life path and to find their way however they most enjoyably choose to live it.

Jefferson: Okay, I see. In our society, we have the institution of marriage. Do you have something that is close to marriage?

Ishuwa: Not of an institutional nature. The ability to recognize our path is very apparent to us. It is a great emanation, a pleasure of life joy. It is very gifted in its guiding intelligent capacity. So we always follow that, in a sense. Because we are in that energy, we know that we will bond with partners only when there is a mutual sensing that is most desirous, most appropriate, and most pleasurable to be doing so.

Neither party is ever left out, in that sense, turned down or forsaken. The length of time that the relationship will remain together is always determined by an unseen quality that will reveal itself to each of those two people by how they are still sensing what is of greatest joy for them to be doing. As the relationship comes to an end, they will both recognize that being together is no longer of their greatest joy. It will be apparent. It will not be something that will be unclear that they will have to question or ask others for counseling about. It will be simply, and is simply, very clear. It is understood. It is accepted. It is rejoiced within that we are able to interact and engage in relationships so easily, so clearly, so mutually accepting of the process. So there is then no divorce. There are no arguments.

Jefferson: Do you have professions? For example, some people are Pilots, some are Cooks, some are CEOs, and some are Scientists. What in this case would be your sort of profession?

Ishuwa: I am an Explorer, a Discoverer, a Traveler, and a Translator.

Jefferson: Oh yeah, indeed, as you mentioned before. Can you talk more about that today?

Ishuwa: Primarily translating languages between two life forms that aren't necessarily able to understand one another. I then will become the third party that learns the languages of both parties and acts then as a translator so they are able to communicate.

Jefferson: Do they pay you for doing that? Well, you don't have a monetary system on your planet...how are you rewarded by your profession?

Ishuwa: By having the opportunity to express that which brings me greatest joy and that which I am designed to be sharing!

Jefferson: It makes sense, yeah; it makes a lot of sense! So what sort of daily tasks do you perform?

Ishuwa: I don't have tasks in that sense that are daily. There is great fluctuation. There isn't the same task over and over from one day to the next that I am engaged in. There are similar functions that I do each day such as observing where I am, what I am experiencing, what I am sensing, and tuning into ideas and opportunities that are of most pleasure for me to move to experience, to be a part of. That type of tuning in will gravitationally place me into those opportunities so I can, in a sense, step in that direction and have those most pleasurable experiences manifested in my physical world.

That then could be considered a task perhaps, tuning in to my self-awareness, my capabilities and what I most prefer doing, what is of greatest joy. I do this to be in alignment with who I am and this is an activity or task, if you wish, that I perform frequently.

Jefferson: Alright. What does it look like where you are?

Ishuwa: At present?

Jefferson: Yes!

Ishuwa: I am at this moment observing a vast landscape before me that reaches out for many miles. There are very colorful flowers in all directions that are approximately one foot to one meter rising off of the ground. They are moving about in a soft breeze and flourishing in the light of the Sun above that is emitting a very warm feeling. I hear a sound coming from a river that is off to my right. It is somewhat different from the water rivers of your world. It has a very buoyant quality about it. It's more bouncy. That is the landscape where I am sitting. I am taking it in and experiencing it. This provides an ability, in a sense, to amplify my connection to the channel and I am then able to have this communication, and I am translating. I am doing what I enjoy, what I am most designed to be doing!

There are off to the left a few birds flying through the air just above the tops of the flowers. They stop ever-so-frequently to rest upon the flowers and they are able to share in our interaction to some degree. There are others present as well, but I won't go into that now. They are simply being a part of this communication. They are like me, taking part in this third reality, experiencing your world in this way and experiencing how our world can communicate with your world in this way, learning through this process as though it were an interactive class. They are off to my left and somewhat behind me. There are some others who are not present on this dimensional-plane that I am residing on, and they are in a sense, networking from a different location. Does that answer your question?

Jefferson: Oh, absolutely! And it reminds me to ask another. Can you tell me about the Association of Worlds or the Interstellar Alliance?

Ishuwa: We have a connection with the Alliance of Worlds. It is something that people and extraterrestrial races are a part of as they choose to be. They can come and go as they please. It provides an opportunity for the sharing of experiences of one race with another, one world with another. In that sense, it can be a very enriching resource, a very wonderful resource to learn about other forms of life, other races, other extraterrestrials, other beings. And we do then, in that process of choosing to share, have various guidelines so we can all communicate on a "similar page," a similar frequency.

Jefferson: I see. We are approaching the end of today's wonderful interaction. Are there any parting thoughts you would like to share with us?

Ishuwa: For now, we sense this sharing is moving along for the ideas and for the intentions set forth in a way that feels good. There is much information yet to come through in our perception.

Jefferson: Yes.

Ishuwa: In time, it will become more clear how to function with the whole of the material that we are creating here together.

Jefferson: Okay.

Ishuwa: And as how to present it, ideas will be provided, shared, to do with as you choose. We feel it is flowing well, fluidly. We thank you for taking part in this process, in this co-creation to bring forth information in a way that your society will have access to!

Jefferson: Great Ishuwa! I thank you very much! Now in regards to a subject I spoke with you about previously that had to do with finding out more about those beings that are very similar to Earth humans. You said you might be able to do a co-blended communication with those two races. When do you think it would be most appropriate to do that?

Ishuwa: Thank you. Realize that it will occur spontaneously.

Jefferson: Okay, cool!

Ishuwa: Thank you for the question, for keeping that in mind, yes.

Jefferson: Very good.

Ishuwa: There will be a moment or two where you will find yourself asking a particular question or two that will then be a catalyst and open the door for that communication to take place or present itself and for those beings to come forth. So the catalyst might be a question you think to ask and you might feel that there is something unusual about the nature of the question before you ask it. That catalyst will be for you to experience then in that timing if it does occur.

Jefferson: Very good. So basically just go with the flow?

Ishuwa: As you feel most uplifted to do, yes!

Jefferson: I was concerned because I thought that we would have to make some sort of appointment with them but from your side and maybe from their side too things can happen quicker?

Ishuwa: Yes. Those beings are present, as we said. There are some others who are participating that perhaps might seem to be on the sidelines like an audience, but they are very active in this process. They are very present in this interaction.

Jefferson: I see.

Ishuwa: When the moment presents itself, they will step forward and you will recognize them in some very interesting ways. That's not to say you will see them before you in person, but you will recognize some different beings communicating with you.

Jefferson: Good! Very well. Thank you very much for today. It has been a most wonderful interaction again!

Ishuwa: Thank you! Always a joy to share and interact with you in this capacity! We look forward to those times ahead in your day and time when we can share in this way with you. Much joy, and much love, and good day to you dear one!

Jefferson: Good day! Thank you! Bye.

Chapter 5

Dismantling the Towers of Babble

"There is within you, and all humans, and All That Is, this understanding. It is as though it is a key that unlocks any "tower of babble" and brings it down to the ground ever so easily and effortlessly without so much as raising a speck of dust. When this occurs, there is no longer a sense that the languages spoken on your world are different." – Ishuwa

August 13th, 2009

Ishuwa: I will say, good day to you this afternoon as you create this experience of afternoon to play within! How are you?

Jefferson: It is lovely to speak to you again! Welcome back to planet Earth!

Ishuwa: Thank you! Always a delight to share with you and to interact in this form in this third reality that together we are able to co-create and thus then explore the infinite realms of Existence and place into this moment of experience that which we find enjoyable, and meaningful, and perhaps even bring forth information that others too will find to be educational, and enriching, and nourishing for them as well. Together we have this moment of time this day of your time. How and in what way would you like to explore this hour of our time together?

Jefferson: Let's talk about you!

Ishuwa: Talk about me you say, oh very well. There really isn't that much to say unless you have all day!

Jefferson: Okay! You said in a previous channeling that your hair is made of tiny follicles placed along your body's skin.

Ishuwa: Yes!

Jefferson: Is the location of your hair similar to humans in the sense that ours is usually concentrated on the head, and the pelvic regions, and the armpits, and rather scattered throughout the body's skin, or is your hair more like cats in our world that have fur covering all of their skin?

Ishuwa: There is a very, very minute follicle throughout most of our integumentary structure, the exterior of our physiology, the skin as it were, including along the scalp region.

Jefferson: I see.

Ishuwa: On the head, the follicles tend to be thicker and longer than other areas, usually at least a quarter of an inch in length. For some of us, there is almost no hair along the eyes and you have to get really close to see that there are some "tiny little forests" of follicles dancing atop the head region.

Jefferson: I see. Does the hair sit on the head the same as on Earth human beings? Does it make a contour over the top of the ear from the back of the neck and then up to and around the forehead?

Ishuwa: There is some similarity to that hair outline that you have suggested, yes. But it isn't that way for all. Some have, even with only a slight amount of hair, what you might consider a receding hairline in which there are almost no follicles in the region from the forehead back along the top of the head for a few inches.

Jefferson: How is it on your head?

Ishuwa: I have a little bit of hair of a very short length, barely less than a quarter of an inch at this timing. It is very fine. It is visible. I suppose some people in your world might refer to it as fuzz. It has a peach-fuzz kind of follicle nature or texture.

Jefferson: Okay, and what's the color of your hair?

Ishuwa: Brilliant blond!

Jefferson: Sorry? Did you say brilliant blond?

Ishuwa: Brilliant blond! It is much like that of those in your world who bleach their hair to a very light blond color. The color is similar in appearance to the bright yellows that you can see in some of your Sun's solar flares.

Jefferson: Okay. Do you have hair right above the eye in the area of your forehead?

Ishuwa: Some, but almost none on the forehead region of my noggin. There are some who do have hair along their forehead, and it comes all the way down into their eye region but that is rare.

Jefferson: Do you have to cut the hair?

Ishuwa: We don't have to do the mandatory hair cutting, shaving, salon styling, trips to the barbershop. No teary eyed toddlers on our world, in that sense, from being forced to have a haircut.

Jefferson: What's the color of your skin?

Ishuwa: It has some sky-blue, and it has light gray with a bit of a flesh tone that is similar to humans on your world. Some Yahyel's have a powder-blue color or a very light sky-blue that is mixed in with some of the flesh tone and some of the gray tone. There is color variation from one to the next of us, but those three colorations are what you would generally see with us.

On some people, some human Yahyelians, there is a blending of these three colors. For example, the arm region may have a flesh tone, and the torso region may have a bluish tone, and the leg region may have a grayish tone. When there are three colors on one person like this, the colors don't appear as three distinctly separate colors. There is a gradual blending within the movement from one coloration into the next. If you were to briefly look at one of us that has the three colors, you wouldn't really notice them. These colors blend in well together.

Jefferson: Can you say the three colors again?

Ishuwa: A flesh tone that's very similar to humans on your world, and a light sky-blue color, and then a very light grayish coloration.

Jefferson: So, particularly with you, how do the colors look on your body? Is it a mix?

Ishuwa: I have some of the sky-blue, and some of the light gray that has whiteness to it, and some of the flesh tone color around my facial region.

Jefferson: I see, nice. Is your face clean-shaven or do you wear a beard and a mustache?

Ishuwa: No beard. No mustache. No facial hair of that significant amount. There are the very fine follicles that are throughout the body, which would include the face as well. The females, the males, and the young children have it. It is very fine hair like what many of you on your world have on your faces.

Jefferson: Okay. Our eyebrows serve several purposes including not allowing sweat to fall into the eye. Do you also have eyebrows?

Ishuwa: I don't have that. No.

Jefferson: Okay, well, maybe you don't need it.

Ishuwa: I don't have anything I need to sweat about.

Jefferson: (Laughter). Okay!

Ishuwa: I am just kidding! We simply don't have that in the function of our biology at this time, but some do have eyebrows.

Jefferson: Okay. How about the eye? How does it sit in your face? Is the part that's closest to your nose lower than the side that's closest to your ear or are they aligned straight across from one point to the other?

Ishuwa: It is lower near the nose.

Jefferson: So they are not at the exact same height horizontally?

Ishuwa: Generally speaking, but this isn't the case with all of us. We do have genetic variations like you do in your world.

Jefferson: For us, the vertical distance of our eyes from top to bottom is generally less than the horizontal distance from side to side. How is it for you?

Ishuwa: The vertical distance?

Jefferson: Yes. The vertical measurement of our eyes is less than the horizontal.

Ishuwa: Yes. This is similar with us, and our vertical is a bit more than yours and our horizontal is a bit more than yours as well. Our eyes' shape tends to be larger in the region close to the nose, and they are more vertical in that region than yours are. Ours are a little bit rounder or not so much of a point in that region where you have your tear ducts.

Jefferson: Okay.

Ishuwa: As you move from the nose towards the side of the face and over towards the ears, that horizontal distance of our eyes is longer than what your eyes tend to have.

Jefferson: Pointy?

Ishuwa: There is a softer curvature than what you have generally on your world.

Jefferson: I see. I discovered that the human eye can exist in over ten million colorations. That's exciting!

Ishuwa: Can you name them for us?

Jefferson: Yes, absolutely! Tomorrow, okay? (Laughter).

Ishuwa: Alright. We'll be there!

Jefferson: You said in a previous channeling transmission that the eyes of people in your society are quite "eye catching." What is the color of your eyes and do they have the iris and the intricacies that make our eyes so beautiful?

Ishuwa: We have a shield that we wear over our eye that is kind of like a contact lens that you have in your world. It serves us somewhat like the sunglasses you wear in front of your eyes. This then, when removed, allows for our eyes' true color to be visible. It is somewhat in structure and coloration similar to humans on your world. There is generally a larger size to the eyeball. It is somewhat less round, less perfectly spherical, not that your eyes are perfectly spherical but that ours are a little bit more not of a perfect spherical nature. The color has similarities. You could say, if you had one of us standing side-by-side by one of those of your world, that our eyes perhaps have a little bit more of an iridescent nature to them.

Jefferson: Yes.

Ishuwa: Generally, that has to do with the frequency of the world that we are tuned in to. Eyes will resonate at the frequency of the world you tune in to and then express or illuminate a particular type of coloration that has a particular iridescent quality, iridescent level, iridescent amplitude to them. Because we are at a higher frequency within the physical world, not necessarily of higher intelligence but of a higher frequency physiologically, our eyes tend to resonate at a faster frequency and have what you would consider a more iridescent coloration to them.

Jefferson: Yes.

Ishuwa: They tend to be larger. The pupil tends to be larger too, but it has the ability to focus down into a very small point when a bright light encounters our space and then the pupil becomes smaller.

Jefferson: I see.

Ishuwa: We don't have the lashes protruding from the eyelid that you will generally find in your world. There are some of the minute follicles that we have around the rest of our body that tend to be a little more densely populated right around the eye lid, but their length is generally the same as the rest of the follicles on the rest of our body.

Jefferson: Can you tell us a little bit more about this thing that you wear which is similar to sunglasses? Is that a contact lens? Can you remove it?

Ishuwa: Yes!

Jefferson: Why do you wear that? Is it optional like in our world where people can wear sunglasses or not wear them?

Ishuwa: Yes!

Jefferson: I see. Do you wear it on a daily basis like we wear clothes or is it just fancy stuff?

Ishuwa: We generally don't go to sleep with them on, and generally we'll remove them during times when we are in a region where the light is low. There are other worlds we have visited where there is not nearly as much light as you experience on your world. In those instances, we usually have no need for that type of protective coating and we will then remove them. There are other occasions where we may choose to remove them such as times when interacting with people socially. When we are wearing them, they are comfortable. They feel very normal, very natural, very organic, very good. We understand there are those on your world who wear contact lenses and can find them to be irritating at times.

Jefferson: Yes.

Ishuwa: At times, some of you that wear contacts can have little bits of dust or other debris get between the contact lens and the eye's surface and cause some irritation.

Jefferson: Yes. How does it work for you?

Ishuwa: We don't have that. We have a particular form of energetic coating that will repel substances such as that in most every instance in our experience. So we do not have that type of irritation as a result of wearing these coatings.

Jefferson: I understand. So you don't, basically you don't ever get stuff in your eyes where you then have to rub them to clear out the debris.

Ishuwa: It is very rare.

Jefferson: Let me make sure I get this information down now, what's the color of your eyes?

Ishuwa: They generally have a bluish quality to them. A very light blue that can fluctuate into a medium blue, into a deep medium blue. They are a very clear blue, and they have a luminary and iridescent quality to them.

Jefferson: Do you see in the dark?

Ishuwa: We do, and there are times when we see more specifically than what most humans can see when they aren't using any of their technological visual aids.

Jefferson: Is that because you have the help of your technology with things such as the sunglass-like lenses you put over your eyes?

Ishuwa: Well, it is just a natural visual embodiment that we would be able to see a little bit more clearly at night if we were on your world. We have experienced planets that appear to have no Sun present in the sky during their "daytime" and their nights are very different than nights on Earth. They have a form of nighttime light that you haven't experienced on your planet, and we are able to see very well in some of those worlds without any technological visual aids.

Jefferson: Do you close your eyes when you sleep?

Ishuwa: Usually I do.

Jefferson: You do?

Ishuwa: Usually I do.

Jefferson: How many hours do you need to sleep?

Ishuwa: I have approximately four hours of sleep over the course of about one week of your time.

Jefferson: (Laughter). Thank you!

Ishuwa: I have micro-sleeps. I usually sleep four to five minutes at a time. If you add them all up over the course of a week, those micro-sleeps, those four to five minute sleep sessions, then it would come out to about four hours that I sleep in a week.

Jefferson: So why do you sleep?

Ishuwa: We sleep to have the opportunity to be more in alignment with our actual nature, that place from which we originate before we incarnated into our physical body. Sleep allows us to, in a sense, regenerate and to reconnect to our higher idea, to our higher heart-mind and that allows us when we are back in the physical expression to be more like that state, that higher-self state of being, as though we bring that energy back with us when we awaken. It is as though we went on a vacation and found wonderful items that we felt were great treasures and we were excited to bring them home with us!

Jefferson: (Laughter).

Ishuwa: And then when we awaken, we can open those treasures. They regenerate and strengthen us and allow us to be more resonant, more in sync with, more in frequency with, more in harmony with our truer state of beingness!

Jefferson: I see.

Ishuwa: Does that answer the question for you sufficiently?

Jefferson: Yes.

Ishuwa: Thank you!

Jefferson: Yes it does. Thank you! Let me ask you something else. The jaw in humans is composed of two opposable structures, the upper and the lower jaw. The lower part we call the mandible. It is the mobile component that holds our teeth and allows enough movement and flexibility for the initial processing of our food intake. How does it work in your human structure? Is it the same?

Ishuwa: We don't have the force that your jaw has to bite down, to chew, to mash. We have much smaller skeletal components that comprise our jaw area. The muscular areas are not the same size as you generally find in your world. We don't do chewing as you do. We don't eat the same things that you eat on your world on such a regular basis.

Jefferson: I see.

Ishuwa: So, we have a jaw, but it isn't nearly as forceful as the jaw that you have in your world.

Jefferson: The jawbone provides definition to our face. How is your face? Is it pointy at the bottom because of the jaw?

Ishuwa: It's much softer overall than you generally find in humans on your world? The jaws are generally not going to protrude as some Earth human jaws protrude.

Jefferson: Okay.

Ishuwa: And overall we have more of an oval shape to our skull.

Jefferson: Oval, okay.

Ishuwa: Not perfectly. You have some people on your planet who have the head structure that is quite similar to what ours generally is.

Jefferson: Would your face be something like the night bird, the night owl?

Ishuwa: Well, no, because that can be on the face quite a vertical up and down quality to it from top to bottom. Our face tends to be more curved.

Jefferson: Okay.

Ishuwa: If you were looking at our head from a side view, it tends to have more of an outward curve or arch.

Jefferson: Okay.

Ishuwa: It doesn't have a straight vertical drop. The back of our head has an outward arch also. It is more of a half circle. It is curved and smooth. If you were to look at us front-on, then you would see the sides of our head are also curved, like a semi-circle, more of an arch that is smooth and more round, but not perfectly so. And we do generally have what you might consider to be a few little lumps and bumps here and there on our heads.

Jefferson: (Laughs). Very good! Ishuwa, because your diet is different I feel interested in asking you the following question. Do you have teeth?

Ishuwa: We don't have teeth like yours.

Jefferson: How do you eat?

Ishuwa: We generally have what you would consider a liquid form of intake and also we don't ingest food in that sense nearly as frequent as humans on your world tend to do.

Jefferson: Oh.

Ishuwa: We don't require the amount of calories, energy intake, in that manner.

Jefferson: I see.

Ishuwa: There is energy in the nature of that which we are, and we can more easily recognize how to tap into that source of energetic nourishment that can then propel our physiology from one moment to the next.

Jefferson: Yes.

Ishuwa: And so often we just, in a sense, live off the energy that is. It fills us. It provides us with most of the energy we need.

Jefferson: Okay. So in that case you guys don't need to go to the toilet then?

Ishuwa: We generally don't have any excrement move through a digestive system like you generally have on your world. So then, the answer is we don't do that.

Jefferson: That's good, but you do pee right?

Ishuwa: There is the intake of the food we have that is more in a liquid state. We eat this way often. It provides us with an ability to interact with a living plant substance. We change a plant-based life form into a more liquid substance. Then we consume it in a way that allows us to have an interaction with that plant and also the region that it grows in. This form of food intake is a type of communication, a type of blending, a type of sharing. It is a type of relationship. We don't do this form of food intake just to keep our bodies going. We tend to ingest food in this way to have a form of interaction with that plant form, that life form, and also with the ground, the planet substance from which it grows in. Do you follow this idea?

Jefferson: I do! So, the liquids that are transformed, do they go out through the same canal as in humans?

Ishuwa: No. They are completely utilized in our physiology. Then the follicles on the skin throughout our body will raise up any matter that the body no longer needs. The matter is brought up onto the hairs, the tiny follicles that we have spoken about previously, and transformed from there.

Jefferson: Okay.

Ishuwa: So we don't need to actually go to a specific room to have a bathroom break. It simply occurs organically, naturally, and there is no scent when these particulates or this matter comes off of the hair follicles as perhaps you might find in a bathroom that someone has recently used on your world.

Jefferson: So, it's basically a transformation of an energetic nature?

Ishuwa: Yes!

Jefferson: Okay, so there's no liquid or matter as we know it? It's more of an energy transformation of some kind?

Ishuwa: There are no bowel movements, in that sense, like you have in your world.

Jefferson: I can only assume then that you —

Ishuwa: There are no urinary breaks either.

Jefferson: Yeah, yeah, that is what I was thinking.

Ishuwa: No trips to the toilet!

Jefferson: Thank you! Ishuwa, do you have nails on your fingers?

Ishuwa: I do not. I do have a material that is a little bit more fibrous than skin. It is similar to fingernails that humans in your world have.

Jefferson: Yes?

Ishuwa: It is a little bit more rugged, rugged in the sense that it can withstand an impact if it encountered one just like the nails on your fingers can, but we don't have something that grows and then we have to clip it.

Jefferson: (Chuckles).

Ishuwa: We don't file it, or manicure it, or paint it. Although we do find this fascinating that in your world this is an activity that is taken on with great interest and frequency.

Jefferson: You said that the nails can withstand impact and so I wonder if you guys ever bump into each other?

Ishuwa: At times we play games like bumper cars with one another for playful interactions.

Jefferson: You do?

Ishuwa: But it's rare that we accidentally bump into each other. It can occur, but it doesn't very often. When it does occur, it's usually not anything that dislocates any of the biology of our body, or our skeletal structure, or our organs. There is no displacement of bodily locations from such a bumping into.

Jefferson: And when you walk, do you walk with your feet on the ground or can you float, or hover, or...I don't know...fly?

Ishuwa: We can relocate, but we don't hover! We can create the illusion of hovering or floating a foot or two above the surface of the ground. But that then is just a moving from one frequency of Isness to another frequency. It is a type of time and space travel. We can do that in a way that makes it look like some of the film characters you would find in your world's movies and cinema.

Jefferson: To go from point A to point D you don't have to walk through points B and C first? You can just relocate or teleport?

Ishuwa: We do have options, other routes! There is no one fixed route that we must take to get from one point to the other. Does that answer your question or were you asking something different?

Jefferson: It does. It does answer the question, but I am not sure I understand. You just...do you have to walk from one place to another or can you just —

Ishuwa: There are many worlds we can explore. On your world, you generally see people walking and we can do that on your world. We have the ability to step one foot at a time, one leg at a time, as you do, which is the general mode of transportation without the aid of any external vehicle on your world.

Jefferson: Okay, so how does it work in your world?

Ishuwa: Frequently, we will just suddenly appear where we want to be. There are those for whom we will be appearing in front of to meet who are aware that we are going to appear. We communicated with them telepathically ahead of time.

Jefferson: Okay.

Ishuwa: They are ready for us to appear before we arrive. Once we are amongst each other in a group, perhaps having what you would call a social interaction, then we can sit together as you see sitting being done on your world. Also, we can simply walk about together if we want to, just like you do on your world.

Jefferson: Okay.

Ishuwa: On other occasions, we might want to rapidly go from one place to another. Generally we won't go from point A, to B, to C, to D. We will just go from point A to Z quickly! We won't make a bunch of intermittent stops along the way. We will just be at the starting point and then we will be at the destination as fast as you can snap a finger or blink an eye, faster actually. That is the way we generally choose to move distances, considerable distances.

At times, we will undertake a more slow movement and, in a sense, take a scenic route where we start at point A and then we move just a little bit into a different time and space pattern of frequency so that we are then at point B, and then we move into a little bit of a different time and space frequency and then we are at point C. We can look left and look right, so to speak, to see the view and to take in the scenery. Then we may go to point D, and E, and F, and so on the same way until we get to the destination such as point Z in this example. So sometimes we will go the slower scenic route but usually we will move from point A to Z. It just depends on our state of mind, our state of play, and where we are at that given moment of our day.

Jefferson: If you are at point A and then suddenly appear at point Z, that could be what I call teleportation.

Ishuwa: It could be similar.

Jefferson: How...how do you do that?

Ishuwa: We just move from one point to another. There is really only one point in Existence and it has an infinite number of frequencies or expressions that are always continuously changing their frequency or their expressive nature.

Jefferson: Okay.

Ishuwa: You can, in a sense, define or create the idea of location. You can define a location within any of these infinite frequencies and thus then you can create the perception of an infinite number of locations. It's really just frequency. There are an infinite number of frequencies, and when you choose to focus on any one of these frequencies you can then have the experience of being in that frequency. It can at times seem like a place like your local restaurant for example, or a mountain top, or a path along-side a river, or a lane of traffic on a freeway. These are all just frequencies. We simply have come into an understanding of this idea and that makes it easier for us to do it. We are, in a sense, born into this understanding. It is so automatic for us. We don't second-guess it. We don't have to think about it. We just know how to do this mode of travel, just as most of you there know whether it is day or night when you are outside. We just know how to change our frequency of what it is we are focusing on, observing, and experiencing, of the place we are creating for ourselves to experience. We change frequencies to that which we tune in to.

We begin at the starting location, say point A for example. We are tuned in to that frequency. When we want to go to point B, we tune into that frequency. When we want to go to point C, we tune into that frequency, and we resonate with it. We become one with that idea.

If we want to take the "fast track," we begin by tuning in to the starting location frequency, and then we just focus our thoughts, our feelings, and transmit the frequency of what is like to be at point Z the destination in this example, and suddenly we are there resonating in and experiencing that frequency.

There are many little components. There are a multitude of little components of what is actually taking place for which your world doesn't even have a language, a vocabulary, a feeling, a mental comprehension capability to understand all of these things. And that is okay. That is perfectly the way it is appropriate for your world to be at this time. So we can't really get into details for you because it wouldn't make any sense. You wouldn't have any frame of reference for what we were talking about. You wouldn't know how to apply it appropriately if we were to try and tell you how to do this.

Jefferson: Okay.

Ishuwa: Because this ability does exist, it does then exist within you. It is just a matter of timing when you and your world begin to choose to explore and tap into that knowledge, and then as you do so step by step, clue by clue, realizational moment by realizational moment, it becomes more apparent what steps you can take to build that understanding until you will reach the point were it becomes an automatic understanding like it is for us. You will just do it. Do you follow that explanation?

Jefferson: Yes. It's very good!

Ishuwa: There are many other very fine mathematical factors that are involved that become second nature as you and your society develop into that ability, develop the understanding to do this.

Jefferson: Yeah, I understand. So onto the topic of communications. How many languages do you speak?

Ishuwa: Over two-thousand.

Jefferson: I am sorry? Would you repeat that? How many?

Ishuwa: More than two-thousand.

Jefferson: Oh my goodness. How did you learn so many languages?

Ishuwa: I can't tell you. I don't have the words to describe it in my language!

Jefferson: Okay! (Laughter).

Ishuwa: I am just kidding! There is within you, and all humans, and All That Is, this understanding. It is as though it is a key that unlocks any "tower of babble" and brings it down to the ground ever so easily and effortlessly without so much as raising a speck of dust. When this occurs, there is no longer a sense that the languages spoken on your world are different.

Jefferson: How so?

Ishuwa: Often, with a particular key "of understanding," we are able to unlock the perception of different languages. Then there is no difference, and it is as though we are speaking with one another in our own native tongue. For example, if I was a French person I could speak to someone from Germany in my native French and it would seem to them that I was speaking in German. I create this effect by going to a deeper level of communication and understanding.

Jefferson: Okay.

Ishuwa: There are unifying languages that exist beneath the idea of a French language, a Japanese language, a German language, a Swedish language, a Portuguese language, a Spanish language and so on and so forth. The unifying languages allow us to communicate with so many different societies; all of them may have their own unique language.

We move underneath the level or layer of language they were raised with, and we speak to them in a place of understanding deep within so they simply are able to get it even if they didn't know before we first encountered them that they could do such communication. They just are able to do it. It is built into the system of Isness, of All That Is, and physiological beings generally have this ability to tap into it. Your world and your people can do this as well even though you have grown up through many generations that have been taught the idea of separate languages. What we are referring to as this unifying language can seem quite foreign to you.

There are those who have spoken of an ancient Sanskrit language or this language or that language as being the oldest language on Earth, but what we are referring to is a language beneath those ideas and is a language that connects to all beings, to all life forms, and brings down the sense of separation in language completely.

There are people in worlds that we can encounter that are so locked into the idea that their language is separate that it can take us time to get underneath their focus on that language and begin to understand what it is that they are using as a locking mechanism, as a blocking mechanism, that is preventing them from being able to understand us on this deeper language. But over time, if we are able to keep interacting with them, they will begin to resonate into this deeper language and be able to communicate with us.

I am able to speak to more than two-thousand different species of what you would consider to be extraterrestrial beings. On the surface, each one of them would appear to be speaking a different language, two-thousand different languages, and yet there is really only one language underneath them all and you can learn to speak it. It is what I have learned to speak, and it is what I do speak when I am in my translation mode as a translator.

The obstacle, or what you might consider to be an obstacle, is getting that other race to be able to let go of the need to speak with us on a language that they are familiar with and to begin to look more deeply within their nature and find this one language we are referring to. There are some worlds that take a little bit longer before being willing to delve into this deeper place. Alternatively, some worlds get it right away and find it quite wonderful, and quite revealing, and exciting because they didn't know language existed in such a deep and more unified state of existence.

So that's some idea of this language that generally isn't spoken of in this way on your world today, but tomorrow, who knows? It could become a language of oneness, awakening within the consciousness of your humanity, and it could arrive as simply as the Sun rising on the horizon. Nobody would have to go to class to study how to get in touch with this deeper flowing current of communicational language we speak of.

Jefferson: Is there an exchange of thoughts telepathically or do you speak this oneness language while the other person speaks in his native language?

Ishuwa: The other person perceives me to be speaking in their language. It is primarily an emotion, a feeling, a thought, a telepathic interaction, a communication that takes place. But they perceive it as taking place in their language.

Jefferson: Oh, I see. It's not like they will think there is telepathy happening? They will see you moving your mouth and they will think you are speaking their language?

Ishuwa: It can work both ways. It just depends on the nature and the place of their consciousness development at that given moment. We encounter other beings that have what seems to be a very, you might say, advanced form of language that sometimes takes us a little bit of opening up in order for us to be able to connect with them and the level of deepness that they are able to communicate from on this one language, this one flowing current of language communication that exists. Do you follow that idea as I share this? Does that answer your question?

Jefferson: Yes, thank you!

Ishuwa: Because we can go into it with greater detail if you would like, but if you got it, very good.

Jefferson: Okay, yes. On Earth, there are so many languages. For example, in America there is English. What do you call the language that you speak in the Yahyel world?

Ishuwa: Yahbwah.

Jefferson: Yabla?

Ishuwa: Yahbwah, Yah bwah. You would spell it, Y, a, h, b, w, a, h.

ISHUWA AND THE YAHYEL - CHAPTER 5

Jefferson: In your language, how would you say, "be in joy?"

Ishuwa: Yah oohm!

Jefferson: How do you spell that?

Ishuwa: You can't really spell it!

Jefferson: A close spelling?

Ishuwa: Y, a, h. H, u, h, m.

Jefferson: Good. Thank you. Now, do you have amongst you —

Ishuwa: No. Y, a, h. O, o, h, m, would be a little closer phonetically. Yah oohm!

Jefferson: Yah hoohm.

Ishuwa: Yah oohm! Take the H out, the second H out.

Jefferson: Okay, yah oohm!

Ishuwa: Yah oohm!

Jefferson: Good! I am getting it! So Ishuwa, do you have amongst you a saying or a hand-sign that you convey every time you meet one another?

Ishuwa: But first, can you tell us what "yah oohm" means in your language, translated into your language?

Jefferson: Oh, in English..."yah oohm" means, "be in joy," and in my native Portuguese language, "be in joy" translates to "esteja alegre contente!"

Ishuwa: Be in joy! Be in joy! Yah oohm! And your question?

Jefferson: Do you have amongst you a saying or a hand signal that you convey every time you meet one another?

Ishuwa: No.

Jefferson: A saying like...perhaps something such as, "hey what's up?"

Ishuwa: No.

Jefferson: You don't? Okay.

Ishuwa: There is a recognition of the person. That is enough. That is sufficient. We understand where they are at, what they are doing sufficiently. That they are present is an acknowledgement that they choose to be in our presence because they find it to be most exciting to be in our presence.

Jefferson: I see.

Ishuwa: Their presence is a greeting in and of itself, and that is a great joy for us to be receiving. They have a similar experience from us as well when we are present in their presence.

Jefferson: So talking about bonding, are there special days of the year that you exchange gifts on?

Ishuwa: No.

Jefferson: Okay.

Ishuwa: Again, being present with one another is a special gift in and of itself for us.

Jefferson: Do you have —

Ishuwa: Now, that's not to say we don't at times encounter an object in a world we are visiting that we know someone from our world would enjoy very much receiving. We might then gather up that wonderful item if it is appropriate and bring it back to that person. That could be considered a gift, but such an interaction would just happen spontaneously and not in the sense of doing it for a birthday or for Father's Day, or Christmas, or Mother's Day.

Jefferson: I see. Ishuwa, we are approaching the end of today's channeling. I have a couple of questions. Do you have a television on your world that's designed to see what is happening on other planets?

Ishuwa: In a sense, yes!

Jefferson: So, do you have —

Ishuwa: It doesn't have any commercials. It doesn't have any news interruptions. It doesn't have a breaking news story. Nothing like that.

Jefferson: Oh.

Ishuwa: There are no sponsors.

Jefferson: That's good! And so can you…do you have a channel that allows you to see what's happening on Earth?

Ishuwa: There are some.

Jefferson: Yes? Okay. Can we revisit the mechanism by which this channeling interaction takes place? Last time we spoke about this you said, or I understood, that the landscape where you were had the ability to amplify your connection to the channel, Shaun. How do you perceive this connection is actually established?

Ishuwa: It is simply a choice to resonate at a similar frequency of conscious awareness and interactiveness and communicative ability. It is something that you can do without being completely aware of all the details behind what makes it possible. The more you then do it, then that will open the door for more of the details to reveal themselves over time. As the details are revealed, you will be in a better position to relate to them, to understand them, to work with them appropriately. Do you understand that idea?

Jefferson: Yes. I see. Good. I also remember you said that you can remove your focus of awareness out of the timeline represented by past, present, and future and by being in the now you are able to resonate communicatively. Yes. Good. So Ishuwa, I think it's time to ask, do you have any parting thoughts or anything else you would like to share?

Ishuwa: Yah oohm!

Jefferson: (Chuckles). Yah oohm! Yah oohm!

Ishuwa: Yah oooooohm! Yah oohm! Yah oohm!

Jefferson: Yah oohm!

Ishuwa: oohm! oohm!

Jefferson: Be in joy!

Ishuwa: Yah oohm! Be in joy!

Jefferson: Good!

Ishuwa: Thank you for sharing and for interacting this afternoon of your time. It is a great joy to have the opportunity to bring forth information that may be useful for those on your world and to bring them the ability to relax into the idea that we are here, that we are brothers and sisters, that we are relatives, that we are children of your world.
    Thus then it is a great joy to have the opportunity to share some of this information awakened mostly through these questions you have been so generous to take the time to formulate. Perhaps you will find new questions for our next session. Perhaps some of the questions will find their way into your awareness in new ways through the given days before the next session, maybe in your dream states again,

or maybe in interactions you have with some people there that you haven't met yet that you will find to be rather interesting and curious in a rather unusual way when you do meet them. With that said, we thank you again and we bid you a wonderful joyous afternoon and evening! Good day!

Jefferson: Good day! Thank you very much Ishuwa!!!

Chapter 6

The ETs of First Open Contact

"The Phoenix Lights is one of the ways we are beginning to present the reality into your consciousness, that yes, you have Earth brothers and sisters that have gone out into space and are now finding their way back for a homecoming with you." – Ishuwa

August 17th, 2009

Ishuwa: Delightful to be here with you in this afternoon of your time and experiencing as you choose to have this experience and create this time! How are you?

Jefferson: Fantastic! Thank you for coming back. Thank you for the sharings!

Ishuwa: Yes! It is always a delight to be here and to have this opportunity to interact with you and your society in this way and thus create a third new reality! How would you like to move forward this day of your time?

Jefferson: Ishuwa, I would like to revisit a few ideas that we spoke about together in some of our previous channeling interactions. Are there animals on your planet like horses that you can ride on for recreation or use for transport?

Ishuwa: We don't have the transport requirement, so we don't use animals in that form of interaction. There are animals that would allow us to share in a riding capacity and have that type of a bonding experience together.

Jefferson: What do animals that allow you to interact with them in that way look like?

Ishuwa: We have some animals that are similar to what you have in your world as a giraffe. They have stronger legs, and they can hold more weight, not that they need to because they aren't carrying anybody around except for the occasional joy rides together. They don't have the same type of small protrusions on the top of their skull that you would find generally on giraffes on your planet. They have a very keen sense of hearing, as those in your world do. The colorations don't tend to be the soft hues of browns and yellows that you have with giraffes in your world. These are more of an iridescent purple with some hues of white and occasionally some orange. There are a few who have a bit of a chameleon ability that can exhibit a coloration similar to the giraffes on your world. These do talk in a more audible way, not really a language as we are speaking, but they themselves converse by making certain sounds that are very clearly present and easily heard and observed. They are more abundant in the locations where we generally go to visit them. There is a world in which they are one of the primary life forms. They have quite a community there together. In a sense, it is as though it is a world of their own, sharing the physical space, the planet surface, and they have an ability to interact with us and with others in a way that lets us know they are acknowledging our presence and that they recognize we are there in a joyful form of interaction with them, a friendship. They greet us in a way that we can acknowledge as a greeting. Often times when we arrive, they will come over to us and, in a sense, catch-up on what has been going on in our world and share with us what has been going on in their world since the last we had a gathering together. It is a bit like a homecoming in that sense, going back and meeting old friends.

Jefferson: Do you have any animals that you can hop on and fly with?

Ishuwa: That isn't really an idea that we undertake. There are, I suppose, creatures that we could have that experience with, but again, we are able to move about quite easily on our own and create the perception of flying. This might be similar to what a hawk in your world does when it floats in thermals of warm air above a cliff-top along an oceanfront.

Are you getting a bit of excitement over the idea that you can perhaps fly on a large eagle or a falcon? Is that something you would like to do?

Jefferson: Yes! That's interesting...or have a winged horse! I thought that could be an idea that somewhere someone might have a winged horse. That would be interesting! But I suppose it wouldn't be fun if I fell.

Ishuwa: Well, in your world you do have the gravity and until you find other ways to interact with the relationship of the gravity, yes, you could fall, but you could have a parachute.

Jefferson: On your world, on the planet of the Yahyel, do you guys laugh?

Ishuwa: Yes we do!

Jefferson: When you laugh, do you move the face muscles?

Ishuwa: Yes.

Jefferson: Okay. You previously said that your eyes don't have tear ducts, does that mean you don't cry?

Ishuwa: Well, we do have an ability to express tears of joy in some sensing, but we don't have a duct that is going to be flowing those types of ingredients that are in the fluids that come out of Earth humans tear ducts when they are in a state of sadness and misery. If you could analyze the liquid, the substance that comes out of our eyes and out of your eyes when we each are in states of joy, it would be similar. But if you were to take and analyze the tears or the fluid that comes out of Earth humans when they are in a state of sadness and crying, you would find substances in those drops that don't come out of our eyes. Your drops of sadness come out of a slightly different duct. We don't have that wired in our physiology. Sadness is an experience that does not serve us and has then no longer any function in our biology and thus then it has, in a sense, just simply been placed aside.

Jefferson: Good! Do people in your society age the way humans on Earth do? Can you maintain physical youth and therefore have no wrinkles or aging marks throughout your lifetime?

Ishuwa: There is some recognition of age, but it generally isn't going to be exteriorly represented through wrinkles as you would see on elderly people in your world where their skin can get a bit flabby and the muscles can be a bit droopy as a person gets on in years on your world. So those are ideas that our physiology generally will not embody, will not express visually.

There is an energetic body, an energy that we give off, and those then who are in our world can recognize, in a sense, an age classification of each one of us based on that energy that is given off. So someone that is quite young in years will have a different vibration or a different energetic body emanating from their physical body than someone of a middle age or of an elderly age that is close to transitioning out of the body and into another experience, what often in your world you refer to as dying and death. For us, the transitioning process out of the physical body is not experienced and perceived nearly the same way that you tend to experience it.

We recognize that death is a great opportunity to move into a new world, a new way of life, and to do so in appropriate timing, in an appropriate way based on what in that lifetime we had chosen to experience and express. As we get older, we more clearly understand that our time to make the transition is coming closer. In your world, it's referred to as death, dying, but for us it is simply a recognition that the time to "close that book" of life experience is coming closer. In a sense, we have read the entire book and we know it will serve us to begin preparing to set it aside with the understanding that a great new book will soon be in our presence for us to begin reading a whole new experience, a whole new form of life expression and incarnation.

We can, from one Yahyelian to another, recognize an age factor, but it is usually done by observing the subtle energetic bodies and rarely the physical body. Does that answer your question?

Jefferson: Sometimes I think of aging as a mechanism that informs us it is time to lose interest in one particular focus of incarnation, in one particular reality, and move forward to explore other realities that can be more in alignment with who we actually are. What do you think of that idea?

Ishuwa: That is one of the ideas, although, there are numerous ways that the aging process provides humans with the opportunity to have wonderful types of varied experiences. The aging process does require certain changes to be made, but that isn't really the main reason why it has been put into the genetics of the body and biology that you have all chosen to work with in this experience on Earth.

There are a multitude of amazing and fascinating opportunities that can be presented to a human given the nature of the biology and the aging mechanism that you have incorporated in this experiencing, into this world, into this physical reality.

Jefferson: I see.

Ishuwa: So the idea you presented is certainly one. Yes. And thank you for bringing that idea up.

Jefferson: Do you think we can stop or reverse the aging process?

Ishuwa: You can lengthen the time that a person lives in their body. That can be done.

Jefferson: Can we make changes to our aging and look young our entire lifespan?

Ishuwa: Yes, that is a world that can be created, but your world hasn't collectively chosen to have that particular experience. There are a few of you that have connected to the ability to remain quite young and appear quite young and to be several hundreds of years old in physiology in your world's time counting process, but as a collective, that really isn't the experience that you were looking to have here. It is an experience that could be had if you were as a collective to choose to move in that direction. There simply are other ideas that humans wanted to explore more and have more experience with than that idea.

For someone to be able to reverse their age and start looking younger, to be exhibiting that level of empowerment over their world, to be revealing that level of their own Creator's creation ability, that would make it more difficult for many people on Earth to continue accepting the age-old beliefs and predominantly desired experiences of limitation and separation and ideas that go with that, such as exploring illusions like, "you are not the ones who are creating your experience." Ideas of limitation and separation have been a primary focus on your world for a number of generations.

If you have several people reversing their age and becoming younger and then telling others they are doing it consciously, this would make it harder for those others to keep on accepting the age-old idea that humans are not the Creator of their reality and that there is someone outside of them that is "running the show."

They might start getting ideas such as, "the people in the town over there say they know how to make themselves younger and they are getting younger. If they can do it, we can learn how to do it too." As more and more people realize this aspect of their actual Creatorship ability, then the old idea that there is some almighty powerful being outside of yourselves that determines when it is your time to go just doesn't "hold the mustard" anymore. Do you see what we are suggesting?

Jefferson: Yes I do!

Ishuwa: In a sense, in order to have your current reality or "world play" remain as the collective has chosen, it's important for it to be able to hold up in its primary thematic story lines. So there still has to be sets, and props, and definitions, and beliefs, and people who are expressing the idea of limitation to great depths in order for your awareness to keep buying into the idea of separation and limitation to begin with.

As more people start stepping out of those old ideas and instead start pointing out that you aren't really so limited and aren't really subject to a Creator outside of yourself, then that whole set, that whole age-old "world play" begins breaking down. In a sense, the old pictures start falling off of the wall and the block walls start coming down and you're left standing in a large studio set with nothing but that green background waiting for you to decide what to put up next, what reality to create next.

There wouldn't be the same degree of belief in limitations on your world if people were flying around on winged-horses and turning back the clock of Old Father Time and becoming younger again, and again, and again.

Jefferson: In this physical world, it seems we have people who are very knowledgeable about Existence. They are able to create the reality they prefer and enjoy, but they usually keep their knowledge to themselves in order to respect other people's desire to continue living in the "play of limitation."

Ishuwa: Often in your history, there have been people that came forward and expressed advanced knowledge to others. This knowledge really demonstrated that humans are the Creators of your reality, but if the collective wasn't ready to go forward yet and expand their awareness of who you all really are as the Creators of your reality, then you can look at your history and see many accounts of such a person whom today is considered to be a genius based on what they in their past lifetime were teaching, and you will see accounts that reveal that that person was bombarded by the opposition of many people in their lifetime. Such "visionaries" have often encountered a barrage of opposition and angry individuals who at times even claimed that such a visionary with the gifts of expanded knowledge was somehow an evil being that needed to be removed from the surface of the planet immediately.

In a sense, they subconsciously thought the visionary needed to be exterminated in order to preserve the collective's desire to keep their "play of limitation and separation" alive so they could keep playing hide and seek, so to speak. At times, the collective doesn't want to stop playing this game, so when a visionary or, in a sense, a parent says it's time to come inside, to "come back home," the kids may instead run away and get lost while playing outside in the darkness.

Jefferson: Yeah, I understand.

Ishuwa: So, only as the collective decides it wants to begin awakening in a particular way, fashion, form, and direction, only then will there be one or more people who start presenting, and expressing, and displaying more of your actual Creator ability. Whether it be through amazing psychic abilities, or some form of levitating demonstrations, or being able to live on light, or being able to live hundreds of years, whatever the talent, ability, or phenomenon may be, it will begin to gain acceptance only to the degree that the collective chooses to accept it.

These kinds of collective choices are generally made on a super-conscious level, and frequently individuals are not aware that they are participating in and making such collective choices.

Jefferson: I see. You mentioned that there are people that "live on light" that don't need any of the common types of food in order to sustain their physical body. This idea has been brought to science where scientists have explored such claims and it's been verified that some people really do it. Yet there are still people who don't believe someone can "live on light" no matter how much proof there is.

Ishuwa: Well, proof is simply determined by somebody's willingness to accept an idea, the willingness to believe an idea as being true for them. Proof is not something that is fixed in the eternal nature of Existence that everybody must look to and accept. There are only three ideas that are, in that sense, eternal and unchanging.

In a sense, the concept of proving something is merely getting a person to accept an idea of yours as being true for them. You can say that an idea of yours is "the way things are," but until the person you are talking to accepts it you haven't proven it to them. What's proof for one person might for another person not be anywhere close to being what they would call proof because they don't believe or accept your so-called "facts" that someone else did accept or believe was true.

Jefferson: Okay! Thank you Ishuwa. Let's move on to another topic now that I have been thinking about lately.

Ishuwa: Yes.

Jefferson: Does the position of the stars and planetary alignments at the moment of birth have any influence on the physical form, on the physical body?

Ishuwa: There will be some opportunity for that to occur, but it isn't something that happens to a person as an effect of having been born at a particular time. It is something that happens as a blending of the energies that were present, and it is something that can remain. The blended vibration of these energies can remain with the person for some time and be a guidance mechanism with them to help them make particular choices and to express a particular personality and particular behaviors and make choices in a particular way. These energies can be a guide in that way. They don't have to be. They aren't something that is fixed throughout a person's lifetime. A person doesn't always have to respond and behave and interact in ways that are based on the energies that were present at the time and location of their birth.

    Frequently these energies that are present for a person at birth can provide such a strong internal guidance mechanism of comfort that humans will hold on to them. A person can become comfortable with that guidance energy, that consciousness, that way of life frequency that was present in the place and timing of their birth. Alternatively, those who begin to get a handle on that idea and are then comfortable with taking other steps and working with other forms of guidance, reconnecting to others aspects of their self, they will more easily be able to shift out of that shaping frequency, that guiding frequency. They will begin expressing themselves in ways that are quite out of the usual for their astrological sign, and they will begin to have experiences that are quite out of the ordinary from those they had when they had been focused on that frequency of the sign language, the internal frequency present on their birth date at their birth place.

Jefferson: As far as the ability of an individual to co-create within this reality, does the collective consciousness limit a person's ability to create whatever he wants once he understands how creation works?

Ishuwa: The idea is that there are collective agreements and you can introduce new ideas that go only so far off the "set," off the "stage," off the collective's "script" for its "world play," not in terms of what you can realize individually, but in terms of what the collective is ready to realize and experience as a whole. It's as though the collective will decide that, "for now, these are the ideas about life and who we are that we are going to accept at this timing, and these are expressions you can share and that you can bring forth in these fashions."

Each individual has the opportunity to tap into and share any of those ideas that fit in with the overall framework that the collective has chosen to explore. There isn't a "sealed-lid" on what can come through for a person, but the collective may not embrace any and everything that does come through. On deeper levels, the collective understands that it is important to allow new ideas to come through. People are free to imagine, and create, and connect to those new ideas and find ways to share them with the collective that will excite the collective or portions of the collective and reconnect those who are excited back to realizing more of who they actually are.

Within the collective's choice to keep some things limited, there are "avenues" that are being chosen by all that will allow the collective to begin coming back "home," slowly perhaps in terms of how you perceive time, but come back home nevertheless.

As you all raise into higher consciousness levels, your higher frequencies begin to act like a catalyst that opens the doors for more expansive information to begin coming into the imaginations of those people who will be more in tune to recognizing the nature of your actual existence. It will come to them through their imaginations and their dreams, their day-dreams, their writings, their paintings, their musical compositions, perhaps intuitively and spontaneously or even through thinking, or meditating, or interacting with other people or other forms of life. These new ideas come through to people who then find ways to begin sharing them with others. If the ideas fit in with the overall "script" and the collective consciousness accepts the new ideas as a format for reconnecting, for coming back "home" in the sense of stepping back into the light of their actual nature, then they will accept those people's ideas and be excited to take part in their events, writings, and musical compositions.

But again, if anyone is connecting to something that is in some sense to radical, then the collective will usually find ways to stamp it out or step on it because the collective just isn't ready. Thus then, such persons will generally be able to share their ideas with others, but they just won't have as great a public audience, or viewership, or readership in that sense for the ideas they are expressing. At some point in your future, their ideas might become recognized by the mainstream of your collective consciousness and then be given more attention publicly. Do you follow that idea?

Jefferson: I do. To a certain extent an individual in our society may have some frustration sink in and say to their self, "Okay, so I can't express all that I am and all that I know I am capable of because other people are just lazy or the collective consciousness just wants to hold on to the old and limiting ideas a little while longer."

Ishuwa: If you can recognize that the collective is an expression of yourself, and if the collective isn't interested in what it is you are trying to present, then it really can strengthen your sense of beingness and experiencing by simply recognizing that there is an aspect of yourself, the collective, that seems to be indifferent to what it is you thought would be so joyful to present. Recognizing this will allow you to move through the illusory experience of frustration.

For example, you might think, "I have this great idea that I feel is more representative of our actual nature but people just seem to be shutting the door on me when I talk about it. They aren't getting on board with me." Rather than getting frustrated, just acknowledge that seeming lack of interest is an aspect of who you are. Consider telling yourself something such as, "Perhaps this isn't the way or the time to bring this information through." Then from within yourself, invite revealings to come through for you of other ways to express what it is you are so excited about. Also, recognize that your information might be just one piece of a larger body of information, so invite other pieces to come in to complement this idea that will then allow you to present more of a whole picture that then more people in the public's eye may be willing to accept it, and embrace it, and share it with others. There are many factors involved here.

If you have something that excites you at any time and you are working to express it with others but they just don't seem to be responding with open arms to you, acknowledge that and find other ways to present it or find new things to present instead of it. Be open to presenting it with the new ideas that start coming into your mind so you can present more of a whole idea. As other people become more receptive, you will know that you are more in the appropriate timing to present the original idea.

Also, if you explore other avenues, you might find people in new places that you hadn't even expected that may immediately embrace the original idea without your waiting for other complimentary ideas to come in to give you that more full picture of what it is you would like to share. Are you beginning to get more of a handle on this idea now?

Jefferson: Yes.

Ishuwa: Do the most exciting thing you can! Follow your bliss to the best of your ability in each moment, to the best of your ability. Do that which you are able to do to the best of your ability that you enjoy the most. Follow your bliss as best you can in each moment.

If you are being confronted by others who aren't welcoming that activity which for you is following your bliss, then maybe you just aren't able to move in your bliss in that direction. So then ask yourself, what can I do that will be perhaps the next most blissful thing in each moment that I can do. Then move in the direction of the most bliss that you can do where there are people who are sharing or want to, if the idea is you are trying to express something you want others to share in with you. So then you would need to find a way to express things to people who are willing to rejoice with you in sharing that. If you can't, then obviously that isn't the most enjoyable thing you are able to do because you can't do it in that moment in the way you are creating your experience in that moment.

As you do the most blissful thing you can do in each moment, you will develop more skills and add new ideas, new ingredients that then will give you a greater maturity, a greater vision, a greater vibration that you will be sending out, a greater excitement, a greater vitality, a greater enthusiasm, a greater exuberance in having lived the blissful experiences. Your maturity level increases. Then those people who in the beginning weren't interested in what you had to say, now for some reason they may become excited by it. In this way, you will be doing the most exciting thing and be sharing your information in the new timing. So timing is a consideration too.

Always do the most enjoyable thing, the most blissful thing that you are able to do. If you encounter people who seem to be, in a sense, closing the door, then move in the direction that you are able to that is the next most blissful thing. That will always guide you into new places to learn the things and to have experiences that will give you the greatest joy and be most representative of your greatest potential, your greatest life path in this incarnation. You will find it will be most effortless for you, most uplifting, most meaningful for you and also have the greatest sense of purpose for you.

There is no all-encompassing purpose that all humans need to follow and do in terms of the nature of your eternal existence. Meaning and purpose is always decided by you, for you, and then can always be changing in the ways you choose to change them.

There certainly are cultures, groups and societies that can create their own definitions of purpose and meaning, but all of those, if they aren't in alignment with the nature of Existence, will be fleeting and will move and change as sure as the breeze changes direction on any given day.

Jefferson: Hey Ishuwa, talking about upliftment, and the breeze, and the wind, and beautiful things, where are you right now?

Ishuwa: Where am I?

Jefferson: Yeah!

Ishuwa: I am located on a planet that is a little different from where I was the last time we discussed this idea. Where I am today isn't too far from that other place. It is the same solar system. It is a pair of planets that have a rotational, gravitational, bond together and share some similar experiences from the planetary experiential standpoint, viewpoint, perspective.

However, this planet sees a little bit less of the sunlight from the star in this solar system. It tends to be a little bit cooler, but I find it very comforting. It tends to be of a little less gravity, a very slight difference, and it tends to be a little bit further away from its Sun allowing for me to step a little bit more bouncingly. I don't always come into contact with the surface. The surface has a very floatational quality to it even when I do touch it. Often, it is easy for me to not touch the surface at all and instead walk a couple of inches above it.

As I lay down now, I can also easily sit up and I don't come into contact with the planet's surface. I am about an inch or two, as you measure an inch or two, I am about an inch above the surface and there is a sense of an electric magnetic current. There is a humming sense between my body and the ground just a few inches below me. The planet surface is very soothing, very vibrating, very soft. It has a slow vibrating feeling to it. I don't have any sense of color, but I feel it. It has a soft slow massaging feeling to it. There is in the sky something similar to the clouds on your world but these tend to be more of a gaseous quality, a little bit more vaporous, and they are far more colorful. They aren't just white and gray as you tend to see at this time of day, for it is close to midday here and the clouds, these vaporous gaseous clouds, tend to exhibit kind of a rainbowish coloration to them but without the high yellows, and oranges, and reds. This rainbowish coloration tends to be more in the blues and the greens with some violets and some soft pinks. The reds, and oranges, and yellows are there, but they aren't visible to our eyes due to the frequency spectrum of this planet's atmosphere.

These gaseous clouds have an ability to actually acknowledge our presence. Thus then if we were to say hello, they will respond to us in their unique way. They are very friendly. They are very engaging. They are very pleasing. They are very enjoyable to have in this experience. We don't see them all the time when we are here, but I do in this moment see them. They seem to be aware that the conversation between you and me is taking place right now. I don't sense they are aware of who I am talking to, but I feel that they know I am talking about them. Perhaps this is somewhat like when you talk about your pet dog or cat and they look at you as if they sense you are talking about them.

AVATARS OF THE PHOENIX LIGHTS

Jefferson: So when you are talking to me from there...oh, before I go there, let me ask you this, how did you get there?

Ishuwa: I simply am aware of the coordinates of this place in terms of sound, and frequency, and light and so I tune in to those coordinates and that brings me into this place, this reality. As an analogy, if you want to watch a particular program on your television or listen to a particular radio show on your radio, you simply push a button that then accesses the precise coordinates for that show that are keyed into the programming technology, the microchips, the semiconductors, the electronics, the computerized instruments that you interact with that hold the coordinates. We hold those coordinates in a different way. We simply are aware of them. If you want to listen to a different radio program or watch a different television show, the new frequency coordinate that you have your technology tune in to when you push its button and thus change the radio station or the TV's channel, its new frequency focus will bring that show into your experiencing. It will be there in the room with you.

Jefferson: Okay, I see! You were saying the clouds have the ability to acknowledge you and even the person you are talking to.

Ishuwa: They do! And I sense they are recognizing that I am talking about them even now as I speak to you about them. Again, it is similar to the way you on your world can be talking to someone about your pet cat or dog and saying how much you love it and while doing that you might get a sense that your pet recognizes you are talking about it. We have that experience with these gaseous clouds, these rainbowish colored clouds.

Jefferson: As we communicate, do you just hear my voice or can you actually see me and see the movements I do with my hands and my face?

Ishuwa: I have a visual system that can view the energetic body and what you are sending off of your physiology, the place that you are focused in. That is primarily what I am observing. So I am not seeing what a video camera would be seeing. I am not seeing you the way someone in your room looking at you would be seeing you. That is something we can do but rarely do. If we do that type of visual viewing, it's generally when the person has agreed to do that. If we are in a group setting with several humans present, we might have that type of observational technology set up.

I am only observing you as an energetic form and colorations in variation that I understand. The colorations in variation are a form of information that provides me with aspects of your personality, your character. So it is like a non-verbal communication that you might pick up from other people when they are communicating to you nonverbally with their biology, with their physical body. I am able to communicate and pick up expressions and ideas that you have just by observing the energetics of your body's being and your subtle bodies, your subtle colorful bodies. In this way then, we do this so it isn't invasive of your privacy. For we feel and understand that if we had some cameras there it could be in that way an invasion of your sense of privacy.

There are some people on your planet that have the natural ability to sense some of these color energies that I am observing of you. They have the ability to observe you and others in this way at any given moment during your day. So this isn't a foreign utilization of high-tech communications and observations that I am working with. It is something that people on your planet are already working with to some degree.

Jefferson: Okay, so as you are communicating with me what do I look like? Do you see any form at all?

Ishuwa: I see an oval light that isn't perfectly round. It has flares of light that emanate outward from it, somewhat like you may have seen in pictures of your Sun that has flares that emanate from its sphere. I see the oval light that is close to the shape of your body and then emanating from that there are flares, but they aren't as sharp and flame appearing as those that come off of the surface of the Sun. They are a little more soft and a little more slow in how they emanate from your body. At times, there are some that are very fast, lighting fast, speed of light fast as you count, and record, and define the speed of light in your world at approximately 186,000 miles per second. So occasionally you do have some lights that shoot off of your body that fast but this isn't so much about your state of being at this moment as it is simply something that occurs with many human bodies in their day to day living.

There is a primary color around your body that has a similar shape to your body. This color is a type of violet with a bit of an indigo blue, but it has a very brilliant quality. It is not a muted color at all. Some indigo colors on color palettes can have a bit of a muted aspect sensing to them. Your primary color at this moment, for it can and does change, but at this moment it is a very deep brilliant hue of indigo and of violet. There are some other colors that are in shapes that change quite quickly. These other colors move location and can be around your head, be around your torso, be around your legs, be around your feet, be around your hands, be around your fingers, be around your toes, be around your hair. They can change shape and size and become very small such as they might focus around the ends of your hair. They might become very large and at times even completely cover the primary violet and indigo blue we spoke of a moment ago. This change has to do with what is going on with you in terms of your feelings, thoughts, biology and also some of the intuitive nature of your being like your psychic nature, sexual nature, and non-physical spirit nature.

At times, these colors have a spherical shape. At other times, an oblong shape. The edges don't take a square shape or a rectangular shape. They aren't edged in that sense. We don't really see a very sharp pointed edge that you would see on a triangle or a square. These shapes and colors tend to be more undefined in that sense. They have the ability to come and go as quickly as your thoughts and feelings come and go because they often are related to your thoughts and feelings. Over the years, we have learned to understand what they mean. We are able to translate them. When we see a particular shape and color around a particular region of your being, we can relate that to a particular thought that you perhaps are having or a feeling that you perhaps are having. Because you can have so many thoughts and so many feelings, there are then so many of these shapes and colorations that come and go. It is quite vast and quite varied.

It really is a very expansive language when you begin to learn to recognize all the different shapes and colorations and where they are located around your body and what they mean or what they are suggesting you are going through in experiencing and expressing. It's a very vast expansive form of language that you express in this way and one you can learn.

Jefferson: So this subtle body is like an etheric body that you see in front of you and it can express various shapes and colors. Is it a projection of myself in a different frequency maybe?

Ishuwa: Yes.

Jefferson: So depending on the colors, and the shapes, and locations around my physical body, you can understand the ideas being conveyed by my thoughts, my feelings, my spontaneous expressions, and anything that relates to my mind's consciousness system?

Ishuwa: Generally, in our experience, there is a connection between what we are seeing and what you are going through.

Jefferson: Are these colorations something you see with the aid of a projection technology that you have built or is it like a holographic image that you can see freely in the air?

Ishuwa: There are devices of technology that have been designed and put together to do this, but I am not working with any technology like that. Those devices are something that I am familiar with, and I have worked with them before. At times we will work with a device like that as a way to get a different perspective on what you might be going through while we are observing these colorations that you are expressing.

Sometimes the technology will be used like an overlay on how we already observe you. It will be a bit like a filter, a coloration filter. There are people in your world that have cameras, and they can take a picture of a sunset and the resulting image is a particular color or hue. If they take the same picture with a filter over the lens, then they get a little different perspective, a little different picture, and we sometimes will apply these technical devices in that way that will give us a little coloration on what we are observing from you. It can give us some different ideas. I usually don't work with any technical devices. Our ability to see these kinds of colorations without the use of any technological devices is basically something that we are born with in my society.

Jefferson: Do you see me right now in your mind's eye, or in your imagination, or do you see me as if I was physically present in the room with you?

Ishuwa: I am not projecting a holographic image of you before me. So it is a bit like imagination, as you understand imagination, generally. You know anything you are experiencing in your physical life is a result of your imagination being projected onto a screen of multi-dimensional spherical canvassing, in that sense. It's a bit like the imagery seen in the "third eye" experiences that people often have when they go into meditations and explore visual worlds with their imagination. It's a bit like that. One of the primary differences is that I know what I am imagining in the connection with you is real. It is every bit as real as if I had just been sitting here in the room with you and observing you directly in a physical connection, physical person to person visual contact in that sense.

Jefferson: Okay, I see. Yeah, I understand what you mean. Now, you said earlier that the planet where you are is in your solar system. Earth is the third planet that is closest to our Sun. Where is this planet where you are in relationship to its Sun and the other planets?

Ishuwa: It is the fifteenth planet.

Jefferson: Fifteenth?

Ishuwa: And the sixteenth.

Jefferson: And what number is the planet of the Yahyel?

Ishuwa: I am presently in a remote region of space in terms of my world, and I am closer to your solar system at this timing.

Jefferson: And in relationship to your Sun, where is the planet of the Yahyel compared to the other planets?

Ishuwa: We are the seventh planet.

Jefferson: The seventh. Okay. In our solar system, we have nine planets as far as we can perceive, maybe there are more. Would it be appropriate to say that the planets that are closer to the Sun are more evolved and the beings on those planets are also more evolved than planets and beings that are farther from the Sun?

Ishuwa: You can create the idea of an evolutionary classification system based on certain parameters and then say that one planet is more evolved than the other based on those classification systems of evolution that you have chosen to create, but that system to other worlds and to other life forms will have no application other than being an idea that you on Earth and humans decided to put together for their own enjoyment, for their own history, for their own scientific studies, to have their own particular type of experiencing.

The planets themselves wouldn't necessarily acknowledge it the way humans would. They wouldn't necessarily feel that one of them was more evolved then another in that sense. They all are expressions in different ways for different reasons, and they all generally get along and understand what's going on. They even understand what's going on with planet Earth.

They realize and understand life in ways that they are willing to begin sharing with Earth humans. The Earth human can begin to have more of an understanding of who the planets are, and more of a connection to the consciousness of the planet they live on, and more of a connection to the planets they coexist with in this particular solar system.

The planets have a lot to say, a lot to share. They have experienced many things in terms of the time line that Earth humans have created. They know they can enrich and enlighten humans with the stories they have to share and with the perspectives and the energies that they hold and carry through your solar system on a daily basis. They are very much alive and awake and in tune to their realm of life and travel through time and space.

Jefferson: In this solar system, we have Mercury, Venus, and Earth, and Mars, Jupiter, Saturn, Uranus, Neptune, and Pluto. Are all of these planets inhabited with life as we know life on Earth but perhaps on a different frequency?

Ishuwa: We haven't observed that kind of life on other planets in your solar system. There certainly are some visitations that can occur. There are some conscious beings that aren't like your physical expression that do inhabit some of these planets at various times. From our experience, it is possible for there to be life forms that we simply haven't encountered. It is possible for there to be life forms on any and all of those planets and we simply haven't encountered them. But again, the idea of an Earth human, or even the animal, or plant forms that you have on Earth presently in your timeline, we don't perceive them living and inhabiting on a regular basis any of those other eight planets you have just spoke of.

Jefferson: I would like to touch on a last question for today. When I asked you previously what would it take for us to meet peacefully, openly, eye to eye, shoulder to shoulder, you said that it might seem to be longer than I expected but that one or two decades away is not really a long time when considering how many thousands of years it's been since we have forgotten about our galactic family. I would like to know why does it take so long? I understand that there is an agreement that goes on with our collective consciousness and in that way perhaps open, peaceful, physical contact today is not a choice that the collective has made, but how does that affect an individual that is choosing to have non-public physical contact. What are the mechanisms as per why an individual would not be able to go ahead and meet you today in a non-public location?

Ishuwa: We have a sensing of appropriate timing that is a little bit beyond the learning state of your world. We understand that in time you will begin to tune in to that frequency of understanding. It is simply becoming more in tune with your nature. Your world has chosen to have public contact with us and you're progressing towards that meeting. When you achieve that place of understanding, when you have learned certain applications of who you are and what life is, there will be a very clear and obvious moment in which it becomes very beneficial for us to meet with you individually and to have open, public, peaceful contact.

So we aren't in any way suggesting that you aren't bright or brilliant now. It's just that you haven't, in a sense, walked in those understandings sufficiently enough for it to have the greatest value for you. You are not yet able to fully appreciate and make the greatest progress and use out of the encounter in a way that would then enrich and provide momentum so your future could move in a way that would be of greater import to you, greater value to you, greater enrichment to you and your collective society.

So, in one sense, we understand your idea of, "why not just have the meeting? What's the big deal? Let's meet now! We can handle it! It will be exciting! There is so much you can share, so much we can learn!" We understand that perspective, but we are suggesting that when the time does come to actually meet you, you will very clearly understand all of the things that indicate why you weren't ready before. You just aren't there yet. When you are ready and the meeting does occur, it will at that time be apparent to you that you weren't fully prepared on this day. There are so many elements, there are so many specifics, there are so many reasons and they have to do with very delicate and very intricate qualities and aspects of the human psyche as individuals and as the collective human race. They are very, very, very delicate, very intricate, and yet of great strength and import to recognize and become once again comfortable with, aware of, and a master of once again.

Jefferson: Can you give us more information about the equation you mentioned before in regards to open contact possibly occurring in a few of our light years as divided by the fractional interest in our Earth's orbit around our Sun. Can you talk just a little bit more about that?

Ishuwa: You have a mathematical formula or component to every experience you have. There is a sound and light frequency that has a particular mathematical aspect to it. You don't need to know what it is now. Some people won't want to. They're not fascinated by mathematics and formulas.

As a bit of an analogy, 1+1=2, is a formula that is complete in the sense that you understand it. It's a coherent formula for you. It makes sense to you. You can put together sound frequencies and then have the experience of one plus one equaling two objects. They aren't really there. You're just creating the experience of them. You are utilizing sound and mathematical formulas to make the experience possible of 1+1=2. One apple plus one apple equals two apples. One orange plus one orange equals two oranges. Those are formulas you understand. Those are sounds you are working with in your consciousness in order to create that image, that physical material object relationship. You set one orange down on the table and you set a second one down and that to you equals two. That's a mathematical frequency, a formula.

There is a formula for when it's appropriate for us to meet. There is a sound, a frequency, a signature, and it is a formula not as simple as 1+1=2. It is a bit like saying, when you're ready plus when we're ready, that equals us being together. When you have the ability to tune in to that mathematical formula, plus when we are in a place to also tune in to that mathematical formula, then that will equal both of us being there together.

Now, as it relates to the fractional interest of your Earth's orbit around your Sun, that indicates that there is an important relationship of where your Earth is in its orbit around your Sun. And also where your Sun is in relation to its orbit with other planets, and its location in your galactic center, and your galaxy's center in relationship to some other galactic centers. These are all then simply mathematical formulas. Each galaxy, and the Sun, and the Earth have mathematical formulas. When you tune in to these formulas, you can experience them being expressed in your physical world.

Because the actual mathematical formula of our meeting is very vast, we wouldn't expect you to begin to be able to write it down as simply as 1+1=2. We perceive there will come a day when you will be able to get the concept and it will then be as simple to you as one orange plus one orange equals two oranges.

Your readiness plus our readiness equals both of us together in contact.

ISHUWA AND THE YAHYEL - CHAPTER 6

Jefferson: Can you push open the door of the future and see the script of potentials and probabilities and maybe give us today some hints about what race of ETs will most likely be the first to openly contact humans here, and around what time that can potentially happen?

Ishuwa: The timing for some contact is before 2020 in our present agreements with our world and yours. For our world, the Yahyel, have been chosen for very many reasons to begin having the contact.

Jefferson: Chosen by?

Ishuwa: Chosen by your world as a collective and chosen by our world also in collective agreement. We perceive some individual contacts will be before 2012, and the individual contacts will begin initially in locations that will relate to some of the power centers on your planet. Some of them are well known and widely advertised, so to speak. Others haven't been revealed in a public way yet. Some haven't been discovered at all by human beings on the present timing of your planet. Some of these interactions will occur in a non-power location.

"Power centers" are very high vortexes of energy, windows for opportunity, in a sense, and they are what we also refer to as "power places." They are locations on your planet where the energy is such that it is like a window into other realities. These locations facilitate a person's ability to open up their awareness which allows them to then encounter and reconnect to more expansive ideas, and other worlds, and other forms of life expression.

Jefferson: Very good! So you are one of the societies that most likely will be one of the first to openly contact humans. That's exciting!

Ishuwa: That is the idea now. Open, public, and peaceful contact with Yahyel. There is already recognition of our presence that has been taking place. You had the "Phoenix Lights" in 1997 over Phoenix, Arizona, and over that region again as well in 2007. These visual contacts are currently documented on the Internet and YouTube.

There are many people who witnessed our presence in that form of presenting our presence into your world's consciousness. We feel, and you as a collective on your higher super-consciousness have felt, this type of visual contact is a way to begin making physical contact more comfortable. So the Phoenix Lights is one of the ways we are beginning to present the reality into your consciousness, that yes, you have Earth brothers and sisters that have gone out into space and are now finding their way back for a homecoming with you.

Jefferson: That's nice to know! So you're saying that the Phoenix Lights sighting, the mile-wide spacecraft that appeared over Phoenix, is a part of the Yahyel family. They actually came from your planet?

Ishuwa: Primarily, although there were other extraterrestrial beings on that craft, and again, that craft isn't the only type of craft we have. We actually don't even need a craft, but it does allow for other forms of life, a vast variety of forms of life, to co-exist in a space together and at the same time be in a form that can be presented to Earth humans so you there can observe it. The craft used is of a form, and shape, and appearance, and material that makes it more conducive for all of us who were on it to be present on it and at the same time have a blended experience together. In that sense, the ship is a facilitator for all of us to be able to have some type of togetherness in the same moment.

Jefferson: Very well. It has been a very enriching day and now it's time to go. Are there any parting thoughts or anything else you would like to tell us?

Ishuwa: Yes! Tomorrow we will be with you again!

Jefferson: Fantastic! I have only one thing to tell you!

Ishuwa: Yes?

Jefferson: Yah oohm!

Ishuwa: Yah oohm!

Jefferson: Yes!

Ishuwa: Thank you for sharing with us a form of language that is rich in our experience. Yah oohm. Be in joy. We share with you in your language! Great joy! Much love dear one! Until we are together in this way again, over and out!

Jefferson: Fantastic! Thank you! Say hello to the clouds!

Ishuwa: Yes! They are listening!

Jefferson: Very good! Bye Ishuwa. Thank you for coming again!

Chapter 7

Earth, 2012, and the end of the ET Quarantine

"The Creatorship is within you, and the ability to recognize that must come from within you." – Ishuwa

August 18th, 2009

Ishuwa: How are you this afternoon of your time?

Jefferson: Pleased to have the opportunity to interact with you again!

Ishuwa: Thank you! It's always a delight to blend, to interact, to share in this way that can be enriching for those who are taking part today and those who perhaps will have the opportunity to share in this information and these energies at some point in the future as you all create your perception of the future to exist. How would you like to move forward this day of your time?

Jefferson: Do you think that as we evolve and know ourselves more, we will start leaving aside prejudices, judgments and belief systems that are based on lack that prevent us from creating abundance on personal levels and as a society?

Ishuwa: Yes! They will be not a part of your function, your vibration, your awareness. They will be extinct, in that sense, completely.

Jefferson: Not because we are trying to exclude anything but because we are including a different way of approaching life, right?

Ishuwa: Yes, the idea is that you choose a different frequency. You know the choice is available. It is the one you realize you prefer. Therefore you choose it. You prefer it. You prefer to be more the frequency that is more in resonance with your actual state of being. When you have the realization that there really are choices you can make that really are more enjoyable, you thus then will find ways to be in that frequency, to be in that experience, to create that type of reality for yourself.

Jefferson: On that same note then, ascension would be a process of including everything rather than excluding whatever doesn't serve. In other words, you don't put fear aside, you include it and through understanding it you can manage yourself.

Ishuwa: You do not have fear the more you realize who you are. Fear is an illusory experience, a misperception of your actual nature. So you are not then putting it aside, you simply are allowing yourself to be free from creating the misperception of fear, the illusion of fear.

Jefferson: Very good! Now let me ask something else. Do individuals in your society fly spaceships freely on their own or is it more like in our world where we must first take classes to learn how to fly a plane that we then are only allowed to fly under the supervision of governing agencies?

Ishuwa: We do not have that type of structure. We do not have that type of a governing body that tells us what we can and cannot do. We all interact together. We are all self-governing and that then allows us to co-exist in a way in which there appears to be a governorship taking place, but there is no body of legislators, in that sense, who are making decisions for our people, for our society.

We do not need to be told or reminded what is or is not okay, what can or cannot be done. We do not get out of line with the laws of Existence, the Four Laws of Creation. We are very much in tune with who we actually are, thus then these universal Laws and the internal heart guidance mechanisms are, in a sense, an automatic, pleasurable, self-governing system. We only need to be in tune with our heart, which is something that occurs automatically for us. We have been aware of these ideas for so long, for so many generations, and they are something that we are born with and operate with at a very young age. Do you follow this idea? Do you understand my response to your question clearly?

Jefferson: I think so.

Ishuwa: Do you think so or are you clear about the answer? Is there something more I could add that might clear something up around that idea?

Jefferson: Yes there is. In your world, are spacecrafts available for everybody that wants to pilot one?

Ishuwa: Well, we don't have very many crafts that are of a metallic structure.

Jefferson: Oh.

Ishuwa: Some people on your world have experimented with flying saucers that are made of particular types of physical material. We don't operate with ships generally of that structural matter or that energetic density, but we have at times. Certainly the "Phoenix Lights" is an example of such a craft. There are very few of those, and we use those types of crafts primarily so that other races, extraterrestrial beings, can come on to one ship and we can then all have a shared experience in a ship.
 One of the primary reasons for having a craft like that one is so we can function as a host for extraterrestrial races to join us and have a shared experience observing and learning about other societies such as your own world, such as we were doing over Phoenix in those experiences in 1997 and 2007. Those events have received a great deal of notice relative to the amount of notice that is generally received by sightings of crafts in the sky.

There are a few crafts that are close to a metallic structure, very few. It isn't the kind of ship that everyone in our society has a desire to get in and, in a sense, captain and be at the command modules.

As for the idea of being able to move about from one planet to another, to have that type of ship, a relationship, is something we all can do generally after the age of three or four years.

Jefferson: So all you need is to desire it and then you can have it? It's not like you have to pay somebody and go to a class and study for a certain length of time on how to pilot it?

Ishuwa: It isn't so much about piloting it. It is more about us just changing our focus of frequency and then being in that other place. Again, it goes back to the idea of formulas. Every formula has a particular experiential expression and so we are able to alternate the formulas of conscious reality that we are focusing on in any given moment. This allows us to go from one point, one formula, to another point, to what seems to be another location, to another place which is another formula, another sound frequency. It is another vibrational reality in that sense.

Jefferson: Okay.

Ishuwa: So we don't have several crafts. We simply are able to focus on one point of experience and go to another point of experience and then experience that reality that we choose to focus on. It would appear to be like we have a time travel machine. But that isn't what we are actually doing.

Jefferson: I see.

Ishuwa: These are ideas, and functions, and forms of travel that you are all moving towards in time in your world. We perceive them as a primary focus and momentum that your society is heading towards. You will all be able, those who desire, those who are of interest in this, will begin being able to do this. For you all can. It's just a matter for the collective consciousness to begin to allow these ideas to trickle back in, to reconnect back into your awareness thus then you can remember how to do it. This is something that will take well over one-hundred years in our perception of your society's current progress before the majority on your planet would be able to do such form of travel.

Jefferson: Well, you said we will remember how to do it. Were you referring back to the time of Atlantis where technology was —

Ishuwa: This was not a form of travel at that time in our observation of your Atlantean periods. They did have crafts. They were able to move about somewhat like you are able to do today with helicopters and your airplanes, but they had slightly different technologies, slightly different shapes of crafts, and sizes, and colorations, and seating patterns within the structure of the craft. But the idea being then that they had an external ship that they would enter and were able then to move from one location on your planet to another location on your planet.

Jefferson: And were those ships run by fuel or —

Ishuwa: There was an external fuel source, yes. It wasn't tapped into the idea of "free energy" in that sense. They were close to that. They were experimenting with some of those ideas, but again, they hadn't reached a level of spiritual soul connectivity or maturity to actually make the necessary jump into utilizing those types of free energy technologies. They couldn't access these technologies appropriately in a way that would allow them to be successful using them. There were attempts or experiments made to utilize crafts that can move about in a free energy fuel sourcing, but they weren't successful because their soul level and their understanding and maturity of who they were hadn't reached the height that would allow for supporting the connection to the frequency of free energy. So those experiments were met with a sense of collapse and failure. The experiments didn't succeed in the ways they had hoped they would.

Jefferson: Is it appropriate to say then that technology will only go as far as the society's mental development, spiritual blossoming, and level of consciousness?

Ishuwa: Those are important components, yes.

Jefferson: It can go far but then it would not be self-sustaining if the society does not have a particular allowing level of consciousness?

Ishuwa: Allowing in the sense of allowing them to be more connected to their expansive nature.

Jefferson: Yes!

Ishuwa: Allowing their truer nature to come through in their aware state and in their feeling state. It's crucial to be accepting of these components that exist deep within you rather than repressing those beautiful understandings and hiding from them and treating them like they were an alien aspect of your psyches. It's vital for the truer understandings to be able to flow and fly freely within the structural frequencies of your physical reality.

Jefferson: Yes.

Ishuwa: When a person is at a frequency of allowing the free flowing expressing of who they are, they do not encounter obstacles. So they are able to fly about more freely, more effortlessly, not only in terms of their feelings and their ideas and inspirations that come into their aware state of being, but also in terms of the way they move their body about and travel from one location to another.

Jefferson: Okay. In regards to having public and peaceful contact here on Earth with you or any other humans that live on other planets, is there some kind regulating mechanism such as the Christ Consciousness that automatically regulates who and what can come here to visit us, or is Earth open to whoever wants to come here and make physical contact with us?

Ishuwa: The frequency of the planet at any given point in your perception of history will have a unique vibration and that vibration then will determine what it is open to receive, what types of crafts, what types of races, what types of extraterrestrials, what types of other life forms that are then able to resonate and come forth and be a part of that blending, be a part of that physical reality sharing and experience. Do you follow that idea?

Jefferson: I do!

Ishuwa: Thank you!

Jefferson: Given the current level of consciousness of humanity, it may be a good question at this point to ask you, are there extra-terrestrial beings that are negatively oriented that are walking among us and within Earth?

Ishuwa: There are some that don't necessarily have your best interest involved, but to their perception it is not a negative act that they are involved in. Negativity can simply be a point of view. What is negative for one person can be positive to another person in that sense. So they aren't necessarily trying to be negative to you, and they are, in that sense, not being negative. They are simply going about putting together experiences for them selves that they feel will be positive and uplifting for them but that exclude you for the most part in terms of what it is they are after, what it is their actions are up to.

Jefferson: I see, okay. I would think that the vibrations we have created on Earth of greed, corruption, misuse of power, warfare, and destruction must have sent out a signal that would create a doorway through which these types of societies could enter.

Ishuwa: Any such societies that would be focused on those ideas of warring would have a very limited ability in terms of interspatial or interplanetary travel capability. They would generally be restricted to metallic craft, incapable of moving from location to location in their heart body, their light body.

Jefferson: How so?

Ishuwa: Well, they would not be able to move through the higher frequencies of effortless flow that are a requirement to be in resonance with consciously in order to be able to become aware of the understandings that would allow them to simply move from one planet to another without the use of a craft. They wouldn't be able to simply tune in to a location and suddenly manifest in the new location they chose to tune in to. Societies of a warring mentality wouldn't be able to access the necessary levels of higher frequency to do that. Traveling without the use of metallic crafts requires that the person be in a higher frequency, a higher fluidity, a higher effortlessness, and be more in the flow of the actual nature of Existence.

There are, in a sense, some barriers that are almost natural within the nature of Existence and its physical structure. They are like a wall of conscious understanding, and they present a barrier to those who haven't achieved a high enough level of understanding of their actual nature. The only way to get through such a conscious barrier is to expand the individual's sense of who they are. When they do that sufficiently, they will be able to move through that wall, that barrier, as though it never existed in the first place.

Jefferson: Okay. And any types that didn't have our best interest in mind, do they have to remain hidden from us when they visit Earth?

Ishuwa: Not necessarily, but again, we are talking about a very few number of individuals. There are enough of you that can focus in ways on positive light and on things you actually prefer, such as following your heart, so that those few will then have no ability to influence you, nor will the media, nor will the educational systems that are of great influence at the present time in your society's method of determining what is or is not real, what is or is not possible.

There are many people who look to the media and TV to determine what is real or not, what can actually occur or what cannot occur. They, in that sense, have not learned to look within their own self to determine what is and what is not possible for them and for others. They have yet to realize they can look within and develop communities that support their dreams. They are still looking outside themselves to the media and the institutions of education and then allowing those resources to tell them what and who they are and what is or is not possible in life.

Jefferson: Some people have said that there is a society of beings called the Reptilians who represent a negative race and that they are biased towards negativity and —

Ishuwa: Can you define the Reptilians please?

Jefferson: Reptilians are a particular race of extraterrestrial beings that look somewhat like a reptile.

Ishuwa: Could you give me an example?

Jefferson: A humanoid that's mixed with a snake-like structure or something like that. Is there such a thing?

Ishuwa: So a human that has a snake's head? Is that the idea?

Jefferson: Not necessarily a snake's head, but it's a form of life that has mixed DNA and therefore it has some attributes that make me think of reptiles.

Ishuwa: Humans have within the physical structure of their brain some base functioning elements that can tune in to the idea of fear for the sake of causing you to escape when there is danger.

There was a time when your physical bodies were very out of step with the nature of your physical environment. So there was built into your biology a system you might call a fight-or-flight response that would function in a way that an individual could either fight to protect itself or run to find cover when real physical danger was present, such as a large hungry animal. This component still exists in your biology today.

In most humans, this fight-or-flight system can be activated when the danger is real and when a person just imagines the danger to be real, such as fear of abandonment, fear of not being good enough.

It is possible to manipulate this mechanism in a way that causes people to perceive the need to either fight or run for protection when they are simply going about day to day tasks in the work place, or in a family interaction, or in an encounter with the unknown, or in a relationship, or in a new situation that they don't know yet how to handle. No large animals need to be present to activate the fight-or-flight action. The person only needs to believe he or she is threatened.

A person can unknowingly activate this mechanism and generate so much fear within their self, flood their thought process to such an extent that they lose sight of what's really going on in their situation and then act out in any number of disruptive ways. They can lose touch with their feelings and their heart.

Jefferson: Okay.

Ishuwa: When they feel threatened, they might hide and protect their self in some way, perhaps by not being honest with their self or with the others in the situation. They might get angry and fight, which is another form of trying to protect themself when they aren't aware of what is actually going on in a situation.

When the fight-or-flight response becomes activated, a person can't easily tune in and recognize that they are defining their self in that situation in a way that is not in alignment with who they actually are. They are only able to recognize the fear and discomfort coming from their biology's fight-or-flight processes. They will try to protect their self by using some type of psychological behavior, or they might actually leave the room or the house for a while, or they might get angry and get manipulative or fight.

This fight-or-flight mechanism can be considered a reptilian quality from the reptilian part of the human brain, but it doesn't mean that you all have to be influenced through this mechanism by another society that may be more aware of it and therefore know how to utilize it and manipulate you if you're not aware of how to use it properly. There are those that you may be referring to as Reptilians who are perhaps more inclined to use this humanoid component to influence you. They have it too in their biology. You can learn more about it and also learn how to not be influenced through it.

There may be some beings that are manipulating your society or influencing people through the mechanisms of fear that then cause many unaware people to be frightened by illusory ideas such as abandonment, loss, lack, depression, anger, or conflict. But this can only occur because so many of you aren't tuned in to it, aren't aware of this mechanism of functioning that can take place within you. It can therefore be like an alien creature, an alien concept within your psyche.

Understand that there are so many people who aren't aware of this component within their biology. They aren't aware of this fight-or-flight mechanism that can be activated in the simplest of social situations. There doesn't need to be bombs going off on your world. There doesn't need to be people confronting each other with their nostrils flared and fists clenched in order to activate this fight-or-flight mechanism. It's very subtle, and it can become activated due to the slightest of nuances of social, mental, and emotional interaction.

This component is like an alien component within a human's psyche if they aren't aware of its existence. Choosing to remain unaware of this part of the human brain can be like having an alien that they are hiding from, an alien component within themself that they have been repressing.

Until people come to terms with this alien within themself and recognize it, it remains possible for those few extraterrestrial aliens who do understand it to continue activating it in people to influence and manipulate them. They will continue creating more fear based ideas like separation and limitation, and the need to build a nest egg, and the need to work to maintain a sense of physical health, and the need to respect some Creator that supposedly exists somewhere up in the heavens so they don't garner its dislike and get lashed at by it in a fire and brimstonian way.

Jefferson: Okay.

Ishuwa: That is something that is important for people to recognize the existence of. One of the ways to do that is to start recognizing more of who they actually are and more of the nature of their actual existence. This recognition will also provide them with the ability to determine what is real and what is not real for themself. They will stop looking outward and allowing their definitions about the nature of reality to be determined for them solely by what the media tells them, what the news tells them, what their professors tell them, what their doctors tell them, what their teachers tell them, and so on and so forth.

People getting in touch with their internal ability to determine what is or what isn't real for them is important. So is recognizing that there may still be living within them an alien component of their own making that is within their psyche. When they get in touch with it, they will begin to free themselves from external influences that any supposedly negative extraterrestrials may be interjecting upon them or your society.

Jefferson: Yes. Some of our biologists have said that when we are in the fight-or-flight mode we shut down the immune system to such an extent that it can cause a person to age faster than they would otherwise.

Ishuwa: And one idea we would like to add to that is if you believe you have an immune system that can be shut off or turned on, we suggest that you explore the idea in which you connect to this immune system and you develop the ability to determine within your own self whether or not it is turned on or turned off in any given circumstance or situation that you are creating for yourself. Approach it this way rather than the idea of only looking to what biologists, or scientists, or doctors, or news anchormen are telling you. Do you understand that idea?

Jefferson: I do! Thank you Ishuwa. Can you name the societies that are here on Earth at this time which are not invited and are acting on self-interest?

Ishuwa: That is not something we are able to do at this time.

Jefferson: Because?

Ishuwa: There are too many overlapping layering realities involved between your society, and their society, and our society, and a few others as well. Thus then you might say there is a little bit of extra sensitivity around these matters, and so by not getting into and talking about them from our perspective it allows us to simply remain removed in a way that we know will bring about the desired uplifting results that we prefer in that way by not engaging in the riffraff.

Jefferson: Oh.

Ishuwa: We don't get pulled down into it.

Jefferson: I see. It makes sense. Okay, maybe we should do that more too. What about this idea that 2012 represents a threshold of energy and also the end of the ET Quarantine in which ETs will then be allowed to land in public if they want to?

Ishuwa: There are many energetic opportunities, many windows for uplifting change opening up. The time has already begun. There are many years yet to go before this window, in a sense, becomes less supportive for making great changes in your perception of who you are and making great leaps into realizing more of who you actually are and what you are actually capable of doing.

There have been many years leading up to 2012 and there will be some years after that demarcation point on your calendars in which this window of inviting and supportive consciousness changing opportunities exist for your world.

One idea regarding 12-21-2012 that the collective Association of Worlds has made a decision about, an agreement on, is that on that date from our perspective it would be okay to make public contact with those on your world. It is a day that we chose for our own reasons, and it also ties in with similar and many reasons that have been written about and spoken about in your Earth human histories. So from our perspective, we felt this date coincided with some of those ideas positively enough for it to be a good date to choose and we also are taking into account your world's perception of your own world.

There are some other ideas that will relate to the 12-21-2012 date. But again, there are many things that are changing and expanding in your world and have been for several years and will continue to do so after that date as well. The idea then on that date for us is that we will be in agreement within our Association of Worlds that it is alright to make contact publicly with your world, peaceful contact, mutually beneficial interaction, mutually beneficial relationship, bonding and sharing taking place between your Earth humans and those in our Association of Worlds.

However, that doesn't mean it will begin taking place that day or the next day simply because we also take into consideration what is going on in your world's collective agreements and the laws that your world has in place. So as long as your world continues to have laws that say any contact with extraterrestrial life forms or substances is illegal, well then, we won't come down and put you into the place in which you could be arrested for having such contact.

Jefferson: Arrested?

Ishuwa: For there are laws in many of your society's countries that state just such a thing can happen to them. So then, only as those laws are changed to allow for the idea of possible contact in a way that will be open, and peaceful, and mutually beneficial between our worlds and yours, only when those laws become enacted will we then begin to make contact after the 2012, December 21st date.

You see...your world has to come up into this growth process and meet us half way. Your society has to begin stating within your legal systems that you are as a collective alright with this idea of open and peaceful contact because the legal systems play a major part in your idea of governing still. In time, even that will change as you all become more capable of self-governing in ways that allow you all to interact positively together without the need for a global governing body that has elements such as your congressmen and legislators seemingly telling you what you can or can't do. Does that give you a little more insight on the idea of the 2012, December 21st date?

Jefferson: It does, thanks. Was this quarantine put in place by someone that is sitting above the clouds to protect humans or is it just a collective agreement that exists within our vibrational state of being at a subconscious level?

Ishuwa: There are several agreements within the humans' collective consciousness on a level from which they aren't necessarily aware of making them. You could call it subconscious or super-consciousness levels.

The Association of Worlds made the decision from a very consciously aware and present state of mind to simply not encounter your world in a public way for a particular period of time, for several thousands of years, so that your world could find its way back into alignment with who you actually are without any interference, in a sense, from extraterrestrial worlds that otherwise might interact in a way that could perhaps influence the human's progress in coming to terms with itself, coming back home to welcome within its own understanding who it really is on its own terms, on its own two feet, so to speak, without having to have its hand held, so to speak.

Jefferson: If we had a more evolved society come down here and teach us, wouldn't we become dependent on them?

Ishuwa: The primary focus of Earth human consciousness was such that it was looking outside of itself for direction, looking outside of itself for its Creator, willing to die to please what it perceived to be a Creator outside of itself. When a person is thinking that their Creator is outside of their self, that person will do anything to please this supposed external Creator. They will even have human sacrifice to please this perceived external God.

If at any time, one of those from our world were to enter into your human conscious awareness in a physical way, that human being would immediately run up to the extraterrestrial thinking it was like a god, a god-like entity. This behavior was done with such great focus and energy by Earth humans so that there was in our perception no way we could be physically present if you were to ever return to the realization that you are your Creator. The Creatorship is within you, and the ability to recognize that must come from within you. So we had to step out of that physical reality experience so that we weren't present, so that you would forget about the idea that there might be an external god that would come down and save you, soothe you, comfort you, protect you, provide for you.

These are all things that you must do from within yourself. You are the one capable of creating the experiences that you choose. Any experience you have is only because you choose to have it, even if you aren't aware of choosing it. If you aren't aware that you are choosing the experiences that you are having, then you made the choice not to be aware that you are the one choosing to have these experiences. You are that powerful.

So, the quarantine was put into place primarily, but not only, but primarily so that Earth humans would forget the idea of looking to the heavens for ships, for extraterrestrials to come down and save them, to provide for them, to protect them. Do you follow that idea?

Jefferson: Okay, so this particular quarantine was put in place by the Association of Worlds.

Ishuwa: Yes.

Jefferson: Who runs the Association of Worlds?

Ishuwa: It is not run by anyone. It is a collective community of extra-terrestrial races in which they come together and share a common bond and a common understanding. They will share stories and experiences they have had in their worlds, and in their travels, and encounters with other forms of life. It is like a communion, a coming together, a very rich time, a very rich community.

We are all self-governing, thus then we know how to interact with other extraterrestrial races without the need to have codes, policies, and procedures of how to interact with one another. There are no laws really being made. The quarantine was simply an agreement that we all recognized would be of greatest benefit for the human race's development and ability to let go of the idea of the external god, the worship of idols, the worship of external beings, and have a chance then to begin connecting to ideas that would re-awaken them, remind them of their actual God Creatorship nature and ability. Do you follow that idea?

Jefferson: Yes, and does every planet have one representative or can anybody from any planet attend the day there is a meeting of the Association of Worlds?

Ishuwa: Anybody can go, primarily, basically, yes. There aren't any appointments or schedule books that have been put into place. If someone has the feeling that it will be of great joy and beneficial support for them to be there, then they will be there in one way or another. Perhaps not physically present, but they will be recognized energetically to be present if they are joining in from a telepathic mode, so to speak, as though it was a group conferencing taking place.

Jefferson: It seems there could be some races that might not agree with all of the things that the association agrees on. What would happen to these nations that would go against a decision?

Ishuwa: Well again, any of those would be of a very low frequency. The idea here is similar to what we spoke of before. They wouldn't be able to have any influence on our world because their ideas and the structures and frequencies of their thought patterns would be too heavy and wouldn't enter into our function of awareness, wouldn't have any impact in that sense. It is as though there is an automatic deflection that takes place. It simply bounces off. It doesn't encounter us.

Jefferson: And those extraterrestrials who break through the quarantine and secretly land somewhere on planet Earth, are they on their own here and have to face the consequences of their actions?

Ishuwa: There are those who aren't of a resonance of understanding that we have. So they are, again as we have suggested, of a lower frequency of understanding, a heavier density, and they aren't, in that sense, getting through the quarantine. It isn't necessary for them to get through because they were already with you and are a part of the reason that humans perceive themselves to be separate in the first place. They are part and parcel of the experiences that took place, the disconnect, the "fall from grace," so to speak, in the first place. They have a part to play in the reconnection, in the re-awakening.

The re-awakening won't occur just for Earth humans. We perceive it will occur for these lower frequency extraterrestrials as well. There is an opportunity that they too will begin to let go of the ideas of dark or less expansive understandings and the ideas of limitation and manipulation and the control that they still fancy and are attracted to. The awakening can be a win-win, in that sense, for them as well. Even if they are interacting with your world, perhaps hidden from your perspective, hidden from your day to day observations, but present perhaps nonetheless.

Do you follow that idea? They didn't get through the quarantine. They are, in a sense, a part of the original reason you are all living in a world of separation and limitation to begin with.

Jefferson: Yes, I understand, thank you Ishuwa! Have you ever been a translator in the Association of Worlds?

Ishuwa: Yes! That is a great joy to have that opportunity! I am one, but not the only one there. When I do translate there, I enjoy it immensely!

Jefferson: How does it feel? What does it look like? I imagine there must be many people there. Do they all look different? Do any of the life forms that attend have an appearance that scares you if you've never seen them before?

Ishuwa: Well again, we have shared with you the idea that we don't experience fear. From our perception of your world's definition of scared, scared is a component of fear. Since we don't have fear, we will not be scared. Do you follow that idea?

Jefferson: Yes.

Ishuwa: We simply will see a physical shape that may be completely different from anything we have ever had the joyful experience of observing before, and we take great joy in having that moment. We acknowledge it, and we will telepathically in one way or another send acknowledgement to that being, send our sense of rich appreciation for their presence and let them know that we have never encountered such a life form before and that it is quite new and exciting for us, simply their appearance. They will be able to recognize and hear our acknowledgement, our granting of appreciating for their presence, and this will be something they can recognize in a way that enriches their experience!

Jefferson: I felt that there was great excitement in your voice when I asked if you have ever participated as a translator. How do you receive notice asking you if you can come today or within a month to one of these huge meetings and be the official translator? How do you receive that note?

Ishuwa: It's kind of like, "there's going to be a meeting and here are some of the ideas that might be focused on." I get a sense what those topics will be and how I feel about them. It's as though someone was talking to me, but it simply is information that begins flowing through my sense of awareness. In a sense, it's as though the middleman doesn't exist. There is nobody getting on the phone and calling me and telling me, "Hey, we are going to have this meeting." Nobody is sending me an email and letting me know, "We're planning to have this meeting." I simply begin feeling it.

There are those of us who get an idea that they would like to share something of value in that forum, in that community, in that fashion, with others, and that idea gets transmitted out. As others begin to hear it, if they feel like it is going to be something they want to be a part of, they will respond energetically, emotionally, telepathically, through thought and through feeling and even through other forms of communication unknown to your perception at this time. As more people respond in this way, the energy can build and build and it becomes in this way an event that simply will then take place at the appropriate timing.

Jefferson: Is there an official place where it happens?

Ishuwa: Not an official place. There are times when it will occur on a craft even such as the one that we had over the Phoenix area in 1997 and 2007. However, it can occur where everyone involved is not physically present with anyone else that is involved. That is a possibility, and that does occur at times as well. There are other locations, other planets' surfaces that it can and has occurred at as well. It tends to be spontaneous or organic in that sense.

Jefferson: How long are these meetings?

Ishuwa: They occur over a period of time that allows for everyone to share what it is they wanted to have shared and to experience the excitement they sensed that attracted them to this event in the first place. There are those that come and go at different timings, as you perceive time. So it isn't a requirement to come at the beginning and to stay until the end. There is an internal knowing of when to show up. When you've experienced what it is you felt would be most exciting to experience of others sharing, when you've shared what you felt others would be most benefited by, then you go. It's a simple knowing, a very simple and delicate knowing that is perhaps subtle in your perceptions of your life today, but you have the ability to begin functioning in this way as well. The more you choose to do so, the stronger this way of functioning grows for you and then the easier it is to recognize these forms of making decisions and following your heart's path.

Jefferson: What is the longest one you participated in?

Ishuwa: From your perspective it would have been a few months of your timing, but to me it occurred in the blink of an eye. It was so exciting and fascinating for me. It was as though it occurred in a time of no time at all. It was over before it started, in a sense, and yet the experience lasts for me a lifetime.

Jefferson: Have you ever been invited to attend such a meeting to translate a language that you hadn't learned yet so you had to learn that language before the time the meeting actually happened?

Ishuwa: Yes, thank you for the question. That has occurred on a few occasions. On one occasion, I knew before I attended, but there have been other occasions when I arrived without knowing that would occur. So it was a complete surprise for me on those occasions. We thank you for the question!

Jefferson: Yes! That story was very exciting! Okay, it's time to say thank you very much for this interaction together today. Is there anything else you would like to say?

Ishuwa: We have been delighted to have the opportunity once again to share and interact with you in this fashion! We are bringing forth energies in a way to support the collective idea that the information thus then will end up in a format, a book or otherwise, that those there in your world who would be interested in it will have the opportunity to read it and to take in this information and to grow from it in ways that will be most enlightening for them, most supportive for them!

Jefferson: Thank you! I am enjoying this so much!

Ishuwa: Thank you for being a part of this idea! Your participation is greatly appreciated, recognized, and acknowledged in many ways, more ways than just in this fashion that we are doing now.

Jefferson: Very kind! Your participation is also a bliss for me and so is the participation of the channeler!

Ishuwa: We look forward to future interactions with you in this format with this intention in mind!

Jefferson: Me too. Yes!

Ishuwa: Is there something more before we go that you would like to share, or say, or ask about?

Jefferson: Well, what's your mother's name?

Ishuwa: She doesn't have a name in that sense.

Jefferson: She doesn't have a name!?

Ishuwa: I have no name for her in the way you use such names.

Jefferson: So when you see her, how do you communicate?

Ishuwa: You are referring to my biological mother in that sense?

Jefferson: Yes.

Ishuwa: Ask me again next time, and I will have a name for you that will perhaps make sense that can be translated in a way that will provide you with a name.

Jefferson: Good! Alright Ishuwa, thank you very much!

Ishuwa: I have a bond with her that goes deeper than that sense of a name.

Jefferson: I see. Can you bring her the next time we meet and perhaps have her share with us a few words?

Ishuwa: It is a possibility that may be.

Jefferson: Yes, let's see. Ask her how she feels about the idea.

Ishuwa: We will leave it up to you to ask about it at that timing.

Jefferson: Yes, good!

Ishuwa: Very well, great joy! Have a wonderful evening of your night experiencings, and if you will, get out a little bit this evening at some point and explore the North Pole region of your night sky.

Jefferson: Yes?

Ishuwa: If the clouds permit some visible sighting of it, then we suggest that could be a fun function for you even if only for a minute or two.

Jefferson: Okay, I will do that!

Ishuwa: Thank you! Much love! Much joy to you! Good day dear one!

Jefferson: Good day!

Chapter 8

Keys That Can Open You to Peaceful ET Contact

"We have always chosen to come forth in ways that your collective has agreed would be perhaps most appropriate in the process of re-awakening your society to their ancestors, their family, so to speak, their interstellar family." – Ishuwa

August 24th, 2009

Ishuwa: I say, how are you this afternoon of your time?

Jefferson: Very good! Thank you! How are you?

Ishuwa: Perfect! We are delighted to have this opportunity to share in this way with you again and create this third new reality and bring forth information that may be of use and service for some others in some way that they will explore and enjoy in that exploration and reveal unto themselves more ways in which they can share their heartfelt joys with others. As though the information could be like a catalyst for them simply from reading this information or hearing it. May they be reconnected to more understandings of who they are and then share it with others in ways that will uplift both them and those others that they are sharing it with!

How would you like to move forward together in this day of your time in this third new reality that we co-create together in this hour of your time?

Jefferson: Ishuwa, you just spoke about sharing. Why and how is someone attracted to reading a book such as this one that shares fascinating and uplifting information? Does it have to do with the thoughts that they are putting out?

Ishuwa: Well, there are the thoughts in combination with feelings as well as attitude and action. These are important aspects that combine as a more complete energy that a human transmits and gives off, in that sense. Thoughts are important, yes, but there are these other ingredients that round out the entire recipe, in that sense.

Jefferson: Can you tell me more about these ingredients?

Ishuwa: Your feelings, your thoughts, your actions! These are all expressions and energies that you are putting out, transmitting. Each is a little bit different unto itself from the others in terms of how you perceive them. They all form a whole melody, a song together, as though a thought is one instrument, a feeling is another instrument, actions — physical actions such as stepping, or moving your hand, or holding your hands together, or raising your arms up — all of these types of physical actions are also like an instrument. Prior belief systems that are a combination of thoughts and feelings are also like an instrument, a more complex type of instrument.

All of these instruments played together by you express particular "notes and songs" that are transmitted outward from your "human radio-transmitter," in a sense. You send out signals to the Youniverse, the Y, O, U, You-niverse. This allows the Youniverse to receive the most prominent, the most dominant, the strongest energy that you are putting off, the strongest song that you are playing, and it then will respond, in a sense, by bringing back to you in your physical world many opportunities, and items, and people. Thoughts come back into your mind and feelings come back into your emotional body. These are responses to what you put out. They are like an echo, in a sense, but they will also have a little bit of a change to them so they won't be an exact duplicate mirroring of what you thought you put out. There is a slight adjustment. They come back to you as though they were building blocks that you build with and manifest the physical reality you experience. They are a reflection of what you were sending out.

"What you put out is what you get back!" This is the 3rd Law of Creation. Whatever you perceive yourself to be receiving is a result of what you have put out, what you have transmitted.

So this then is a beginning of giving you a bit of an answer to your question. So how now, if at all, would you like to explore any of these ideas, any of these instruments more specifically?

Jefferson: At this point, I am observing that perseverance can be important in the sense that it will help me get what I am asking for. When I ask for something, it is always given if I am able to persevere and keep myself in the place of receiving rather than giving up or being distracted and moving on to something else. It's like sending out a boomerang. If I don't persevere, then by the time it makes its way back to me I am not there anymore to receive it. I will instead be focused on something else, and I may even start thinking, "Well, the things that I asked for haven't come to me so maybe it's because I don't create my own reality after all?" Do you agree?

Ishuwa: Persistence for what you want, having what you want be the strongest energy or the strongest "song" that you are playing outward, is important. Also, if someone believes that they don't create their reality and if that is the strongest "song" or energy that they are putting out, then because "what you put out is what you get back," they will get back thoughts, feelings, behaviors, attitudes, and opinions that will seem to confirm for them the idea that they don't create their reality, but the paradox is that they are then creating the experience of not being the one creating their reality. By sending out the idea that they don't create their reality, they get back a reality that seems to confirm for them that they don't create it. They are then actually creating the experience that they don't create their reality.

Jefferson: I see. So it can be like saying that the Universe works like a mirror.

Ishuwa: Yes, in a sense, a multi-dimensional mirror.

Jefferson: Very good! So Ishuwa, if I prefer to believe that the Universe doesn't help me or that is doesn't support me, then I will get back experiences that confirm that. And if I do that, I am using my free will. I am the one that's choosing to believe and thus then experience the idea that the Universe doesn't support me. I am being the Creator of what I experience. When will more people understand that they are the powerful Creator of their reality?

Ishuwa: In time more people will begin to recognize that they are powerful Creators. In the past, people have been taught, and their parents, and their parents, and their parents before them, and generations before them, were taught that they were not the Creator of their reality. So they have been constantly putting out that idea for a very long time, and they are thus constantly receiving experiences that confirm that strongest energy that they have been giving off, that idea that they are not the Creator. In time more people will begin to explore the idea that they are the Creator of their experiences and thus then they will begin getting back more experiences that let them know, yes, they are the ones doing it!

Jefferson: How about the idea that there are no victims anywhere and all experiences that people are living are those they have chosen, maybe not consciously, but still chosen from a different level of their consciousness where they saw some value in living a particular experience. Would someone choose to experience the idea of being a victim because they believed they would benefit from it by becoming a better or stronger person somehow?

Ishuwa: Somehow they were defining those choices as being the most pleasurable and least painful based on the belief system they had.

Jefferson: And if the pleasure outweighs the pain then they go for it?

Ishuwa: All choices are based on how they are currently defining pleasure and pain, and what pleasure and pain are isn't written in stone, in the sense that we don't all experience pleasure and pain in the same way. It is always something that can change.

As a person chooses to get more in touch with who they actually are and what it actually feels like to be in resonance with All That Is, unconditional love, loving all things and being loved by all things in each moment, as a person chooses to define their self as unconditional love and wants to experience more of what that pleasurable feeling feels like, the more then they will begin adjusting their belief system and how they define pleasure and pain. They will realize they can begin defining pleasure in ways that are more in alignment with their actual nature, their infinite divinity of ecstasy, and thus then they will also begin to realize that choices which involve experiencing pains such as discomfort, displeasure, and depression are completely unnecessary for them to consider choosing anymore. They will begin to enlarge the choices that they perceive are available to them in terms of what is pleasurable. As they expand the list of potential pleasurable experiences they can choose from, the more then they begin making choices that allow them to let go of pains and displeasure completely.

Jefferson: Regarding the idea that there are no victims —

Ishuwa: Anyone can create the perception of victimhood, but everything simply "is." Within All That Is, you can create a play, a drama within a family, or within a relationship, or within a human interaction and create the misperception of a victim, of an attacker and a victim, but these are simply characters that the people involved are choosing to create in that particular play for their own reasons.

Jefferson: Why do people decide to play the role of a victim?

Ishuwa: Each person's choices are made by a very unique set of beliefs, circumstances, and reasons and there are a multitude of reasons why people make such choices. If you want to understand why a person has chosen to play the role of a victim in a specific set of circumstances, then you can ask questions related to that person.

Jefferson: Yes, I see.

Ishuwa: The reason why anyone is choosing to experience being a victim will be unique to them, but at the core of their physical life experiences they will have a belief system in which they are defining that choice as being the most pleasurable and the least painful for them. Because you create your belief systems, you can change them.

When a person chooses to begin letting go of a belief that they are a victim and wants to move into more pleasurable experiences that are more in alignment with their actual state of being, then they can begin getting in touch with how they are defining their self in a way that is preventing them from making more pleasurable choices. When they get in touch with their old beliefs and recognize how they had been defining their self in limiting ways, then they will immediately begin letting those old beliefs go. It is almost an automatic system in which they become aware of old limiting beliefs and realize there are other more positive and pleasurable choices now available to them. They will automatically replace the old less pleasurable ideas and belief systems with the newly discovered ones, with more pleasurable definitions and beliefs about who they are and what is possible, what Existence is, and who is actually responsible for the experiences they are having.

Jefferson: Is that like saying that a person makes decisions based on what they believe will be the best for them?

Ishuwa: People make every decision based on what they perceive will be most pleasurable and least painful for them. That is the motivation behind every choice that everyone makes.

You have an inherent subconscious mechanism to experience more of your actual nature and less of that which is not in resonance with your actual nature. So it isn't so much to make choices to be a better person, it is simply to make choices that allow a person to experience that which is more in alignment with their actual nature in terms of what they believe their actual nature to be.

Jefferson: Okay. Bringing together the idea that there are no victims and then the idea that we are all powerful Creators, can a powerful Creator influence someone else's life and make that other person's life turn out to be negative or detrimental in some way?

Ishuwa: No one causes any other person's life to be any less than that other person chooses for it to be.

Jefferson: Thank you! This is what I wanted to clarify. Great, what a satisfying thing to hear! Awesome!

So let's continue. In our last interaction, you said something that was really thrilling to me, you suggested that I go outside my house at some point on that evening and look towards the North Pole region of the night sky because there could then be some fun function for me and —

Ishuwa: One moment.

Jefferson: Yes.

Ishuwa: The idea just spoken of previously.

Jefferson: Yes.

Ishuwa: You can, on the stage of human creation and playfulness, create the idea or experience that one person is causing another human's life to be somehow less than. You can create the idea or experience that one person is somehow bringing down another human and causing that other human to have a troublesome or less than desirable moment or life journey, but again, that is just an illusion. It is just a part of the drama of actors on a stage for their own reasons coming together to create the idea or experience that one person has power over another human and can somehow determine that other human's fate in such a way that the other human will have a good life if they obey but will be required to suffer in some way if they don't follow some person's wishes, desires, commands, and so on. Okay, back to the idea of the North Pole suggestion.

Jefferson: So yes, you suggested for me to go outside at some point on that night and look in the direction of the North Pole and that there might be some fun function for me. So I did. I went outside that night, and I witnessed a shooting star that was different. It was somehow closer to me, and it had a blue turquoise color to it, which is different from the shooting stars I have seen in the past. This was thrilling for me!

Was this sighting event activated by you and your friends or was it just you knowing ahead of time that a particular event would take place at a particular point in time?

Ishuwa: It's a combination of these ideas. We knew there was the potential for this in your atmosphere to take place and given that the possibility was very high we then suggested that you go there. Thus then with your energy present and your willingness to take part in something that would be a little bit different, with that energy added into the mix so to speak, it was more possible to manifest the experience that you observed take place.

There was intention coming through from yourself into the celestial objective bodies of life conscious beings that were floating over your atmosphere in that region, over the sky at that timing. They, in a sense, received your consciousness that were transmitting out there and, in a sense, they gave you an acknowledgement of your presence. It is fun for them to do that in that way. So that was something then that manifested, in that sense, in that manner.

The way that you saw the colorations of the shooting star were unusual in the night sky in that region. How you perceived it was something unique for you even though there may have been others out there in your city that were able to see it as well.

Jefferson: Were you involved in that in any way?

Ishuwa: We had our own intention, yes, to have some kind of an experience like that to come forth. Our intention mixed with yours and with those of the beings that live life in that form. They then expressed life in that way, as an object flying by in your night sky.

Jefferson: Can you tell me exactly what that thing that I saw was?

Ishuwa: It was a being of life, an inter-spatial life form, an organism. You have many of them living in the primarily non-gravitational region, primarily the first region outside of your Earth's atmosphere of gravity.

Jefferson: Okay.

Ishuwa: They generally float about on a field, on a sphere, that is just outside of Earth's main or primary gravitational field. They are able to bounce off of this field. At times, they come through it very slightly, very delicately and, in a sense, pierce the membrane of this frequency, and in doing so they light up the sky of the night which you are a participant of, not just visually, but consciously as well with your thoughts, and feelings, and observing. Usually they will have created such a trajectory of speed and momentum that they will then exit that membrane and come back out, thus exiting your visible field. They seem to you to thus then just disappear.

Most of the time, they don't fall to Earth. Usually they will, as we said, come back out and continue living but carrying with them the experience that they had at that moment of interacting with that form of your Earth's atmosphere and also with those who in a moments glimpse, in a flash, in a sudden almost blink of an eye moment, interacted with their consciousness, those humans who sighted them as that light, that streak of bright sharing, a blending of interaction, of energy, a form of existence, a consciousness. And so they are then a little bit different in how they experience themselves for having taken that journey. They are able to share their experiences with those other beings that tend to propagate just above this first atmosphere field, sphere, that is just outside of your Earth's primary gravitational field where they usually hang out, so to speak, It's where they propagate and flourish.

They have been filmed by your NASA space shuttle cameras, although it has not been identified exactly what they are. In some instances, the astronauts have spoken about sighting them, spoken with the individuals in mission control at NASA space center. These lighted beings and conversations about them were filmed and shown live on your national television screens and recorded by others who later put the footage onto your YouTube. The astronauts and those in NASA space center were asking each other what the images were. Both parties didn't understand what it was that they were seeing, and they didn't have a chance to, in a sense, cover up the images that were being broadcast live. But at the same time, because of the unique nature of these life forms, it didn't in any way raise any sense of concern or fright from those who were viewing it. For the life forms where expressing themselves in way that was in no way threatening.

They looked somewhat like microbial life forms floating about in the light Sun rays, almost like something seen under a microscope, very tiny and seemingly without any capability of causing any harm, and therefore they were not at all threatening to those who were viewing them.

Jefferson: It made me think of...somehow it reminded me of a dragon.

Ishuwa: How so? A dragon? Like something with a big fiery flame shooting out of its mouth?

Jefferson: No! It is like —

Ishuwa: That is too threatening?

Jefferson: Right!

Ishuwa: Describe, explain, share with us this idea. Like a dragon? How so?

Jefferson: No, not like that kind of dragon. Like a dragon expressed in the Chinese culture. It looks like a worm that is long and it doesn't really have wings. It's like —

Ishuwa: It looks like a what? A worm?

Jefferson: Yes, a worm, like a little squiggly line.

Ishuwa: A little squiggly line, a worm, with wings?

Jefferson: Without wings! It reminded me of a symbol of the Chinese dragon. Yeah. It is shaped something like a hose. That's what I saw. You described it before when you spoke about what the astronauts saw in space. It's like what you described. It is more like that, and then I have seen —

Ishuwa: One moment! One moment!

Jefferson: Yes.

Ishuwa: Can you share with us where you have been at the night sky and visualizing stars and seeing a bunch of worms with wings flying around? I'd like to go there and share that experience with you!

Jefferson: (Laughter). Yes. (More laughter).

Ishuwa: Please share! Where to go? When? Date and time please!

Jefferson: Okay, it was after the last time we spoke.

Ishuwa: We're just having some fun!

Jefferson: Yeah. I thought so. Fun! It was about 10:00 pm. I went to the Cal-Train here in Belmont, California, two blocks from my house.

Ishuwa: To view the North Star and the North Pole region of the sky?

Jefferson: Yes.

Ishuwa: Yes.

Jefferson: I stayed there for a while and kept looking at the night-sky, but I have to tell you that I was expecting you would at least give me a clue about your ship.

Ishuwa: A clue about our ship?

Jefferson: Yes. Show it! Blink it!

Ishuwa: Blink it?

Jefferson: Yeah. (Laughter). How does that work? What are some of the mechanisms necessary for a sighting to happen?

Ishuwa: Yes, one moment! Keep that thought, that question!

Jefferson: Yes!

Ishuwa: We would like to explore a little further the idea of the Chinese dragon with you, for we feel it is a little bit revealing in an unusual way.

Jefferson: Yes? Please enlighten me!

Ishuwa: How for you is it like a dragon?

Jefferson: It was more like a... I say a dragon and the Chinese dragon because it was long, and it was round just like a worm, and it made me remember the movies that I saw with those kind of dragons, and it made me remember as well pictures that I saw on the Internet of seeing these things that look like microbes on a microscope. Then I just connected all the ideas together, and I thought of talking about it with you.

Ishuwa: You saw microbes, but they were objects in space that you saw?

Jefferson: Yes.

Ishuwa: Okay, we follow, yes!

Jefferson: Okay.

Ishuwa: And the connection to the Chinese dragon for you is that it seems to be a little bit similar in appearance to what you viewed that night?

Jefferson: Yes! And then at the same time it was for me —

Ishuwa: How do you feel about the Chinese dragon symbol?

Jefferson: I find it to be very exciting! It may represent many things for many people, but for me it represents freedom and power. No, not power, it represents strength and freedom for me.

Ishuwa: Have you been to the Chinatown area in San Francisco that is near where you live?

Jefferson: Yes, I passed by!

Ishuwa: And have you stopped in for a little visit at any time?

Jefferson: Whenever I go to places like that, I have some memories of being sort of a...someone that works close to an emperor...as an advisor. It makes me remember these things for some reason. I have no idea why, but it is exciting. The Chinese culture for me...it's something that excites me. I don't know why.

Ishuwa: May we suggest an idea?

Jefferson: Yes!

Ishuwa: There are some awakenings available related to this idea, and they will have a greater opportunity to be unlocked and thus then enter your awareness in a way that we feel you will enjoy and find useful.

Jefferson: Oh yeah?

Ishuwa: If you will, have a few visitations to that Chinatown region. Visit one afternoon when you feel it might be rather busy with a lot of people and visit another time on an afternoon when you feel it might be not so busy. Perhaps the weekend might be more busy and during the week not so busy.

Jefferson: Okay.

Ishuwa: One visitation at each timing. Allow yourself to simply walk around for 15 to 25 minutes. If you feel drawn to something, explore it, perhaps to have a snack, to have a drink, to see some kind of clothing that is very connected to this culture and has a very strong deep connection. It could be some form of clothing. There is also the idea of food that is very strongly connected to this culture. Just a snack or a bite. It doesn't have to be a whole meal or anything of that sort. Perhaps a drink, a tea, a cup of tea. Something very light and easy.

Visit once in the afternoon, or it could be in the morning, or it could be in the evening. But the idea is to visit sometime when it is a little bit more light out, not so much late at night. More when there is light, daytime. Visit once when it is not so busy and once when it is perhaps quite busy. You can decide which you will take first, if you choose either.

Jefferson: Okay.

Ishuwa: The choice is yours to explore as you choose in your own timing. We may ask you at the next channeling or the next if you have had time or the interest to schedule such an outing of adventure.

Jefferson: Are you going to be there disguised as a Chinese person?

Ishuwa: We don't have that on our calendar, no. Our suggestion relates more to, as you were saying, a past life and the sensing of working with someone in some capacity. That is where it will be more of use for you.

Jefferson: Very good. So, Ishuwa, you said that the idea of the Chinese dragon could unlock something as it relates to my sighting, what are your thoughts about that particular symbol?

Ishuwa: It has many meanings. It has many origins. There are some species of extraterrestrials that resonate strongly with it from the place of their heart center, and they work to nourish your Earth. They have had some interaction with those people on your planet that would call themselves of Chinese origin. Thus then, this is one of the ways that symbol came into the Chinese culture and became, in a sense, a representation or a symbol for them. Not that it still carries the same understanding with people who acknowledge this symbol's presence in that culture today. It has changed a little bit over the generations. That was several thousands of years ago when the extraterrestrials had an opportunity to interact with those humans in that region. There are still a small number people today who carry with them this understanding, but for you to uncover that isn't what we are suggesting you try and do.

If you choose to explore the culture a little more and this symbol that has come into your awareness as a result of visualizing the "comet," it can help open up and pave the way a little bit for the next step of this adventure, however unusual it may seem to be for you. It will allow you to become more connected, to shine a light, to become more enlightened around the idea of that life and the energies of your Chinese heritage. We aren't suggesting you try and understand the origin of the symbol itself. It is a symbol that conveys a particular understanding and thus then with that frequency of understanding it can begin to open up within you some new doors, some new rooms of understanding and, if you will, libraries of experiencing in lifetimes you have had with a similar culture that can be useful for you in your present world and lifetime.

Jefferson: Very well. Thank you very much! I will take that to heart. There is no doubt within my being that I have had those interactions you mentioned in past lives, although, I have up to this point chosen not to be consciously aware of further details. I am focused on sharing knowledge in ways that inspire our collective and help our human race step up in consciousness. Whatever openings can help me bring back ideas that I have shared in the past is exciting for me. Thank you for the insights! Now Ishuwa, let me ask you this, what are the mechanisms or the intricacies that need to take place before this kind of comet or shooting star sighting can actually occur?

Ishuwa: There are atmospheric conditions of the planet you have your opportunity to live on. There is a particular region of the space, a spatial conscious region that your Earth was moving through that allows for a particular type of these light streaking beings to be more willing to, in a sense, dive into the atmosphere and to show off their existence in a streak of light. In a sense, it's kind of like the public events you have that are televised wherein someone unexpectedly takes their clothes off and goes streaking in front of the camera real quick and gets everybody's attention. It is, in a sense, a little bit like that. These beings or life forms suddenly go streaking into your atmosphere. They are like a light streaking presence. On the night you were watching, your Earth was in that region of spatial consciousness that made it more inviting for them and more probable that they could do it successfully because, in a sense, there wasn't anybody waiting for them at the end of the grandstands to take them off to security and start questioning them or give them a ticket or a fine for their behavior. They were able to more effortlessly enter and show off their streak of light and then exit and all was well in that sense.

So these are a couple of ideas that make it more inviting for it to take place. To understand how it can happen, it isn't that different from how you can open a door and enter a room where other people are talking and then if you choose to you can walk back out and close the door behind you. From those people's perception, you opened the door, looked in, they saw you, you exited and closed the door and they no longer see you. It is similar to that idea. It is just a different life form doing it in a different physical expressive way. Instead of a door in a room, it is coming out of the atmosphere of the night darkness into your light visible spectrum for your eyes to see it and then exiting as though they were, in a sense, closing the door and no longer visible to you.

Jefferson: Is there any danger for a race that would do that to be shot down or be intercepted or anything?

Ishuwa: This will not occur. Your world's physical mechanisms would not take that as a target, would not be able to target it. The technology isn't sufficient to be able to make that connection. It happens too quick, and the light beings aren't considered a threat from those who have weapons on your planet. People don't really understand the mechanisms of what is taking place to begin with, and they don't consider it to be a threat of any kind at this timing in your world's collective consciousness.

Jefferson: If I were to ask you to give us or give me the opportunity to see the metallic crafts that you have, what would have to happen on your end for that to take place?

Ishuwa: We would simply have to sell you a ticket through PayPal or something like that.

Jefferson: Okay, and then just schedule the time and take a seat, have some popcorn, relax, and enjoy the show?

Ishuwa: Yes. We'll just land on your 405-freeway, or the 101, or any other interstates and you can hop on and we'll go for a ride. It will be business as usual.

Jefferson: (Laughter).

Ishuwa: We understand you have expressed a desire to interact and contact us physically. What we would like you to consider doing is to take time, perhaps we have suggested this before, and really imagine having contact like that. Really go through it with as much detail as you possibly can come up with in your imagination. Make it very real as though it is really taking place, as though you do have a time appointment to meet us in a craft, landing, to come along and come aboard, you are meeting us, talking to us, interfacing with us face to face, body to body. Really imagine that.

See as many specific details as you possibly can. See our body moving with heart beating and our lungs in the chest breathing. See the veins that we have here and there protruding from our skin and pulsing from our heart's beating. See yourself in some way, see your own hands, see your own feet, see your own clothes that you would have on. Take note of how your breath rate is, how your heartbeat is. Is it normal? Are you breathing more quickly? Are your thoughts going in this direction or that direction? Are you calm? Are you a bit scattered or a bit unsure of what is taking place? What will happen next? Are you really going to ever come back? Are we going to return you? Do we really want to take you off into some experimental laboratory where you will never see your family again? What is going through your mind in those moments of actual contact?

Imagine as best as you can all of the details and the entire voyage whether it takes half-an-hour or five minutes. Try to imagine every detail as though it was really occurring. When we bring you back, imagine that too. When you exit, imagine as clearly as you can all the details as though it actually is happening to you. Then imagine going home. Look around your house and let the experience of what just happened blend in with the new reality you are thus beholden of. See your refrigerator, see your computer, see your couch. See out your window with this new understanding of the world that you have taken into your consciousness, taken into your bodily being, taken into your belief systems, taken into your biology and begin allowing it all to digest.

This encounter is a meal unlike any other you have had at this point in this lifetime. As you know, every meal you have takes some time to digest, to move through your digestive track and through your body's digestive systems to take down, to work through that meal, to take it in, to take into smaller quantities, to share it with other components of the biology, to bring about that food consciousness, to share it with the heart, to share it with the blood cells, to share it with the caloric cellular mechanisms of your body. Really allow for the experience of your encounter with us to be digested. Take it in. Drink it in. Allow it to be real for you. In this way, have the experience be real in your imagination. This will go a long way, if you do it, if you really go through it in great detail, it will go a long way in bringing forth your ability to have the meal for real, so to speak.

Jefferson: (Laughter).

Ishuwa: It will go a long way towards manifesting an experience of that nature with us for real. In the way you define real, for if you do it in your imagination, it really is just as real as if it was occurring in what you define as physical reality. The only distinction between the two is the distinction you have been taught and continue to create. The experiences you have in your imagination, in your mind, are every bit as real as what you experience in your physical day to day reality. You only have been taught to create the idea that there is a difference between the two and thus then you continue to experience there being a difference.

Often, if something is experienced only in the world you think is your imagination, you've been taught to create the idea that it isn't as important or as meaningful as the experiences you have in physical worlds. We understand this distinction that you have chosen to create as a collective. It is a very wonderful way to create two separate worlds, but the more you begin to allow yourself to recognize there really is no difference, you will more readily begin giving equal value to what you can more easily imagine at any given moment in your mind's eye, in your heart's world of playfulness, and then you won't be left out, you won't feel as though there is something missing that you haven't lived yet because you can more easily manifest it in the imagination of your heart and mind's eyes and really relish and enjoy those kinds of experiences and have a sense of them as being of equal importance to those you have in your physical world.

Your physical world is the result of your world's imaginations and "make believe." You have all chosen to imagine certain beliefs and to "put them out" together with such great strength and magnitude that they have "come back" as your physical world. Your make-believe system of belief systems has made those shared imaginations into a physical reality that seems real to you, but it is all the result of "make believe," your pretend and imagination.

So to expedite your physical contact with us, we suggest you explore with your imagination the idea that it has actually occurred and make it seem very real. Flesh it out, mock it up, give it lots of detail.

Jefferson: I think I understand that by doing this it will put down my part of going half way, in other words, it will bring my vibrational frequency or my energy signature closer to a point of resonating to yours so that then the particular experience of meeting in person can take place, right?

Ishuwa: Yes.

Jefferson: So, that would be my side, my going half way. Now, as a part of my curiosity here, what happens on your side then once I am done with this project of imagining meeting you? When I go through this, as I imagine, as I make it really real, as I resonate, and as I sort of lock into that frequency, what happens from your side, from your point of view?

Ishuwa: We are then able to begin coming closer to you in your physical world, in the physical contact sense.

Jefferson: When you say, "closer to me," does that mean in a way that other people would not necessarily be involved in the contact if they were not wanting to?

Ishuwa: Correct.

Jefferson: Creating a sort of vortex or a sort of reality in which something can take place without actually intruding on other people's free will?

Ishuwa: Yes!

Jefferson: I see. Very good! So give me something that can help me with my imagination. What does your craft look like or at least a craft that you would use for that end?

Ishuwa: Imagine a large triangle.

Jefferson: A triangle.

Ishuwa: A little bit of a deep purple.

Jefferson: Deep purple. Okay...triangle...deep purple...and do you have a beam of light that will make me float that nullifies gravity or do you have to land and open a door? How does it work on this particular craft?

Ishuwa: We would, in your case, allow you to have your imagination work with either idea that is most attractive to you, most pleasurable for you to imagine, to play with. You can explore both ideas and see which one feels most exciting to you. We will take note of whichever is most exciting to you from our perspective to the best of our ability to do so.

Jefferson: How big is this particular craft?

Ishuwa: It is approximately, in terms of this encounter, in terms of the idea in which you are asking about for there are different crafts we have, we would be suggesting you think of one that is approximately 55 feet by 55 feet from one point to a second point and then from that second point down to a third point. The shape we are referring to is an equilateral triangle.

Jefferson: Okay!

Ishuwa: Approximately 55 feet in length along each of the three sides. It has a very deep iridescent purple quality of color to it, and there will be a slight bit of white and an iridescent blue around the exterior of the sides emanating anywhere from one to three feet in a non-linear form. The light will not have a sharp edge, in that sense, it will have soft edges that will change quickly, fluctuate. Seen from a distance, this can create the appearance of a light blinking off and on, but it is just the flickering flare of the light against the craft's sharp lines creating the perspective of turning on and off. When you are in a close approximation visually, you can see what is actually taking place. There are no lights turning on and turning off. The lights are simply fluctuating in the output and the length of the flarings they send out, which can be from one to three feet.

This is similar to how the Sun has flares of light that adjust their lengths at any given moment. A short flare can suddenly change to a long flare, then to a medium flare, and back to a long flare, and again to a short flare and so on and so forth. The white and iridescent blue light shifts in this way too. If you see them, it can look like they are emanating from behind the craft. This type of craft that I am describing is what we generally will use for this particular function, for contact with one or two individuals.

Jefferson: And does it have a window?

Ishuwa: We don't have any glass windows on this particular craft, but we can create something that would allow us to look out that is like a window. It is not a form of glass like you use and call a window in your vehicles there on Earth, but it can serve as a similar structure to look out of.

Jefferson: And this is going to be sort of a metallic craft?

Ishuwa: It is not of a metal format that you are familiar with on your planet. You wouldn't find it in your chart of elements, if you understand the idea of chart of elements?

Jefferson: Yes. What element is it?

Ishuwa: It is one that we will not refer to at this time.

Jefferson: Okay, surprise then, good! I like surprises! So I wonder if this is a living craft or does someone actually have to pilot it.

Ishuwa: It is alive, in a sense, yes. It requires the conscious thoughts, and awareness, and feelings of a person in order to function. It is a co-crafting, a co-maneuvering, a co-piloting form of relationship that takes place.

Jefferson: And have you ever done some piloting of this particular craft? Do you know how to pilot it?

Ishuwa: I have done so at times, yes, but it isn't something I do very frequently.

Jefferson: So you would come and someone else would come with you?

Ishuwa: Quite possibly, yes!

Jefferson: Very good!

Ishuwa: There may be some others that would be more comforting for you to meet first. But that we won't talk about at this time.

Jefferson: Okay, another surprise, huh?

Ishuwa: Just to let you know.

Jefferson: Very good! Okay, I will keep that in mind. Now you said that the craft serves the purpose of hosting other races aboard and enjoying, in a sense, a relationship. How does this process take place? I mean, do you write their addresses down and then you go pick them up by parking the ship at their front door or can they simply teleport to the interior of the spaceship?

Ishuwa: There are those who have a teleportation-like system and arrangements are generally made through a telepathic mode of communication. Sometimes it can be scheduled through some forms of instruments, kind of like a computer that you have there?

Jefferson: Yes.

Ishuwa: There are those others who will simply begin to come into a particular region of the ship without the use of teleportation in the form of electronic technological shifting taking place. They come from an understanding of how to, in a sense, move through space and time. They understand the coordinates of this particular location within the craft. They focus on them and thus then materialize in the craft and usually we know in advance that they are coming. If we didn't, it's understood when they arrive that they are present. They will arrive generally at a time that is of greatest appropriate timing for them in their adventures that will also allow us to most beneficially enjoy their presence as well.

There is a mutual enjoyment factor involved that simply occurs with, and through, and from, our higher realms of beingness. It's a part of the mysterious realms of who we are that we simply honor and know is capable of bringing to us experiences of great joy without having to plan them all out in advance. We simply know that they will begin coming into our experience in the appropriate timing and so without any need for advanced planning.

Jefferson: So —

Ishuwa: When we have an idea to hover over a particular city such as we did in Phoenix, Arizona, on a couple of occasions in 2007 and 1997, it was something that was understood would be of value. The timing was appropriate. The consciousness on Earth as a collective had agreed to it, perhaps on a super-conscious level so not then thus aware of making these choices in their day to day awareness level.

As excitement for such an event begins to grow, other extra-terrestrial races that would also be excited to be onboard will simply become aware of the event within their own state of beingness and will thus then be there at the appropriate timing and appropriate day. They will be present on the craft to have the experience with your world and with all of the others who are in our craft as well, and they will contribute in some way to the whole experience.

Jefferson: Why did you only show a few lights of your spacecraft? Was this done to allow some people to believe and allow others to continue not believing in the idea that there are intelligent life forms from other planets? Was that your way of respecting people's free will and their individual process of re-awakening to the reality that you really do exist?

Ishuwa: We have always chosen to come forth in ways that your collective has agreed would be perhaps most appropriate in the process of re-awakening your society to their ancestors, their family, so to speak, their interstellar family.

Jefferson: Very good! So, Ishuwa, thank you very much! We are approaching the end of today's channeling. I remember the last time we were finishing our channeling and I asked you about your Mom. Could you at this point come up with a sound vibration that would come close to a way that you use to refer to your Mom?

Ishuwa: Yahh!

Jefferson: Yohch?

Ishuwa: Yahh!

Jefferson: How lovely, thanks. Very well Ishuwa. I appreciate that! Tell her she has a beautiful name. Perhaps you could conclude our communication today by sharing with us the place where you are?

Ishuwa: My present location?

Jefferson: Yes! There is always so much wonder and magic on the places you visit and this awakens my curiosity whenever we speak to find out more about where you are speaking from and what it may look like, feel like, and smell like.

Ishuwa: Oh, very well then! We have a table today that is made of a form of living tree. It has chosen this shape for reasons having to do with the water table on this ground where it has taken root. It mimics the flow of the stream that is just bellow it, and it is a rather flat surface and very smooth. We are able to sit at it as though it was a desk or location where we could set some objects on the top of it and our legs underneath it, as though we could pull a chair up to it, right beside the stream, very shallow, very thin flowing stream, more like a brook. A trickle of water.

This table-like tree extends about 12 to 14 feet from left to right. To the right is where its trunk comes up from the ground to a height of about two feet. Then it makes a sharp left turn and grows parallel to the ground surface for about 12 to 14 feet, as I said before. It goes over the narrow brook. Then it turns upwards towards the sky for approximately three more feet. It has very soft, very easily floating in the breeze leaves, very round green leaves with a bit of orange exterior border on the leaves. There is a very bright orange exterior border that goes around each of these round leaves. They aren't perfectly round. They are shaped a bit like a half of a heart, half of the typical symbol you have for a Valentine's heart, shaped a bit like half of one of those. At times in the breeze, two of these leaves will come together, in a sense, and visually appear like one whole Valentine's Day heart.

We also have here very rounded rock-like objects around us. They have a crystalline quality to them in that they can hold some energy, some consciousness, and they emanate a little bit of a message for us. They don't really talk to us, but they are about three-and-a-half feet in diameter. They aren't perfectly round in shape. They are soft on the exterior. There are several hundreds of them clumped together. They are very close together with a few even stacked on top of one another. They have a bit of crystalline quality to them, as we said. Their coloration is a bit of a pink, and blue, and a light purple.

Overhead we have bit of a, not quite a black sky, it has a bit of a tangerine in it, and it seems to be very close to us. It feels as though we could reach up and touch it, but it is a little bit too far to do that. It gives us a comforting sense, but it is actually high above us.

I am relaxing here, taking in the day, watching the leaves move about very easily in the breeze. There are a few others of us here off in the distance, in a sense, gallivanting around the countryside of some rolling hills that have a soft golden brown and green coloration. They rise up to about 50 feet in height and are very soft rolling hills. There are a couple of very sharp protrusions that come up about 1,000 feet in height that are made of a particular form of red granite-like material. These protrusions are somewhat like a monument, although natural to this location, and they serve as a marker for us as a place we come and frequent from time to time and visit.

Jefferson: Nice, and what planet is this?

Ishuwa: It is quite different from a planet, more like a moon.

Jefferson: Oh, so you are definitely not in the same place you were last time?

Ishuwa: Well, this is quite different from our last location. We like to explore different spaces —

Jefferson: Wonderful!

Ishuwa: And see how it changes, the interaction with you there.

Jefferson: Yes! Well, very good Ishuwa. I thank you very much for all that you are doing, for taking the time, traveling around, and sharing with us all these beautiful things! I sincerely thank you!

Ishuwa: Thank you! We also thank you for your presence, and interaction, and willingness to explore with us, to move out and to venture into the skies at night, to see these celestial beings as they streak across the night sky. We look forward to our next encounter of this form. This third new reality can continue to expand and grow and take on greater momentum and frequency that then the day can arrive when we have physical interaction effortlessly and comfortably. Much joy! Much love and appreciation! Until next time, "Ah yuha umka." {Ishuwa spoke a phrase in another language}.

Jefferson: That was a good one! Yah oohm for you! Thank you!

Ishuwa: Yah oohm!

Chapter 9

The Ego, the Heart, & Masters of Creationships

"The Youniverse works effortlessly within its ecstasy of being and you can experience that when you let it show you how, when you let your heart-mind show you how." – Ishuwa

September 2nd, 2009

Ishuwa: Very well! Once again with you in these blending moments together in this day of your time as you create this experience to exist and together we are able to co-create a third new reality in which we can experience those fascinating realms of the infinite Existence in ways that we choose, in the moments of our own timing. How are you?

Jefferson: It's lovely to speak to you again!

Ishuwa: Yes and you as well!

Jefferson: I am living in a world of perfection, experiencing life from within a human physical body. Oh, how delighted I am!

Ishuwa: Exciting for you! Thank you! We have an opportunity to share one idea with you before you begin asking questions in the fashion you have before.

Jefferson: Please!

Ishuwa: How are things going with the idea of visiting the Chinatown region?

Jefferson: How? Oh that's true...how is it going...I haven't had the opportunity to go there yet, but I will Ishuwa. I promise you!

Ishuwa: Very well. The dragon is coming very close!

Jefferson: Yes!

Ishuwa: At this timing, there are some interstellar planetary energies that are orbiting in a particular pattern, some of the solar system brothers and sisters, some of the planets, as they're often spoken of in your world's frame of reference, and this will be an opening and a very strong opportunity of illumination and ability for you to connect to this idea more strongly when you and if you choose again to venture off into that location in both of the ways that we suggested before.

Go once at a time of day when it is very busy and once at a time when perhaps there are only a few people there. It will be very soon, very shortly, that the planets, in this sense, will be more lined up or more in alignment to, in a sense, nurture, foster, and strengthen the ability for you to have more of an experience within your aware state of being and begin to pick up information more clearly and more readily.

If you do go there, we suggest you bring a piece of paper and a pen or perhaps something so you can record your voice, so you can record your experiences. Record those that may be a bit different from what you have had in your day to day life experiences. In this way, you will be able to bring back on paper or in a vocal recording information to review regarding what that took place for you there. Do you follow this idea?

Jefferson: So you are saying that there's going to be some sort of alignment. What consciousness is involved?

Ishuwa: You will discover more of that in the days ahead. It is related to the idea of the dragon that we spoke of with you previously that was, in a sense, something that you were attracted to for reasons that will become more apparent to you as you, if you, choose to make this adventure.

Jefferson: So the specific information that I will access or remember through this enlightening experience will become revealed to me as I go to and explore this area you speak of?

Ishuwa: You will be more successful with this since the alignment of certain planets is coming into place very shortly. So you might just ask yourself each morning or evening when you wake up or before you go to sleep, is today or tomorrow a good time to go into town, the China region of town, to explore the idea if only for a half-an-hour of your time. You do not need to be there more than a half-an-hour. Give yourself time each day to check-in this way to see if it's today or if it's the next day that would be best and most optimal for you to be in this place for this revelation, this reconnecting.

Jefferson: I see. It seems like it is something really big that is about to happen because it's worthy of your mentioning it.

Ishuwa: A dragon is very big would you not agree? A dragon flying through the sky is quite large. Those dragons can get very large. A big idea.

Jefferson: No, not the fiery winged dragon you mentioned. I meant this whole idea of Chinatown and these things that you brought up. Apparently it's something important because it is worthy of your mentioning it again. You came back to it without me bringing it up! Well, thank you!

Ishuwa: It is up to you to check-in and to be the one that makes the steps if it feels, when it feels, most optimal for your state of being. You also have to take into consideration the other daily activities that you have scheduled already.

Jefferson: Yes! I will find time! Let's start. Are you ready?

Ishuwa: Yes!

Jefferson: There is apparently a difference between what we feel and what we can create as far as mental concepts in our mind.

Ishuwa: The difference is only that which you create there to be in your perception.

Jefferson: Very good!

Ishuwa: So, back to the dragon. The idea of the dragon is a very large idea! Consider scheduling it into your day. Check-in everyday and see if it is appropriate to go out there that day, or the next day, or maybe even two days out into the future. Do this each day. It will only take less than a minute to check-in. You will feel it. You do not need to weigh the perceptions that come back to you when you ask these questions. It will be simple and apparent for you if it is appropriate. It will take less than a minute to do each day. You can do it in the morning or the evening.

Jefferson: Very good! Thank you so much Ishuwa!

Ishuwa: Regarding the idea about the difference between feelings and mental concepts in your mind?

Jefferson: Yes!

Ishuwa: Do you have a question around this idea?

Jefferson: Yes. Apparently there is a difference between things that we feel and thoughts that we can conceptualize in our mind. In other words, it seems that there is "us," the consciousness that feels within our body, and it seems there is another part of us that some people call the ego aspect of us that is the mental mind that can only conceptualize or relate to things that it has learned. Can you talk a little bit about these two different facets we have for expressing ourselves in this physical world? Talk about the ego and also about the feeling presence within us?

Ishuwa: Yes, thank you! A feeling is something that you create and the idea of thoughts is something you create as well. The difference between the two, you create that difference as well.

Jefferson: Okay.

Ishuwa: We thought this was the first part of your original question, and now it seems the question has changed a little bit.

Jefferson: Yeah.

Ishuwa: It has changed to more of the idea of the ego-mind and the higher-mind of your Creator self.

Jefferson: Yeah, what about that?

Ishuwa: In a sense, you have created a mind that comes from the heart, the heart-mind, and then there is the ego-mind.

Jefferson: Okay.

Ishuwa: These two can be spoken of more generally as the higher-mind and the physical-mind. That is, we can give this specific idea of the ego-mind a broader label. It can also be called the physical-mind, and the heart-mind can be called the higher-mind.

Jefferson: Okay.

Ishuwa: So now we have two labels for both ideas.

Jefferson: Right.

Ishuwa: The ego-mind thus then has been created by the heart-mind or the higher-mind. The heart-mind did this so you could have a specific kind of experience here on this planet, in this physical world.

The heart-mind isn't really in a physical state of expression, not really, but you can create the idea that it is.

The physical-mind or ego-mind has really been designed so you can experience the perception of physical worlds, physical objects. Because the physical world isn't your real state of being, the collective higher-mind or heart-mind of all of you has had to create many veils or filters with your belief systems that serve, in a sense, like costumes and forms of make-up on your face so you can play certain physical characters on this seemingly physical stage of your "Earthian play."

You create certain filters, which you do with definitions and beliefs, and because of the nature of Existence, "what you put out is what you get back," when you collectively "put out" these definitions and beliefs about a physical reality, you "get back" the idea of this physical world. You have even created the belief or "costume" that you have an ego-mind or physical-mind that allows you to perceive yourself as being separate from your source, separate from your heart-mind or higher-mind.

We want to share with you that nothing is actually detached from anything else. You are just creating these masks, these costumes, with your collective definitions and beliefs so you can have this particular kind of physical experience, this type of "play" here on Earth.

The idea of being detached from your higher-mind is one of the main focuses that has been explored for so long here on Earth. The physical-mind or ego-mind has been given the "reigns of power" for a number of generations, for thousands of years. In a sense, your society has given these reigns to your ego-mind by teaching it and telling it that it's the one in charge, that it's the one that knows how to make the decisions that are important for determining your happiness, and future well being, and what you will achieve in life. However, the physical-mind or the ego isn't really the one that's in charge. The higher-mind or heart-mind is the one that is more connected to your actual nature. It realizes the love of All That Is.

For so many generations, the ego-mind has supposedly been in charge. With it in charge, you have ventured off into realms of darkness, and separation, and limitation, and despair, and lack, for so long. You have now chosen as a collective to begin letting go of those ideas. Therefore, having the ego-mind in control is something that will not support your ability to come back into more of your aware state of wholeness. Having it in charge prevents you from realizing who you actually are, prevents you from experiencing more of the infinite and unlimited loving being that is your actual nature.

As the ego or ego-mind becomes more spoken about, more talked about, more written about and observed, it can become something you learn to let go of in the sense that you let it know that it isn't really in charge. It can let go of trying to control everything and it will not cease to exist. Because it is eternal, it will not die. It cannot be taken over.

In a sense, the ego has been taught to protect itself and the idea of survival is something that it feels is very important. It will protect itself, in other words, you will protect yourself when operating from the idea of your physical-mind, your ego-mind, because from it you can create the perception that you can be killed and thus terminated. For another example, with the ego-mind you can create the idea that you will go to some evil place such as a hell if you don't "follow proper procedures." Of course such concepts are just illusions that are part of the play of limitation and separation that the ego is very good at creating and playing within. The ego-mind has created so many filters, so many beliefs, so many masks, so many costumes. It has been like an amazing actor or an amazing actress and it has been doing a great job of pretend and "make-believe" for you.

Now it is time for the ego to start taking the old masks of illusory beliefs off, taking those layers of make-up off and letting the costumes drop so the "naked body," the naked mind of the heart-mind can be revealed once again. Eventually the "clothes" will begin coming off. People will become more comfortable walking around, in a sense, naked. What we mean by that is living with their heart open and being able to interact with other people's hearts simply, easily, and without any sense at all of threat, or provocation, or problematic experiences being brought into the person's daily life as a result of becoming more open hearted, more in tune with their actual natural state of beingness. This letting go can take some time. Each person will have their own way of letting go of their costumes, their make-ups, and their belief systems that are out of alignment with their actual nature. It will take each person time, their own time, in their own ways, to process and let go of the "old ideas."

Ideas of separation and limitation are primarily what we are referring to when we say, "old ideas." Ideas that you are "limited," that's an old idea. The idea that you are not the Creator of your reality, that's an old idea. We suggest people begin letting go of these old ideas, that they begin letting these "costumes" fall to the floor, that people become more "naked" and allow for the infinite and heartfelt ideas to become more their new clothing of choice.

The ego has served great purpose. The idea now is to allow that portion of your beingness, the ego, to more fully and more simply experience the ecstasy that you are, to be more naked on the stage of this worldly play and to be willing to allow others to be naked, to allow them to express their heart in their own unique ways. When you allow others to be "naked," they then will allow you to be "naked," to express your unique qualities. In allowing others to be naked, to be more true, to be more simple, and ecstatic, and playful, then you will by their perception be allowed to also be more playful, more naked, more effortlessly expressive of your true nature, and in doing that, the heart-mind will always know what is most appropriate for you to do next, what choices are most loving and feel the best to make and thus then will be the most purposeful and have the greatest sense of support and service. You will find that your world and your life will become more enlightened with what you prefer. Opportunities and synchronicities in your life will begin occurring more effortlessly, more fulfillingly, more spontaneously, more abundantly. The ego-mind will be able to thus then simply experience this joyful journey to a greater extent. It can just sit back and enjoy the ride and not feel it has to get in the way and start making tough mental choices. Having to make tough choices isn't the way of your actual nature. The Youniverse works effortlessly within its ecstasy of being and you can experience that when you let it show you how, when you let your heart-mind show you how.

The physical-mind or the ego-mind begins to realize it isn't going to die, it isn't going to go to hell, it isn't going to be sentenced to an eternal prison of pain by some exterior and all encompassing, all knowing, all powerful being. That "make believe" being is just an illusion that was created to support the idea of separation and limitation from your actual all encompassing, all creating, eternal, heart-mind nature.

As the ego-mind begins to explore the idea that it will not become extinct, that it will not suffer purgatory eternally when it begins to allow the loving sensations of the heart-mind to come forth to the forefront, when the ego-mind allows itself to become more naked, to become more "make-up free," then it will gradually begin to feel that it can act freely and breathe easily and not be labeled as an outcast, or a devil, or a devil worshiper, or some satanic type of individual, or a witch, or a crazy insane person. It will begin to recognize that the heart-mind knows the way that is of greatest eternal life and of greatest joy and it will then begin to just sit back and enjoy the experience of this physical life. It will let the heart-mind guide the way through your life's true joy filled life purpose.

These points of view that we have been sharing about your ego-mind and your heart-mind are, in a sense, just a drop in the bucket, just the tip of the iceberg of what we could be sharing on these ideas, but perhaps that is enough for this moment to answer you question.

Jefferson: Thank you! It seems to me that as more light or information starts coming to the body, the physical vehicle starts receiving more data and then old paradigms of limitation and separation are shattered.

Ishuwa: Yes, shifted, transmuted.

Jefferson: That's very interesting.

Ishuwa: You are all very interesting Creators.

Jefferson: Right, the masters of limitation?

Ishuwa: Well, you are masters of all that you create and when you create the idea of limitation to such a degree as you have in this world then yes, you are masters of limitation, but you are also the ones creating that mastership of limitation. Therefore you can create the mastership of revelation, and that's where your society is beginning to move as you all let go of the mastership of limitation and begin stepping back into the helm as the master of unlimited joyful creationships in your relationship with one another.

Jefferson: Yesterday as I was talking to a friend, an idea occurred to me that everybody actually has the potential to be either wonderful or horrible.

Ishuwa: They are just perceptions, opposite sides of the same coin, in a sense. Which do you prefer? Neither is better then the other as far as the y, o, u, Youniverse is concerned. They simply are experiences that you are choosing to create in that way. They are both valid. They are both in existence. They are both validated, in that sense, brought into existence by All That Is, the Universe. Being brought into existence is the indication they are valid. They are validated. They are of equal value. Neither one of them is more valuable to the Youniverse than the other.

A person can, in a sense, step out from this eternal understanding of Existence and create the illusion or misperception that one is more valuable or more worthy than the other. Which do you prefer? You have the choice. You create them both. Which one do you prefer to create more of? It is your choice!

Jefferson: Perhaps expansion of our awareness happens when we are experiencing contrasts in life. I can give birth to new ideas that make me want to experience something more even if this more for me means going more into darkness or more into light. By living with contrasting experiences, I feel I am able to come into more of an understanding of that which I do prefer.

Ishuwa: Yes, after living the contrasting experience.

Jefferson: Yes, alright. So Ishuwa, what was the last planet you have been at?

Ishuwa: Rorkin.

Jefferson: Okay. Is that near you house?

Ishuwa: No. It's quite far actually.

Jefferson: And what did you go there for?

Ishuwa: We had an adventure. There is a society there that was beginning to come into contact with our world. So we felt it was time to acknowledge that. We had a sense that the resonance of vibration was of a good frequency, that they would be ready. They seemed to know that we existed. They didn't question it at all. They were, in that way, very in tune with the idea that there was a world such as ours, a society of human extraterrestrials such as us that could communicate with them, that could visit them.

Because they were so self-assured in their imaginative state of creative beingness, they transmitted out to us a signal that we received over quite a number of orbits of our planetary's timing around our Sun. We monitored it, and we felt it was time to go to Rorkin and visit. It was quite an occasion and quite an opening for them. It was a very celebratory experience. Celebrations of a very deep kind within their innermost being were expressed outwardly towards us, and we were able to express from our inward heartfelt state outward to them. It was a very warm embracing and sharing and there are some of us still there. Shortly, there may be an opportunity for some of them to come and visit us on our world but that wouldn't be for a few decades.

Jefferson: Oh.

Ishuwa: And that would be in the appropriate timing. For now, they know we do exist. We visit with them on their planet in that way and that is quite an amazing opening, in that sense, for them in their world's perspective of what is possible in life.

Jefferson: Okay, that's interesting! Can you repeat the name of the world?

Ishuwa: Rorkin.

Jefferson: Were they in a state of mind like us, at the same level of awareness that we are at here on Earth today? Like, was there —

Ishuwa: Not really. They weren't exploring the idea of limitations in the way that your world does. They were living in a world that hadn't had contact with many other races. They have the awareness that there are some, and they have had contact with some. They have been exploring the experience of knowing their connection to All That Is and having the opportunity to experience the idea of, in a sense, being far out in the country where there aren't many travelers that come and visit and they don't very often go into the big city where there is more action taking place. It's as though they are way out there in the country of space's physical worlds. In a sense, they sent us a letter. We are more in the city, so to speak, in terms of having interactions on a regular basis with other planetary beings. We are more active at this timing interacting with several races simultaneously day to day. They tend to interact with very few.

Jefferson: When a person is following their highest excitement by bringing you a gift from another planet, where do you keep the gift after receiving it?

Ishuwa: Well, it isn't something that we store away in a building behind walls of cold steel with a padlock on the entrance.

Jefferson: (Laughter).

Ishuwa: It simply nourishes and enriches us and becomes something that is always a part of us, "always a part of us," in the sense that is a part of our experiencing in that lifetime, something that adds color to our beingness in that lifetime. The experience has a vibration, a frequency, a signature, a perception, an understanding of who we are and what the world we interact with is like. In a sense, it gives us a platform or a foundation from which we can share that experience with others that we come into contact with. We can explore and share new possibilities within our self and have new inspirations come forth.

We know that because we've had the interaction with them that it will be with us and be in our awareness and color our beingness in a positive way and in the timing that is most appropriate for us and for others who then later come into contact with us in the ways that will be most uplifting, most encouraging, and most fascinating. It simply becomes something that we do not need to, in that way then, capture like a photograph. Not that there is anything wrong with that idea. We simply know that it will be an image that will flow through our awareness and touch others in the appropriate way and appropriate timing.

Jefferson: So, basically it's energy that you transform and keep? It's like energy?

Ishuwa: Yes, that unique signature. It is an energy, in a sense, yes. It allows us to have more colors, more perceptions, and more ideas thus then to share with others.

Jefferson: What was the last gift that you received?

Ishuwa: I would say this one of interacting with you in this moment but perhaps that is not what you had in mind. Could you ask the question a little more specifically?

Jefferson: That's kind of you! I will be more specific. If someone you see says, "Hey Ishuwa, I was visiting another planet and I found this really cool object that I brought back as a gift for you!"

Ishuwa: Yes, well then, first of all there are the gifts that are not physical objects. The beings that live on Rorkin were very delightful. They had understandings that were amazing gifts for me and for those with me. A few of our world are still there visiting with them. In terms of a gift that is a physical object, there was something they did offer me that I have since placed into an archive. They understood my choice to place it in this archive. They where very welcoming and, in a sense, they look forward to the time when they will be able to visit the archive to see the object there.

Jefferson: Sweet!

Ishuwa: The archive is something that is an energetic melding of many objects that have been gathered from many worlds. They are easily accessible. They are not put away in a building in the sense of being padlocked away for only a few to see. It is a bit like a museum that's open to the public of extraterrestrial beings to come and visit as they feel attracted to it, to the idea. So they will then, those who come to this museum of interstellar physical objects, they will be attracted to various objects that are on display there and receive what they need to or what they feel would be most uplifting for them simply from exploring this archive, this complex, this interstellar museum.

So there was an object, thus then, that was given to me from this being on Rorkin that I then placed into this interstellar museum that is open, in a sense, 24/7. It is never closed.

Jefferson: How lovely!

Ishuwa: The object that was given to me has a scent that is very unusual, but it is attractive to me, something I enjoy. It has the size of approximately a half-a-foot in your world's measurement system. It is shaped a bit like an egg that you have on your planet, but it is about a half-a-foot long.

Jefferson: Okay.

Ishuwa: The longest part is about a half-a-foot, and it's not perfectly round. It is rather hard in some areas while in others it is a bit soft, and you can push it in a little bit. It's a bit forgiving in that sense. The interior has a life energy to it that suggests that this object is alive and has its own consciousness. It has an ability to share the scent as a form of dialogue, as a form of spoken word, but it hasn't spoken in this way yet to me in my experience with it, not yet in a word format. It seems to communicate with the scent, and I have yet to explore it further. Those who gave it to me said that it can communicate at times in some other ways as well that we sense will be most enjoyable when that occurs.

Jefferson: Okay.

Ishuwa: We aren't aware just how that will be. We don't have scientists that are studying it. It is clear to us that it is something that is of a positive vibration in any way, shape, or form that it will at any moment or time choose to express itself.

Jefferson: Cool!

Ishuwa: So for now, the only form of communication that we have had, that I have experienced, is the scent that comes off of it at times. It doesn't always have the scent. There are times it seems to have no scent at all. It's a very comforting feeling to be around the object. It has a warm feeling to it. It has a medium brown coloration to it and some light brown too. These two colors seem to change. The medium brown changes to a light brown and the light brown changes to a medium brown. Then they both change back for no apparent reason.

There are sections of this object that have abrupt changes between the two colors. It's as if a line is drawn separating the light brown area from the medium brown area. On some sections of the object, there is more of a soft blending that takes place as the light browns gradually become medium browns, like a thin white cloud floating before a blue sky. There is some of that kind of soft shading that takes place as well. The object's shape doesn't seem to change, but we are told that could occur. It won't grow larger. The mass or the weight won't gain or become less. It will simply have the ability to change shape and remain the same weight in a sense.

Jefferson: Okay. Was it given to you or to your society?

Ishuwa: Well, it was handed to me, but it is also a gift to our society.

Jefferson: Did they tell you why they chose you? Why did they give this gift to you?

Ishuwa: I was the one interacting with the communication, the translation, the dialogue, the interpreter. I perceive they chose me for that reason.

Jefferson: Well, that is nice! So what was the last gift that you gave and to whom?

Ishuwa: We had a form of food that we felt the Rorkin society, based on our observations, would enjoy. It's a bit of modification on something they already have there. The modified version is something that our society brought, and I was the one who handed it to them.

Jefferson: Okay.

Ishuwa: It's a little bit like you have on your world, a green bean. It's about two inches long, and it can grow about a quarter-of-an-inch in diameter. It can grow a little bit wiggly in its shape. It's about the same size and weight of a green bean on your world, and yet it is something that is a little bit different then the green bean on your world as it is a little bit leafier and a little bit softer. We thought that it was something that they would find to be a very positive and nourishing food to add in their dietary sustenance. They were quite excited by it. We were very happy to see their response. They are having success with it and slowly bringing it into their world's dietary intake.

Jefferson: You said your diet is more based on liquid and you don't have much by way of teeth, how do you guys work that out with this green bean stuff as part of your diet?

Ishuwa: We are able to transform it energetically and turn it into a more soft substance.

Jefferson: Ah, okay!

Ishuwa: You have blenders on your world?

Jefferson: Yeah! Right!

Ishuwa: So we work with it in that way.

Jefferson: Ah, okay. Well yeah, that makes sense.

Ishuwa: But it isn't actually a blender like you have as a physical object. It's a little bit more about adjusting the energies around that object with our hands and our thought processes. For this form of food is very open to that idea of transformation and very willing and able then to hear us and to follow-suit as we ask it to transform into more of a liquid format.

Jefferson: In what circumstances can you say no to receiving a gift or has anybody in your society ever said no to a gift?

Ishuwa: It does occur. There are times where the gift is something that just isn't going to be placed in our world's frequency. It isn't going to resonate with us, and we will explain that to the individual or individuals who are presenting it to us so they will be able to understand and acknowledge this in a way that is agreeable. The interaction won't cause them to feel neglected or rejected. They will be able to understand the idea.

Jefferson: And what was the last gift that you guys said was not appropriate?

Ishuwa: There was an object that's rather unpredictable.

Jefferson: How so?

Ishuwa: It has the ability to create something like pollen that you have in flowers on your world that are released into the air.

Jefferson: Yes.

Ishuwa: This form of pollen that was being released from this plant-like object, it was rather erratic and could thus then interact with some of the plants in our world in a way that wouldn't be supportive for their highest productivity, proliferation, and growth. So with the people that presented it to us, we all found another world for it to be placed upon. They are now the ones that are the gardeners of that new planting on that world. It's a world that is new for them as well.

Although they didn't have the opportunity to give us an object that we took back to our world, they did have the opportunity to offer it to us and they understood why we couldn't have it on our world. Thus then, they had the opportunity to experience a whole new planet. They were able to bring their gift there and thus introduce it into that world and become guardians in a whole new world. It is a world that they found to be quite enjoyable and they still do in ways that are quite unexpected for them. So they are very happy with the present that we said no to.

Jefferson: Right!

Ishuwa: They are happy with the end result that has taken place as a result of that whole interchange.

Jefferson: I see. Has your society ever received a present that changed the way you experience life for the better.

Ishuwa: Well yes. We had a present of understanding.

Jefferson: Ah, okay.

Ishuwa: Understanding more about our nature. The present was brought forth in ways that we could all really easily connect to and make sense of and grasp. It wasn't just an idea that was presented. It was fully realizable, connectable, a present that we could, in a sense, plug into. Not that we were physically plugging into anything, just in the sense of plug into and understand and really see how the present fits into the world that we interact with, how it fits into the nature of Existence so we can be able to apply it instantly and to then be able to utilize it effectively in very whole and comprehensive and meaningful ways everyday! Yes, quite a gift indeed! In a sense, it uplifted us. It was a step up in our world's energy vibrational state of conscious being. It helped us step up quickly, in a sense, from one-dimensional realm of consciousness to another.

Jefferson: Great, thank you. When you interact with us, I would say that what you are giving us here is a gift of knowledge, of care, of love, in this sense. When people get exposed to gifts such as the ones you are giving us through this book, does anything happen as far as activating DNA or opening them up to new ideas and possibilities?

Ishuwa: This does occur, but only at the willingness and acceptance of that person, especially from their higher self's state of awareness and choosing.

Jefferson: To the extent of their allowance?

Ishuwa: Yes, which would be generally something the higher self is aware of.

Jefferson: But the fact that synchronicity brought the book to their hands is already a hint that they were interested and that it could be uplifting for them.

Ishuwa: Yes. They have attracted the book into their presence and so there exists within their higher self the potential that it is time for them to begin exploring and expanding in that direction, to begin exploring the information that is in that book.

Jefferson: You mean they —

Ishuwa: They are ready in that sense. When their vibration puts out the readiness, the book's information that will support the growth comes forth. The idea you've heard before, "when the student is ready, the teacher will appear."

Jefferson: Yes, right.

Ishuwa: When a person has reached a certain level of consciousness and openness, then a book, or a person, or a teacher and information will become present, will be attracted to them.

Jefferson: Fantastic! Now, talking about teacher, do you have a school of wizardry where you can learn magic in your world?

Ishuwa: We don't. From your world's perspective, we are able to do things that would appear to be very magical, as though we were pulling a rabbit out of a hat, so to speak.

Jefferson: Yeah.

Ishuwa: But to us, it is just a part of our beingness. It is something that has existed in our society for quite some time. So for us to be able to do such things is simply a part of who we are. In each instance of creating something magically, we certainly are able to be aware of and acknowledge that it is, in a sense, magical to be doing that. We experience it as being magical and acknowledging that brings in a very heightened sense of joy. Being aware that we are magically creating this or that is very joyful for us to realize.

Jefferson: Can you give me one or two examples of something that you did yourself that could be perceived as magical?

Ishuwa: From your world's perspective?

Jefferson: Yes.

Ishuwa: Well, yes. For us it is all magical, but the idea of a magic show from your world's perspective, if we were on a stage in an outfit presenting ourselves as a magician, we could certainly pull a rabbit out of a hat, but it would be done differently then how magicians in your world tend to do that idea.

Jefferson: Oh.

Ishuwa: So that would be magical. We would be manifesting the rabbit in a more time and space transitional format.

Jefferson: Ah, okay!

Ishuwa: It wouldn't be like we were hiding a rabbit in our coat and then simply using a fast sleight-of-hand trick or pulling a rabbit out of a hidden compartment in a hat. We would take the rabbit out of a different time and space location and then have it suddenly appear on stage in the time and place that those people watching the show would be able to see.

Jefferson: Are there things that you do that would be like shows for entertainment?

Ishuwa: We do have entertainers that are capable of doing some things that are similar to your entertainers, your magicians. Our performers do shows that we all realize are things any one of us could do too, the rest of us just hadn't thought about doing it. There are those of us who are more focused on bringing forth new visual expressions that are fascinating and pleasurable for the rest of us to see happening. These artists are masters at that form of expressive Creatorship, of showmanship.

We will at times gather in the presence of one or more of our artists who are masters of this form of creation and thus then we take part in being like an audience for them as they present shows of exciting and previously, from the audience's point of view, previously unimagined creations, magic tricks in a sense. But again, once done, any of us in the audience could have done a similar thing, but we just hadn't focused on creating that form of visual expression. We hadn't thought about doing it.

Jefferson: Are there any plays or shows that the children themselves organize for others?

Ishuwa: They are able to do this, yes. At times this occurs.

Jefferson: Do you live in houses similar to the ones that we live in, or is it more of a cave community, or if you don't have houses or caves do you just lean against the first thing you find in front of you and go to sleep? (Laughter).

Ishuwa: It depends on the planet we are on. In some areas it's easier to hold our presence in the gravitational field and to be able to enjoy in comfortable ways that planetary surface. At times we will reside in something you would consider to be a house, but it would be built out of materials that are quite different than what you use to build your buildings and houses there on your Earthian landscape. At other times, we are simply able to exist in a non-physical state to some degree and just be in the space of a planet without having any walls, or ceilings, or floorings around us. Somewhat like a tree in your world or a flower in the sense that we are able to simply sit or stand on the surface and exist. That can be a way that at times we can, in a sense, sleep in that format of just standing, or sitting, or lying down on the planet's surface, and we will be completely taken care of through the shift from day to night and night to day.

There are many variations of light and darkness that can exist on planetary surfaces. Some planets have more than one Sun. Some have variations of Suns and sunrises and sunsets that can cast different qualities of light in the atmosphere.

Jefferson: On the planet of the Yahyel, do you live in a house such as the ones we live in?

Ishuwa: We tend to have more oval shape structures that are very in tune, and alive, and aware, and conscious with the atmosphere and the ground, with the substance they tend to be resting upon that we walk on. They do not need to be secured with bolts and nails to a foundation. They do not need that form of securing into the ground. They are able to consciously adjust their electro-magnetic field, in a sense, and hold onto the surface of the ground. If we want to move them, they are able to follow us. They can adjust the frequency that has allowed them to hold that space on the ground and then let it go so they can easily move about to some other location. Once at the new location, they are again able to "hold" themselves on that portion of ground in a way that gives them a sense of stability and prevents them from being moved about like a water lily on the surface of a pond.

Jefferson: I see. We are very particular here about our houses, and I guess most of us can relate to the idea of having a house. Tell me something about the houses that you have. Can a person have two, three, or more houses? How does it work?

Ishuwa: We don't, in that sense, have ownership of our houses, of what you call a house, the abodes that we tend to live in.

Jefferson: Oh.

Ishuwa: In our world, we can easily live outside if we want to.

Jefferson: Oh, how lovely.

Ishuwa: In terms of the abodes, we have the ability to access several of these abodes. They are interchangeable in terms of who will at any given time be inhabiting them. For example, if I am in one today, then I might move out from it to a different one the next day. The one I had been in might then become occupied by someone else.

Jefferson: Oh.

Ishuwa: Each abode has a particular vibratory frequency that can be serving for some period of time. When it is in our sensing appropriate, we will move out into another abode that is of a different vibration. We will then experience being in that one for a while. The one we had been in will perhaps become more attractive to another person, and they will move into that abode.

So it is very interchangeable, very flexible in that way, moving about very regularly, continually, in a way that we enjoy, in a way that feels like being at home for us, energetically at home, sensorially at home, vibrationally at home.

Jefferson: The idea that you are giving me seems more like a hotel than a house.

Ishuwa: It is a bit more like that in the sense that you can move from one hotel to another and after you vacate one hotel room at that hotel somebody else perhaps will be residing in it that night while you move into a hotel room that someone else had been in the previous night.

Jefferson: Okay.

Ishuwa: It can be similar to that, but again, our energies and our biological nature is such that there isn't anything left behind that needs to be cleaned up. There are no maids that have to come in and vacuum and dust.

The energy or the vibration that we have left — only because we interacted with the abode, and the understanding of the place, and the vibrational consciousness of its space — our energy is then added to that space in that place. It is a positive addition, a positive vibrational state of our consciousness that is blending now with that place, with that abode. When we leave and go to another location, the abode that is now vacant will have a new vibrational frequency that will attract those who will be most guided to be in it in ways that will be most nourishing and nurturing for them, most enjoyable for them. They will, if they want, be able to blend with or take on some of the energy consciousness we left behind. There will have been others before us who have stayed there whose energies will also be available for newcomers to take on if they want to. They can do so in a way that they just know internally will be more supportive for who they are. It is always a positive form of sharing, growth, and exploration.

Jefferson: What is the abode you stayed in the longest? What is the longest you stayed in a particular abode?

Ishuwa: When I was growing up with my family of birth, there was one that I was in most of the time during my first five years. It was one that we generally didn't move in and out of, but we did at times.

Those of us that are supporting the raising of a young newborn will generally maintain residence in one place for a regular period of time. We generally don't move in and out as frequently during such times, but it can occur. I was briefly in four other abodes by the time I was of the age of five.

Jefferson: Okay.

Ishuwa: Occasionally we would go from the main abode to one of the others for a very short period of time. There were four others that we lived in briefly at that time of my development as a newborn in the world of our Yahyelian society.

Jefferson: And in these houses, do you have like we do, a kitchen, a living room, and bedrooms?

Ishuwa: It is primarily one large space. We have the ability to create the sense of partitions if that serves us in some way. The partitions are of a thin light frequency that can then appear to be a fabric and create some appearance of spatial separation. We can in that way create the appearance of more than one room.

Jefferson: Oh, I see, and this particular one where you grew up, how many rooms would it appear to have?

Ishuwa: Anywhere from two to three.

Jefferson: So, one room where your parents would sleep and another where you would sleep?

Ishuwa: Usually we would all be sleeping in the same room.

Jefferson: How cozy.

Ishuwa: That room would be our main focus, to reside in that space. Occasionally, for various reasons, it would be time to go into another room. For example, at times some interstellar communications would take place when I, as a young one, wasn't prepared or ready for the interaction and the visual experiencing of.

Jefferson: Okay.

Ishuwa: That is one idea why we would have a different space in the same abode.

Jefferson: And do you sleep inside your house on the floor or is there a comfortable thing like a bed prepared for you?

Ishuwa: We have an energy, a construct of energy, that is very soft and it can change color as I choose for it to.

Jefferson: That sounds very interesting! Now, on to a different topic. I don't think I have ever asked you this, are you the only child or do you have brothers or sisters?

Ishuwa: I am, in a sense, the only child. There is no other that my biological parents have had.

Jefferson: Very well. What about the outside of this house, do you have little gardens or fences or is it just open land?

Ishuwa: We do have the idea of gardens. There are no fences though in that sense. We can sometimes grow things in such a pattern that it might appear to be a fence, in a sense, separating the other abode that's closest to the one we reside in, but that isn't done in any way to keep out someone or to keep in something.

Jefferson: Okay, great. Well, we have just a few minutes left to go. Do you have streets in your community like we do?

Ishuwa: We have thoroughfares that we frequent which are the result of energetic choices. They feel like the fastest, and most effortless, and most enjoyable way to go. They also tend to be the places where we will come into contact with others that are most appropriate for us to meet with on that day.

We are able to venture off and travel in many different directions. The roads aren't built in a pavement or concrete freeway in that sense. They tend to manifest energetically as being the most powerfully uplifting passageway to progress upon at any given day, and it is the passage way that many others will feel most guided to. Thus then we can meet up in that way at the appropriate timing with others to share a moment and to be enriched by each other's presence before we then move along the path to our next location.

Jefferson: Is your vehicle something like our double-decker buses or more like a train?

Ishuwa: We do not have trains or buses.

Jefferson: Ah, okay.

Ishuwa: There are many other shapes and many other types of crafts. There is also the option to create a non-physical type of craft that is entirely of a vibrational frequency that many of us can resonate with and use to travel to other locations as well. You wouldn't be able to see it with your physical eyes in the way that you can see objects in your sky today that fly through the air. It is a type of craft that exists at a higher frequency of being. You would be able to see it only through your mind's eye, so to speak, in more of a telepathic ability of visual perception that more and more of you are learning to develop today on your world.

Jefferson: I understand. Very well. What about the large spacecraft you had over Phoenix, Arizona, in North America, when do you use that?

Ishuwa: It provides a place where people from many other worlds can come together, many people who have different ways of travel and different forms and shapes of craft. So rather than having a big parking lot, in a sense, with all of these different spacecrafts, we can all just join together in this one space and place. It is a craft that supports a common frequency for communal gatherings. It provides a place where people that come from planets and civilizations scattered lovingly throughout this Youniverse can come together and share a vast number of ideas, and experiences, and also create together.

Jefferson: Fantastic! I enjoyed this interaction immensely!

Ishuwa: I as well!

Jefferson: So, I have to say thank you very much for coming back, for being with us, for holding this lovely energy and sharing with us this knowledge which is really, really enriching from my perspective!

Ishuwa: Thank you for sharing! For us it is a joy to be with you in this blending way as well and to have this opportunity to bring forth information that can engage the inner most realms of consciousness within the readers in ways they may or may not be aware of occurring, but will always be occurring in ways that their higher self knows and feels will be of their greatest support and nourishment in positive and uplifting ways in their development as interstellar heart enriching beings on planet Earth. We look forward to our interaction with you in this way again, and we will be with you tomorrow of your time! Much love and remember the dragon of delight!

Jefferson: Yes, I promise you. I will go there at some point in time. It's going to happen. Thank you very much again for bringing this to my attention. I am sure that all of these unfolding experiences that might take place, like me visiting Chinatown, I am sure that you are to some extent involved in and helping to hold the frequencies and vibrations so we will be able to enjoy even more interesting ideas together!

Ishuwa: Yes. Thank you. Wonderful! Most delightful! Always a joy! We will say goodbye and step aside now, but together still we are whether we seem to be or not I assure you. Good day dear one!

Jefferson: Yah oohm!

Ishuwa: Yah oohm!

Chapter 10

Existence is Actually Amazingly Magical

"You are all great magicians creating a show in which many of you have, in a sense, pulled your heart out of a hat and made it disappear. Some day soon as a collective society you are all going to make your hearts reappear, at which time the audience of humanity will applaud to no end. There will be a standing ovation the likes of which has never been recorded in your history, your herstory, whichever you prefer." –Ishuwa

September 3rd, 2009

Ishuwa: Alright I will say, most wonderful to be here with you in these moments together! How are you this day of your time?

Jefferson: Oh, I am flying like a kite being blown ever higher by the winds of this knowledge! Knowledge that, as you mentioned Ishuwa, does not come only from you but from many civilizations.

Ishuwa: Thank you for recounting that idea that we have shared with you before! Yes! Wonderful to be in this expression in this blending moment with you this day of our time together as we co-create this experience and create a whole new third reality that together we can explore more of the infinite realms of our nature, of our beingness. We can do so in ways that we enjoy and find uplifting, and revealing, and comforting, and that can also present ideas for others that they too may connect to that inner most realm within themselves in the

moments and in the ways that bring them joy and ecstasy while they are reconnecting!
Today we have for you one idea at this moment to bring forth before the question and answers segment. Are you ready?

Jefferson: I am starting to like it! Go ahead!

Ishuwa: We have begun to see some movement in the region of California, Northern California, with some groups that are choosing to move into light and are beginning to find ways to incorporate light within this area of the media, within this area of your television, within this area of your newspapers. They are beginning to get a bit of a grasp, a bit of an inroad into those areas. So there may be a little more revelation coming through in those areas in terms of information distribution through the media of television and newspapers that could begin to get people's attention regarding ideas such as the extraterrestrial worlds that are real and that will thus then become a little more in the spotlight, so to speak, for the people living in those coastal regions who are reading those newspapers and seeing those news telecasts however brief the articles and shows may be.

It is something you may or may not yourself connect with and experience. Either way, we sense that there will be more opportunity to read and to hear about extraterrestrial presences and existences, and also more opportunities for people to get in contact with ET consciousness in ways that can be peaceful and uplifting for your world. We perceive people will soon begin seeing more of these ideas in your newspapers and television media in that region, particularly at this timing and for some months to come. That was the idea to share. Thus then it is so. Where would you like to go now with this time together? Questions perhaps?

Jefferson: Thank you Ishuwa. Regarding the idea of magic and a being in our world called Merlin, do people who perform real magic do so by holding an image of an idea in their mind with such great focus to the point of having that focused idea finally materialize in our physical world?

Ishuwa: Are you asking how magic can occur?

Jefferson: Yes.

Ishuwa: There are many ways it can occur from the perspective of your society. What magic is for you is up to you to define. So let's start with that idea. What is your definition of magic?

Jefferson: I would say that magic is the ability to have something manifest in a way that is out of the ordinary by using phenomenon of things that exist in nature that are not actually seen. For example, taking something that exists in an unseen light-realm and having it lowered in its vibration until it materializes in our physical world.

Ishuwa: You have an idea of magic as something that occurs that is out of the ordinary. Are you suggesting that is a definition of magic that works for you?

Jefferson: Yes.

Ishuwa: Existence itself is not ordinary. Anytime a person is able to have an experience that to them seems not to be ordinary, then they are having an experience of their actual nature in some way. This is another way to define magic. They would be experiencing something that is not ordinary by simply experiencing something that is in alignment with their actual nature. For as we said, Existence in its true state of being is not at all ordinary. It is quite extraordinary! It is quite amazing! It is quite magical! Do you understand that idea?

Jefferson: Take Jesus for example. He could be in two places at the same time.

Ishuwa: But do you understand that idea?

Jefferson: Um, let's see.

Ishuwa: And, take Jesus? Where are you going to take him? To the department store to get some lunch?

Jefferson: (Laughter).

Ishuwa: Where would he like to go? Perhaps his hair is getting a bit long. Maybe he needs a shave?

Jefferson: Oh, by the way...no...take Jesus...it's been said that he could be in two places at the same time. That's magical! Walking on water, that's magical.

Ishuwa: You all are simply in one place and there is no time in that space nor space in that place.

Jefferson: Okay.

Ishuwa: But you can create the perception of being in a particular place at a given time. So you can thus create the experience of being in two places at the same time. You create the perception of time, and you create the perception of place. So you can create the perception of being in three places at the same time. However, for the most part, your society has chosen not to be functioning with that application of your Creatorship ability, your master Creator ability!

Generally, you all have chosen to create the idea of only being in one place at one time. So any time there comes along an individual that can express more of your actual state of being and capability and create a more expansive expression by being in two places at once, it can seem like a miracle, but it is just moving more into that place that is more representative of your actual nature where you are capable of creating an infinite number of ideas and experiences including being in more than one place at any given moment of time as you create your perception of time.

Jefferson: What about this idea of "creating the perception?" What do you mean by, "imagine yourself somewhere else?" That would just be imagination!

Ishuwa: It's all imagination! A nation of images! Your imagination, image nation. That which you choose to focus on continually and put out thus then will draw back to you what you are experiencing. The idea of "Law of Attraction" or "what you put out is what you get back" is the 3rd Law of Creation.

The world that you perceive is all a reflection of the images that you are projecting out from inward of your being, from your heart, from your mind, as though you were functioning somewhat like a film projector. Your thoughts, and ideas, and feelings, and images, are products of your imagination. This nation of images within your heart-mind is what you project outward, somewhat like how a film projector projects images in a movie theater. You project out your images onto the "screen of life" and then you sit like an audience member and experience these images as they are being reflected back to you in life's surround sound multi-dimensional movie screen.

Continuing with the analogy of a movie theater, the film projector projects images onto a screen of which then the audience can look at the screen and have an experience from the moving pictures, from images in motion, motion pictures, motion images, a projection reel with thousands of images projected out for you to then experience.

Making a movie and then watching it is a way of mirroring what you all are always doing in each moment of your life. You are all projecting images from the nation of images within you with your thoughts, and feelings, and ideas, and attitudes, and opinions, and actions. You project all those things outward like a movie projector and then you become like an audience member in a movie, so to speak, as you begin living in your 3D physical reality theater the results that come back to you from all of the images you were projecting outward. You are able to then live in and experience your very own motion pictures that are filled with energy in motion, emotion.

Activity through your imagination comes from that internal and eternal place of you. It is an infinite connection you have with All That Is, and it brings through a nation of images. There are an infinite number of images within this nation, so you have infinite potential in terms of what you are capable of bringing through and projecting which means you have infinite potential in terms of what you can get back and experience as your physical reality, as your personal life "movie" being projected onto a "multi-dimensional screen" of life experiences. In this sense, imaginations are what you experience in your physical world. It is all a product of what you are projecting out with your imagination through your thoughts, feelings, attitudes, ideas, actions, behaviors and so on. Thus then, it is all simply the result of your imagination, and in that sense, it is all imagination.

In general, many people have the misperception that experiences they have while watching a film in a movie theater are just the product of their imagination and so aren't really real. But actually, in terms of the Universe's perspective, those experiences are just as real as the physical experiences you have when you step out of that movie theater and go about your daily activities. It all simply "is." Neither type of experience is actually more real than the other. This is similar to the universal understanding that one idea is not better than or less than another, more holy or evil than another, greater than or lesser than another. Neither type of experience is more real than the other from the Youniverse's perspective, from the perspective of that which eternally "is."

Human beings have chosen to create a "world play" in which they have the perception that what is going on in their physical world is somehow more real than what they can imagine in their mind's eye, or more real than what in a book is a product of the writer's imagination, or more real than what in a movie theater on a movie screen is a product of the director, the actors, the producers, and the cinema photographers all working together.

It is all imagination, but so many of you have for so long been taught to believe that your physical daily activities, which are a product of your imagination, are somehow more real than your imaginations and thus then you tend to place more importance on the physical world and less importance on the ideas that come from within your heart and your mind's eye.

As more of your society learns to give their imaginations equal importance to what is happening in their daily life, you will then be able more effectively to grasp those imaginations and access them more fully and focus on putting them out more predominantly, more powerfully, with greater focus. Thus then it becomes easier for you to utilize your imaginations and with them manifest what you prefer to experience in your physical world. Do you follow this idea?

Jefferson: Yes, thank you!

Ishuwa: Is there something about this idea you would like to ask further in particular or is it clear for you?

Jefferson: I always like to ask further. You just never know, right?

Ishuwa: You always know, but you can create the idea of "never knowing."

Jefferson: That's so true! Okay, what is the difference, if there is any, between mind and imagination?

Ishuwa: In the physical world, it is simply the difference that you create there to be.

Jefferson: Oh.

Ishuwa: How you perceive it to be different is a result of your own belief systems. The way you define the two. When you put out a definition for what the "mind" is and you put out a definition for what "imagination" is, if those two definitions you are putting out are different, you will thus then get back different experiences of what the "mind" is and what "imagination" is for you.

In terms of the actual nature of Existence, there is no difference. But in terms of having the ability to create a "play" and have "performances" and experiences on a "stage" of physical reality, you can create the misperception, the illusion, that there is a difference. And again, the difference is determined by how you define the two and the difference in the definitions that you then create and put out will determine how you will experience those two ideas as being different.

So, for you, how do you experience the mind and imagination as being different? Become more aware of how you are perceiving the idea of the mind and the idea of imagination as being different and then you will start to get a clearer picture on how you must be defining the two as being different. Do you see that idea?

Jefferson: Yes, I understand! Basically, we are only as limited as our ability to expand our definitions.

Ishuwa: You limit yourself by having limited definitions and beliefs, and when you choose to expand your definitions and beliefs you can then begin to expand your awareness of Self in a way that is more in alignment with experiencing your whole, infinite, unlimited potential.

Jefferson: In order to have more expanded definitions, we would need a frame of reference and that may not always be available.

Ishuwa: Yes, and that was a key element in making it possible to live in a world in which your society could perceive itself as being limited and disconnected. You had to find a way to limit your awareness of your actual unlimited, expansive, nature. So you created the idea of limitations and separations within definitions and belief mechanisms that you could then "put out" knowing you would start "getting back" more and more limited perceptions until you would reach a point where you wouldn't remember that you actually have an infinite number of choices from which to create your definitions and beliefs from. For example, it's as though the "buffet of life choices" has an infinite number of items available to choose from, but you chose as a collective society to limit the number of buffet items and pretend that there were only a few styles of food available. As a collective, your society found ways to limit the number of dishes available at the buffet.

Jefferson: Yes.

Ishuwa: And gradually, over generations, you were able to get it down almost to the point where there was no food available, to the point where as a world there are many people who seem to have no food and who are, in a sense, dying of starvation from a lack of food, as though there are no choices for edible foods from which they can consume and nourish their body.

If you take that idea into the spiritual heartfelt realms, many people have found a way to create, in a sense, a buffet in which there is no food available of a heartfelt kind, no ideas about reality that reflect your true spiritual nature. So they are, in a sense, dying from within their hearts. Their hearts and their minds are, in a sense, starving. They are dying from malnutrition of the heart, in a sense, due to a disconnection from their heart's actual nature. Many people, thus then, are developing cancers and illnesses of depression because they haven't been able to find dishes at the buffet table of life possibilities that reflect their more expansive heartfelt nature. They haven't been able to find and dine upon true ideas that would nourish them and give them more awareness of their infinite, unlimited nature in which there can thus then be no heartfelt starvation and no physical dying from starvation as well, for the two go hand-in-hand, the physical starvations and the heart feeling starvations.

Many people have much money, much food, but their heart is lacking in feeling, nourishment, and awareness of their whole nature. That type of nourishment and those types of food and ingredients are still not being found in the restaurant of "beliefs and definitions" about reality that they "dine within" daily. Even with fat wallets, five star restaurants, and multiple course meals that are available, there are still few foods for the heart that they are yet aware of that will remind them of their actual, whole, divine, unlimited nature and their true Creatorship awareness.

Jefferson: I loved that explanation, thank you! Can you talk about abundance, perhaps with or without the idea of money? How do you think a person can be abundant within this life where we are today using the powers of their imagination?

Ishuwa: Abundance can be defined in a multitude of ways. For example, you can have an abundance of money or an abundance of lack of money.

Jefferson: Okay.

Ishuwa: It helps to get specific, to get clear, and many people simply aren't really very clear about their ideas around money and having an abundance of money. So, this is one of the key factors that come into play for those who don't have money. They simply aren't that clear around this idea.

More importantly, they aren't clear and aware of the idea of "what you put out is what you get back." This 3rd Law of Creation is eternal and never changes. This is something they haven't been taught. In fact, quite frequently they are being taught things that are the opposite of that. The media and the institutions of "higher learning" have, unknowingly perhaps, been teaching ideas for many generations that prevent people from getting into contact with the understanding that "what you put out is what you get back." The other three Laws of Creation have been glossed over too, filtered out, rarely taught, and in many instances even considered heretical teachings. Often, these universal understandings that reveal the nature and the structure of Existence are something that many people will be frightened by when they hear about them or when someone suggests they are "dishes" of knowledge that are available for people to consider "tasting."

In your society, it is as though there are these "dishes" of eternal universal understanding at your daily "table of life choices," but somehow many people still feel if they "take a bite" by considering these understandings that they will then somehow turn into a strange forgotten creature or be cast out into the depths of isolation and despair. This type of fearful response that causes so many people to quickly disregard the universal understandings often grows out of so many of the religious teachings that have been taught in your world in frightening ways and in threatening modes for generations and generations. So many religious followers have become conditioned to automatically repress the universal understandings due to their fears.

Many people think it's important not to stray from religious teachings so they won't get laughed at, or cast aside, or tortured. They have been afraid to consider that these "dishes" of universal understanding that are on the "buffet table" of eternal life might somehow be very nourishing, and nutritious, and enlightening, and revealing for their heart and sense of joy in life.

It's almost as though the universal understandings have been growing like fruit of knowledge on a tree of life, but somehow many people have felt internally that they are being told by the so called higher institutions not to "taste of that fruit" for somehow if they did they would be cast out of the "garden of eden" forever and perhaps then be placed into a world of despair, or placed into a world of depression, or perhaps placed into a world of pharmaceutical dependency, or perhaps placed into a world of fear, and anger, and disagreement, and arguments, and frictions, and inability to get along with others, and even an inability to get along with and communicate comfortably with their self.

However, contrary to their fears, it appears that by not choosing the fruit of knowledge, by not choosing to share and to teach the information about the Four Laws of Creation that exist in All That Is, it appears that quite the opposite has happened. It appears that without the fruit's heartfelt knowledge being consumable by them, not being accessible from the tree and consumed due to their fears that if they did they would then be cast into a dark burning hell, it appears that they have actually limited their awareness of who they really are to such an extent that they have ended up creating a world of experience that contains all of the ideas they initially feared.

Look at your world today. You will see so many people are actually living despair, living limitation, living with the illness, living with anger, living with wars, living with conflict. All of these things would not have come into place if everyone had been taught where the tree of life was and how to consume this fruit of knowledge, how to find it within. For it is always within. It cannot ever perish, but shadows from fearful beliefs can be placed over this understanding to such a degree that individuals are no longer able to find it, recognize it, realize it, or even consider that it really does exist. They instead go about their worship of the old limited ideas and abstain from feeding upon their tree of heavenly life to appease unseen gods they fear.

They have thus then become like stone within their beingness and become absent of the nourishing internal understandings that the tree of life provides them. They have done so to such an extent that they are now at a loss in many given moments of their day. They may feel as though they are missing something, as though there is something not quite right in their life that they would love to reconnect with, as though there must be more to life even though they might have millions of dollars and are living a life of luxury and traveling all around the world. Somehow they still feel as though there is something missing. We suggest that the thing that is missing is their knowledge of who they are.

Metaphorically: they have yet to taste the fruit of knowledge that grows on their tree of life. The fruit that comes from the tree is like an apple of infinite understanding and realization of who you are. It grows upon the four Laws of Creation that are like a tree of life. This tree has roots that go very deep within the Earth and into the eternity of your actual heartfelt beingness. No matter how much abundance you have of money, without some level of understanding of this tree and its fruit of knowledge about life, there will always be a sense that there is something missing, that you're incomplete, that there is something much more meaningful to life that you aren't yet getting in touch with.

The common feeling that "something is missing" from life is thus then one of the mechanisms that has so many people going about each day "chasing a carrot" that is being "dangled in front of them" with constant temptations suggesting ideas such as: this job is what you are missing in life, or this lavish lifestyle, or having this much money in your bank account, or being able to travel to exotic places or eat at extravagant restaurants is what you are missing.

These types of "dangling carrots" have been hanging in front of so many people for so long, and no matter how many of these types of "carrots" a person "grasps" they still feel that meaning and purpose in their life is deeply missing. The experience of realizing fulfillment in each moment is left dangling just out of their reach because, again, only with the understanding from their tree of life and it's fruit of infinite knowledge — the Four Laws of Creation — only in understanding this will a person fully feel like nothing is missing.

It is all within you. The feeling of fulfillment that they have been chasing is within. It can only be found when a person chooses to go inward and accept that they are the one that is creating all of this and realize that it is an infinitely beautiful place. As they choose to allow themselves to accept that, then they will thus begin bringing back experiences that confirm that understanding. And they will do so in ways that will be very fulfilling for them, very meaningful to them.

They will have a sense of abundance that they are very delighted with, and they will feel in tune with this abundance. They will feel incredibly abundant in ways that they always enjoy. They will realize this abundance can never be taken away from them. They will thus then never have a lack of any of the experiences that they truly, from within their own nature, prefer to resonate within and be able to thus then manifest in ways that will be absolutely magical beyond that of any magician performing on a stage in Las Vegas or any concert theater hall. Do you follow some of this idea or perhaps all of it?

Jefferson: Thank you! So there is a sense of lack that creates a need for security and —

Ishuwa: The sense of lack does not create the need for security.

Jefferson: What does?

Ishuwa: People create the need for security. You are infinitely secure in your infinite existence within the ecstasy that you are. However, "what you put out is what you get back," and because people in your world have been taught to create and put out the idea that you are disconnected from your Creatorship and you are disconnected from your infinite eternal abundance and ability to experience it securely, people are thus then getting back experiences of having lack and of having to work to secure their existence here.

Remember, your existence is eternal. The more that people accept and understand that idea, that tree, the more then they will begin to grow branches and leaves on this understanding. And then they will begin to grow flowers and fruits of realization on this understanding. They will begin to grow, many, many, many, many trees and they will have a whole orchard of trees, many of them "fruit trees," many of them will provide other forms of meaningful nourishment. For there is within this understanding the ability to create an infinite number of trees. That is the nature of the tree of life, the fruit of knowledge. When a person is more in tune with this, realizes it is real, they will begin more and more effortlessly to create in their physical reality experiences that support this, for "what you put out is what you get back," and thus then they will let go of the idea that they need to work hard at something in order to create a sense of security. There also will be no more "false senses of security" being manifested, for presently there are many people who have done and followed the ways of your society's teachings for so long who still end up jobless or feeling unfulfilled.

Many people go to church. They do what the "good book" says. They do their best to follow the good book terminologies even though this book has been interpreted in so many different ways on your world today, even in ways that are contradicting one another and that itself is a clue that something isn't in alignment. There are hundreds of different versions of the good book. There are so many people that are interpreting this book in so many contradictory ways. Perhaps people will begin to get to the core of how it can be that they are interpreting anything in any way to begin with. It is in understanding that, that they begin to get into contact with their actual nature as the Creator of everything they are experiencing. "What you put out is what you get back," which makes it possible to create several different interpretations of that book or any other book.

As people begin to understand how it is they are creating all these contradictory ideas, they begin choosing to create one whole resonant idea and let go of the book. The teachings that are within it that are aligned with the infinite nature of Existence will remain intact in a way that everyone can agree resonantly and peacefully with for there are some teachings in there that are in alignment with your eternal nature and only those will remain. All of the other teachings within it will simply perish.

Jefferson: It seems that when we talk about creating abundance, if our intention is clear then the desired result appears!

Ishuwa: And if the desired result has not appeared then the intention is not yet clear enough! Is that clear?

Jefferson: Very much so! Thank you!

Ishuwa: Rather than giving up by saying, "I studied some teachings about creating abundance by using the Law of Attraction, but the abundance hasn't shown up yet so this Law of Attraction stuff must not work," rather than questioning its ability to work for you, just acknowledge that it really does work and acknowledge that you must not yet have gotten clear enough yet in what it is you are putting out.

Whatever you are "getting back" will let you know what you are actually "putting out." When you are getting back abundance in the ways that you prefer, then you are being clear with what you are putting out.

Jefferson: I would assume that there are infinite ways that the Youniverse has to manifest what has been asked for?

Ishuwa: Yes! Yes, an infinite number of ways!

Jefferson: Is one of the ways related to our spirit guides that can arrange synchronicities?

Ishuwa: Yes. Spirit guides can provide a form of support in the manifesting of something an individual is choosing or intending to create for their experiencing in physical reality.

Jefferson: Are these guides part of the person that is being guided or are these guides like an individual with a separate identity?

Ishuwa: It simply depends on how you choose to define them, for "the one is the all, and the all are the one."

Jefferson: Okay.

Ishuwa: So they can be seen as you from a different frequency, a different perspective of you that is helping you. Or you can, if you want to, choose to give them a definition that somehow they are different in some particular way. You can choose to define them as being different from you.

Jefferson: Yeah, but then in that case are they like yourself because I can also say that you are a part of myself since we all come from the One, but still you are an individual and you have your consciousness and you are a separate individual, so to speak, so are spirit guides the same?

Ishuwa: Creating the experience that I am separate from you gives you the opportunity to have this experience. If you were aware of everything that I am as being everything you are then you wouldn't be having this experience because I and you would be completely in alignment as one in how we are perceiving ourself in any given moment. So you wouldn't be able to have this interaction in this way, this play, this performance, this kind of experience.

That's all it really comes down to. You're choosing to play and to interact in this way. You have to have some, in a sense, companions in order to have this experience. So you create in your imagination some other characters to talk to, to play with, somewhat like how a child living on a country farm might choose to create one or two imaginary characters to play with in a way that would give it's parents the perception that their child was simply talking to itself. In a sense, that's what you're doing now. You are just taking to yourself, me. I am you from a different perspective. This allows you to have an experience. It can be fun, or you can create the idea that it is exasperating, or challenging, or frightening, or life threatening, or uplifting, or joyful, or expansive. You are the one that is creating the experiences you have, always, always, always. You create the experiences that you have. You are the one responsible for all of your experiences without exception.

So, are you enjoying this play you are having today in this way with your imaginationary beingness?

Jefferson: If everything that I am experiencing here in this physical world is a product of my imagination and my physical senses are interpreters of vibration then I can also see you as something separate from me the same way as I see this table or this computer as separate. Regarding the idea you shared earlier that if I were to see both of us in unity then perhaps I wouldn't be in physical form anymore since I would be in full alignment with the One, it seems that there has to be some sort of space, and time, and physicality, in order to have separation to begin with otherwise everybody would be the total being of God.

Ishuwa: Space and time is simply something you are choosing to create. It isn't representative of your actual beingness, your actual nature. You choose to create the idea of time and space. There are many different worlds that create time and space in different ways than your world is used to. There are an infinite number of ways to create the perspective of time and space, the experience of time and space. There are worlds that can be created that are not concepts that include time and space as well. There are different ways to create experiences that are entirely incomprehensible to you in your physical state of awareness and being as you experience yourself to be in this moment.

If you, Jefferson, were aligned and focused in the eternal state of being, then you aren't really going to be having a physical experience. You aren't going to be talking to me in this way particularly.

In physical reality you choose, in a sense, to take your focus out of the infinite non-space, non-time state of eternal being so that you can create the perception of a physical realm of experience filled with life explorations. You create the experience of other people. You create the perception that they are different and separate from you so you can have a play, but you simply are All That Is. You simply exist eternally.

You are all things, and if you were to focus on this state of infinite awareness you wouldn't be having a physical experience because, in a sense, all things exist here and now. They are all Isness. You are all of those things here and now, in a sense. You simply are everything simultaneously. There is no sense of yesterday, no sense of tomorrow, no sense of what you did five minutes ago, no sense of what you're going to do five minutes from now, because you already are all of those things, aware of all of those things already right now. So there's no way you can go from here to there because you already are here and there. You can't go from five minutes ago to five minutes from now because you already are five minutes ago and you are five minutes from now. You already are all of those things. You can't be born and have the experience of being five years old and growing to six years old and growing to ten years old because you already are five years old, six years old, and ten years old now!

Jefferson: Interesting.

Ishuwa: You can't go in the kitchen and cook eggs to make an omelet and watch the cheese melting because you already are the eggs, you already are the cheese melting, you already are the omelet, you already are you consuming the omelet, you already are you as the consumed omelet, you already are all of those things here an now, in a sense. So you can't, when you are functioning from that level of infinite awareness where you would be aware of all these things existing simultaneously, you can't then have an experience of the egg cooking, or of growing from five to six years old in age development, or of yesterday, or tomorrow, because you already are yesterday, and you're today, and you're now, you're all of those things because everything simply is here and now, in a sense. Do you begin to get an understanding of this idea?

Jefferson: I am, but it doesn't seem to be fun. If you already are everything, what's the point —

Ishuwa: Well then that is simply how you have been taught to perceive this idea.

Jefferson: Oh.

Ishuwa: For the state of infinite awareness is a state of absolute ecstasy beyond anything you have ever imagined in your physical lifetime I assure you!

Jefferson: I have been told that before!

Ishuwa: There is no way we can prove it to you. The proof, in that sense, is in the tasting of the pudding. Only as you begin to be willing to define this as an aspect of yourself, as a reality for yourself, and also then ask to begin having more experiences that will be reflective of this idea, only then, because "what you put out is what you get back," only then can you begin getting back experiences that will begin confirming this for you in a way that will be like you tasting the pudding. Thus then you'll begin getting the proof. More and more you will feel more of this ecstasy and the more you will then begin to be willing to acknowledge, "Yes, to be more in alignment with my actual nature is more what I prefer. It feels magnificent to me!"

As a human living in this world that you have on Earth, you have so far only experienced ever so slightly the actual magnitude of your infinite nature!

Jefferson: And that was the idea right?

Ishuwa: That was, in a sense, a choice that you all as a collective chose to make for various reasons.

Jefferson: Okay.

Ishuwa: So the you that is listening to me now is seemingly choosing to step out of the eternal, all knowing, all omniscient state of your actual nature so that you can have this physical experience. With that idea in mind, we aren't suggesting that there is a goal to get back into that place where you are being all omniscient, all knowing, because you actually already are there. If you focus back into that state of awareness, then you will seem to have to step out of this place where you are focused now, and you will not then have the awareness of living this life you are having now because this life requires you to have the perception of past, present, and future. So then that wouldn't be the thing we suggest you do.

The idea again, we are not suggesting you set a goal to get back where you can be in this omniscient state of awareness. You already are in that place, but you, Jefferson, are choosing to create the idea that you are having a physical experience on Earth because that in this moment is actually what is really most preferable for you. So as you realize this and are willing to let go of the idea of trying to get back to that place of the all omniscient state of infinite beingness, forget trying to get back there, you already are there. You already are all of those things.

The idea we suggest is to learn to acknowledge that you already are all things and to also realize that you are a master of creating interactions in your physical reality and thus can remember how to create in ways that can be delicious, revealing, tantalizing, and a joy for you to have experiencings of in your world, in your life, in ways that will for you be fascinating, and enjoyable, and meaningful, and purposeful, and enriching, and feel like the great abundance that you prefer. You will be without any sense of the need for security for you will recognize that your security is infinitely secured for you already simply because you are an infinite being.

To simply be willing to follow your heart is what we want to suggest here for it knows what is most enjoyable for you to experience in this life without question. It does not hesitate to move forward in ways that will be of greatest joy for you, that will provide you with the greatest joyful experience in this lifetime, that will be the most meaningful and give the greatest sense of purpose, the greatest sense of secured abundance in the ways you prefer.

Your heart can guide you in these ways because it is simply more in alignment with your actual infinite state of beingness. It is the guidance mechanism that will not fail you. It will, for many, take time to learn how to get back into contact with this internal heartfelt guidance system, for it is so simple. It is so effortless that it can be hard to locate for many people who have been struggling for so long, who have been carrying so much mental weight and feel weighed down, who have been taught so many heavy serious concepts that have filtered and fogged up their ability to see more clearly, more easily, more effortlessly.

Learn once again how to recognize delicate beautiful sensations and feelings that come from the heart, the infinitely knowledgeable guidance system within that is like an internal tree of life, fruit of life, that has knowledge and infinite understandings that are always fruitfully available for you to realize, to taste, to dine upon, in ways that are always available and in ways in which that fruit of heartfelt guidance will not and cannot perish and need not be zipped up in a plastic baggie and placed into a dark frozen box of ice crystals. It is eternal so it does not need to be secured. Its existence within you is infinite.

As more people are willing to define their heart as being the guidance mechanism that will allow them to be more in alignment with the path and purpose of their truest self in this incarnation in their current physical life, it becomes easier for them to then open the "mental ice box," in a sense, and take out the plastic baggies that contain old frozen crystallized ideas and beliefs. They can easily unzip and dispose of those old frozen definitions of limitation and separation and then enjoy the fresh fruits of eternal knowledge that their heart can guide them to continually and remind them of consistently so they will be able to enjoy more of their life's actual flavors, aromas, and ingredients that have, in a sense, infinite vitamins and minerals that will boost the body of physiology, the body of feeling, the body of thought, the body of psychic abilities, the body of psychology, the body of your spiritual beingness, and do so in the most nourishing ways, in the most healing of ways everyday!

Jefferson: Ishuwa.

Ishuwa: Yes.

Jefferson: What are the main differences between your society and ours in terms of the ability to perceive time and the oneness of time?

Ishuwa: We define ourselves as being that which is the Creator of our reality, that which is thus then connected to All That Is, creating All That Is. We will share with you again that your world has chosen to explore the idea of separation and limitation. In order to do that, you realized you had to create the concept that you were separate from the Creator and that you were not the Creator of your reality. So you created the concept that there was a Creator outside of you. Because you actually are the Creator of your reality, this concept is then the opposite of your actual nature, and because "what you put out is what you get back" you began in your experience to develop this other world, this illusory world in which you were losing contact with the awareness that you actually are the Creator. You began losing contact with this fruit of knowledge and its tree of infinite life.

Over many generations of putting out these ideas that are actually opposite your actual nature, you cast your aware selves out of the garden of your eternal knowing, your eternal Eden, the eternal heaven of your ecstatic actual nature. In a sense, you forgot your eternal nature and seemingly became disconnected from it.

Your actual state of being is where the real Garden of Eden is. When you are aware of your real state of being, you are connected with the garden and the fruit of knowledge on your tree of eternal life. You are aware of it. You understand your actual nature in that sense. You have this knowledge of your actual nature.

But, again, in the past you chose to cast out that information from your state of awareness. You chose to believe you were separate and that your Creator was outside of you. Over time, that created the movie, the play, the experience that has been projected back at you for so long of being separate, of being without something that would nourish you, complete you, and provide you with the sense that you are whole, complete, fulfilled.

Your society as a whole began to feel as though it was missing something and it began thus then creating ideas that, "this will complete you," or "that will complete you." Many of these discordant teachings can be found in the good book and they are all simply variations of the carrot being dangled in front of you. The more you listen to those, the more you put out those ideas, the more you will get back experiences of not ever actually getting into contact with the carrot. For those ideas and beliefs are out of alignment with your actual nature. And when you put out things that are out of alignment with your actual nature, you continuously get back experiences or reflections on the "movie screen of life" that are out of alignment with your actual nature. You continue to be a participant in a play that is disconnected from its actual nature. This feels uncomfortable, especially when done over thousands of years like your society has been doing. It feels like something is missing, yes.

That which is missing is the true knowledge, the true fruit, the true Garden of Eden, which is in most simple of terms that you are the Creator. You always have been. It is not outside of you. It is you. It is within you always. It cannot ever be taken away from you, but you have found a way to create the perception that it isn't who you are and, in that sense, you did create the idea of separation. In that way, you created the perspective that the Creator had been taken away from you, but it was an illusion. So many people are still living in this maya, this illusion that their Creator is outside of them.

We in our society do not create that idea of being separate from our Creator. So regarding your question, we would say that is the primary difference. We know who we are. We know we are the Creator, and we know that everything that we are experiencing is us and is also the Creator, even if it is coming from a different point of view, a different perspective such as a different creature, a different life-form, a different thought, a different feeling.

We know who we are! This doesn't mean we can't experience aspects of ourselves in new and fascinating, and exciting, and loving, and nurturing, and heart embracing relationship ways. To know who we are doesn't exclude our ability to have those types of joyful surprises. They happen more often is the actual truth of the nature of that understanding.

The more you know who you are the more you have enriching, joyful, and fascinating experiences, for fascinating, joyful, uplifting experiences are infinite. There is not a limited supply of them. There is no lack of them in the actual nature of Existence. So we know who we are. Your world chose to create a world in which you have not known who you are. That was the choice that you made in order to have a particular type of experience, a particular physical world of experiencing, that of not knowing who you are. That choice is the primary difference, and it allows for you to create the experiences of lack, of needing to do things in order to be secure for the rest of your life, and so on and so forth.

We in no way are trying to demean the choice that you have made. It is a fascinating choice. It is of equal value to the choice that we have made to know who we are. It is a choice that is of equal value to us and also as far as the Y, O, U, Youniverse is concerned, as far as Existence is concerned. It is an equal choice, and we find it a fascinating choice that you have made.

We are grateful to have the opportunity to explore and experience how you encounter that idea. We also are grateful that you have chosen us and many other teachers to come back and reconnect you to the understanding once again of your actual nature so you can let go of the limited old idea that you are not the Creator, that you are separate. For that old limited idea will no longer serve you in any way that you are preferring. It will only serve you to experience more pain, more fog, and less clarity, more guilt, more devaluation, and less joy, less worth, less feeling of worthiness.

Your actual nature is of infinite worth. To create the concept of separation and of a Creator being outside of you will only support and bring back experiences of worthlessness and lack of honor, lack of respect, lack of worth, lack of love, and then thus the need for security follows suit in a world that continues to create such plays, such acts of illusion, such magic tricks, such magical illusions. You are all great magicians creating a show in which many of you have, in a sense, pulled your heart out of a hat and made it disappear. Some day soon as a collective society you are all going to make your hearts reappear, at which time the audience of humanity will applaud to no end. There will be a standing ovation the likes of which has never been recorded in your history, your herstory, whichever you prefer.

Do you get what the main difference is between our society and your society?

Jefferson: Yes! Thank you very much! I enjoyed this exchange immensely Ishuwa!

Ishuwa: Are you sure?!

Jefferson: I am positive! I am sure, and I can repeat it! I enjoyed this exchange immensely!

Ishuwa: Can you count the ways?

Jefferson: Yes, but then we would remain here until next month!

Ishuwa: Oh very good, thank you!

Jefferson: Thank you. It is always comforting to have the opportunity to exchange knowledge with another facet of yourself right? With another aspect of Creation!

Ishuwa: Yes! We agree with you!

Jefferson: So, are there any parting thoughts you would like to share with us today?

Ishuwa: We thank you for this interaction. It is a great joy to be with you and to have this opportunity to share these ideas. We appreciate your willingness to take the time to ask these questions and to explore these ideas and concepts that we may then bring forth our perspective as it relates to these ideas and questions that you share with us. We feel the information can be of value. It has been a value for our society and many others that we feel are enjoying their understanding and their experiences within this ecstatic Youniverse that we are all the one of which we are the all.

As to your presence and participation with us today, again, we acknowledge and understand the time that you set aside. We appreciate it and so that for us is a great joy, to blend, to share, to interact with you in these ways. Is there something else before we say good day that you would like to add?

Jefferson: One thing Ishuwa, just one thing. How many nations do you have in the Association of Worlds?

Ishuwa: There are approximately four-hundred. They do change, the numbers. For various reasons.

Jefferson: Okay, that was it. We will continue with many other questions for you on another day. Sure enough this is for me a joy. I recognize and I thank you immensely and your society and everybody that is here interacting with us who also have the willingness to share these points of view of creation!

Ishuwa: Thank you dear one! Much love and joy for you and in your experiencing of your day!

Jefferson: Thank you!

Ishuwa: We will see you very soon. Don't forget the dragon of great joy is flying about in the realms of your neighborhood these days.

Jefferson: Tomorrow morning I will be there!

Ishuwa: Wonderful! Good day!

Jefferson: Good day Ishuwa! Thank you!

Here is a portion of Jefferson's conversation with Ishuwa after visiting Chinatown in San Francisco, California.

Ishuwa: We bring through the following idea. Before Arch Angel Michael, before the Suns of your heavenly experience on Earth, before you came to see this world, before you came to explore this idea of life here, there was a beautiful idea about the nature of life and how it all works and you understood this idea. You have brought this idea with you.

Jefferson: Okay.

Ishuwa: For you, the symbol for this idea had a very large wing. It had a very large neck. It had a very large tail. It had a very large eye. It seemed to be able to move through objects at will. It seemed to be able to fly at will into every idea, into every moment in this place that you were in, in the space. Now, in your world today, you would think of it as a dragon, but that shape is just a symbol for the idea that you carry within you. Accessing the idea is the key!

We perceive you have lost some of this connection around that idea and what the symbol was originally all about for you. What can you tell us about your experience with that street-side culture in Chinatown that you visited so recently in the land that is symbolized in some ways with dragons?

Jefferson: It made me think about elements like the wind, the fire, the water, and the earth. It brought me more into the idea that we are benders in the sense that if we realize the truth about life then we can bend physical matter with mind and heart.

Ishuwa: And how does that feel for you?

Jefferson: It feels great! It feels like I am an alchemist, and I can perform those things if I want to!

Ishuwa: And are you doing that now?

Jefferson: In subjective ways, like in dreams or in my imagination, but not necessarily in the physical world.

Ishuwa: Why so?

Jefferson: Because I still believe that this is true!

Ishuwa: That what is true?

Jefferson: The matter.

Ishuwa: The matter?

Jefferson: The physical matter, the walls, the buildings, the computer.

Ishuwa: But you are the one being the alchemist that is placing form into those shapes!

Jefferson: So, you're saying that before I came to Earth, I had a tail? That's interesting.

Ishuwa: No, that is part of the symbol.

Jefferson: Oh.

Ishuwa: You did not have any of that form at all. That was simply a symbol that you could use to retain your connection to the idea of what that energy was all about.

Jefferson: I see.

Ishuwa: You came into this physical body here on Earth to explore certain elements: the earth, the air, the fire, the water, and ether or prana. You came to explore such elements and to be, in that sense, an alchemist to see how you could shape them and shift them as an alchemist, as a wizard, as a magician.

Jefferson: Okay.

Ishuwa: You came here with others to work with those elements. You knew before you came here that you would likely lose some awareness of your true Self but you wanted to come here in order to be an alchemist in a whole new way. The symbol was a way to remind you or reconnect you to your inner awareness that you are an alchemist. The symbol of the dragon was like a heartstone that you could think of and thus be reminded of your truer Self.

Jefferson: I see.

Ishuwa: You felt the symbol could prevent you from getting lost and losing hope in the strange and limited world that you all were going to explore together on Earth. You wanted to come to this new world to create new things, to see life in a whole different way. Those you came here with felt the symbol could remain within your awareness and act as beacon to always call you home when you meditated upon it. You felt the energy within that symbol could connect you back to the understanding that you have the whole picture within you at all times.

Jefferson: Okay.

Ishuwa: This is one idea around that symbol, not the only idea.

Jefferson: Oh.

Ishuwa: Meditating on the symbol and connecting to the idea within you that it symbolizes will help you in this timing. It will help you in matters that relate to topics you have spoken about earlier with us. It will help you with matters that relate to your work and interacting with others in the way you spoke about in the conversation you have had recently with your mother. You spoke to her about people at work and why you have the perceptions you do in regards to them. You also spoke to her about friends. Where they all are, how many there are, and how many there aren't. As an alchemist, you must understand how to blend your sense of awareness about these matters more fully. As you do, old beliefs will begin to unravel for you.

You have a long chain, a very long chain that you have wrapped around yourself. It has been around you for some time. It is ready to unwind. It is ready to unlink. It is ready to be removed so you may be more aware of what your shape really looked like before the symbol of the dragon came forth.

The flame that comes from the dragon's mouth is that which allows you to evaporate the chain-links. You can melt those links. They will then be altered alchemically through your wizardry. Do this and you will thus then find blooming in the "garden of realization" of yourself two entirely "new flowers."

Jefferson: Okay.

Ishuwa: When that occurs, you will know more easily that it's time to make a move in your life; moving either in regards to your apartment that you live in or in regards to the work that you currently find yourself at. It will be very clear to you when the two "new flowers" are blooming. Until that time, we ask that you be patient so that you can begin to feel that the flower is already present and that its aroma is surrounding you. It too will be another guide that will be around you. The "scent of understanding" you gain from this process will expand your realization of life and you will then perceive the types of friends you spoke about with your mother and the workplace interactions in a more understanding and playful way. You are very close to this way.

Jefferson: Nice! Truly good!

Ishuwa: Sweet to have had this interaction with you!

Jefferson: Yes, and me with you too!

Chapter 11

The First Time Ishuwa Heard About Earth

"Surrender to the idea that your heart knows the way and will guide you sensorially with feelings of great joy. The more you do this, the more you will be able to effortlessly experience that you have all you need to have and also that you know what you need to know when you need to know it to be supported in the ways that create the greatest sense of joy." – Ishuwa

September 7th, 2009

Ishuwa: Most lovely to be here with you in these afternoon blending moments as you create this afternoon of your experience to exist! How are you?

Jefferson: I am fantastic, great! Thank you very much. Welcome back!

Ishuwa: Good to be here this afternoon in the presence of your day! How would you like to play in this interaction, in this creation of a whole new third reality together that can thus bring about new ideas that can be shared with others and in that fashion and in that form meld a higher frequency and bond a relationship most strong with greater strength that some day we can actually come together and meet one another in a physical way, in a form of physical contact, peacefully, joyfully, upliftingly, enrichingly, yes. How would you like to interact?

Jefferson: Ishuwa, of all the recreational activities of which you are involved in or have been involved in, which one do you or did you like the most?

Ishuwa: I don't have a sense of one more than the other, in that sense. Life has always been an ongoing expansive sensation of growth and enjoying. I don't create then the apparatus to function in a way, to compare in that way, something as being more enjoyable then another, for in each moment each has been the most enjoyable I could possibly bring forth in my experience.

I know that in each seemingly successive moment into what you would call the future, I will be having a new joyful experience that will be fully satisfying. So I won't go back and compare it to something I experienced in the past to create the idea that one is somehow more enjoyable than the other. I don't, in that sense, create a frame of reference of going back to a past time and asking, "Was this present moment more joyful than that one on that day or in that period of my growth and experience in my life journey?" I simply allow for each moment to be that of most joy while knowing that what will come in the future will certainly be joyful for me. I let it be at that without the need to go back into the past and try and compare and contrast that idea in that way. Do you follow that?

Jefferson: Yes! Thank you! Ishuwa?

Ishuwa: Yes.

Jefferson: In what dimension does your planet exist in? Is it the fourth dimension?

Ishuwa: Our planet does have a fourth dimension existence. I am primarily in a fifth to sixth dimension transition state of consciousness at this timing. So, fourth for the physical planet and transitioning from fifth to sixth for the state of consciousness.

Jefferson: Okay, I see. So what are some lifestyle changes that your race or perhaps you need to make to accommodate your planet moving into the fifth dimension frequency?

Ishuwa: We know that whatever changes need to be made will occur in the appropriate way and in the appropriate timing. So then we don't have, in that sense, some kind of a plan or goal that certain ideas need to be met so that we will fit in with the new dimension. We don't know how the new dimension will be, for we haven't, in that sense, been there in our present state of awareness. When we do become aware of getting there, whatever it is like in that new dimension of consciousness, it will be completely different from anything we could have imagined in our present place, our present dimension of awareness. So we don't, in that sense, make plans to accommodate the new dimension other than to always be in the place of greatest joy!

We allow ourself to be stepping along and taking the path that is of greatest joy for us in each moment. Because we do this, we know that as we progress into that next dimension it will be what it is. It will be most joyful for us. We will be prepared for it simply because we have been doing the most joyful thing that we could do along the path of greatest joy, in that sense. Choosing this path is what then we know will provide us with everything we need to know when we arrive at that new dimension to be most prepared, to be most able to appreciate it, and acknowledge it, and recognize it, and interact in it in ways that give us the greatest sense of meaning, and purpose, and playfulness, and excitement!

Jefferson: What do you think may be some changes that our society will need to make to accommodate our next move up in dimension?

Ishuwa: Surrender to the idea that your heart knows the way and will guide you sensorially with feelings of great joy. The more you do this, the more you will be able to effortlessly experience that you have all you need to have and also that you know what you need to know when you need to know it to be supported in the ways that create the greatest sense of joy.

Let go of the idea that you need to plan for that movement into the next dimension, and instead allow yourself to be more in your heart, to be guided more in that sensation of your heart, what feels like the greatest joy for you that you are able to move in. Take the steps of greatest joy that you can take.

Your society will do great service to itself by beginning to more fully educate that idea, to accept that idea, to follow the heart.

Jefferson: What are the main differences from your perspective of a human body that exists in the third dimension and a body that exists in the fourth dimension?

Ishuwa: You are working with more semantics in how you define these words. You have the idea of physical space where you can move about left and right, top and bottom, forward and backward. These give you a sense of having dimensions of movement in that regard, as though there are three dimensions of space: left/right, front/back, and top/bottom. This can be a X, Y, Z axis, 3D. You can then consider a fourth dimension as that of "time" with the perception of past, present, and future. So this can be an idea of the four dimensional physical reality in which you exist.

However, your consciousness can have a whole different framework of dimensionality to it that is different from this idea of 3D or 4D physical spatial time dimension. Your consciousness can have a whole different experience of dimensionality, of frequency, of the consciousness in which it is tuning in to.

You are, in a sense, moving more into a fifth dimensional consciousness as a society now in which the heart has a greater connection to your state of awareness and is more then allowing you to be in tune with consciousnesses that are more in alignment with your actual nature.

You have been in a very thick third dimensional consciousness that allows for a great sense of separation from the heart. Again, this third dimensional of consciousness is different than the idea of physical "3D" dimensionality with the X, Y, Z axis of space: left/right, top/bottom, front/back. So it is, in this sense, important to recognize the distinction of dimensions, the dimension of your physical space and time that you are most focused in and the dimension of your consciousness.

You can still have 3D experiences of space-time dimensionality with time as the fourth dimension while you are moving into a fifth dimension of consciousness. They can co-exist. You can have a three dimensional physical world with a fifth dimensional consciousness.

This will give you the ability to then be more connected in your heart while interacting in the idea of 3D. You can become more aware of how you apply the idea of time in the world of three dimensionality, physicality, and you can get a better grasp on the idea of a fourth dimensional physical reality, that of spatial X, Y, Z axis plus time, four dimensions within physical reality. However, remember that your consciousness doesn't have any, in that sense, physicality to it.

Jefferson: I hear you.

Ishuwa: It does allow you to create the perceptions of 3D objects in physical reality, but that is an illusion.

Jefferson: Were you on your planet when it changed physically from third to fourth density?

Ishuwa: I was not present in my current incarnation in that transition.

Jefferson: Have you heard your elders talk about it? Are there books that describe it? How did it happen? How did people change?

Ishuwa: There are a few in our society who are focused on holding that information. This is not something that I focus on simply because I don't resonate with it, but for those who do, it does serve a function. It gives us a vehicle of consciousness and language that allows us to then interact with a society such as yours so we can make translations of the language, the vocabulary, of how you create the world you are perceiving yourself to live in. So it certainly serves a function for us.

Those that are very skilled at doing this provide us with the ability to connect with your world. They are like telecommunication experts of the networks, in a sense, that know how to link us up effectively with your society and then we are able in that way to simply communicate with you as I am now. But myself, I am not focused on that transition the way they are. It simply isn't something of great need for me to work on while we have others who find great joy tending to those ideas of transitioning from one dimension to another.

Jefferson: Do you have any idea what the main differences will be in your physical body when it moves from fourth to fifth dimension of physicality?

Ishuwa: I imagine it will be lighter, and it will be moving at a faster vibration. Anyone who was in a lower dimension might see me and get the impression that I was becoming very ghost-like and somewhat invisible.

Jefferson: Ethereal?

Ishuwa: Yes. I imagine I would not feel like I had made much of a change in that regard. I will still have a perception of my body and being in the body, but I will understand that a change is taking place. I will understand that it is a higher frequency body that is capable of doing things more fluidly and flexibly. It will be less static and more adaptable.

I will then at certain timings have new ideas come into mind of how to go about exploring life while in this body and doing things that before I couldn't do. I will move about a physical landscape in slightly different ways. I will be more mobile and perhaps be a little bit more capable of flight, in a sense, without focusing on the ideas of moving from one frequency of location to another one. The body can become a bit lighter and more flexible, more malleable, and I can thus then in some worlds of physicality, I can simply, you might say, walk on water. That wouldn't be extraordinary because there would be others there who had already been doing that their whole life. They would understand it is remarkable, yes, but they wouldn't then get up and start praising me or worshiping me if I was to walk on water, in that sense. It wouldn't be remarkable in a way that they would then kneel down or start bowing to me.

Jefferson: Perhaps that could help other people to find that particular ability within themselves.

Ishuwa: Others could learn, yes!

Jefferson: Have you ever interacted with any fifth dimensional beings that are from other planets?

Ishuwa: Yes, certainly! We have and continue to on a regular ongoing basis in my experience in this lifetime.

Jefferson: Ishuwa, what do you consider to be the most significant experience on your resume?

Ishuwa: Every moment is! Again, it's like the idea you asked before about what moments do I most enjoy. It really is quite that way for me.

Jefferson: I see.

Ishuwa: I don't, in that sense, have a "most." I don't create something that I compare things to in that regard. Do you follow that idea?

Jefferson: Yeah, yeah, yeah. So, as far as civilization then, in regards to accomplishment, what is the biggest accomplishment for your civilization?

Ishuwa: We will let you describe or define accomplishment from your perspective and then let's go from there.

Jefferson: Alright. From my perspective, an accomplishment has to do with working on something until I have completed it successfully.

Ishuwa: Yes, thank you! Ask the question again please?

Jefferson: What would be your society's biggest accomplishment?

Ishuwa: We have many accomplishments every day, but to ask then "what is the biggest" suggests that there are some that perhaps were not as big. So again, the idea is that they are all of equal accomplishment. A goal is always of equal value to any other goal to us.

Jefferson: I hear you.

Ishuwa: So we don't, in that sense, value one as being biggest, or more important, or more significant than another one. To us they are all of equal value, equal significance, equal importance, and this allows us to have a more fulfilling experience of each moment whatever we are accomplishing in any given moment.

Jefferson: As a space brother, perhaps you have come across a variety of issues in many different ways. So what issues have you found to be uncomfortable to handle?

Ishuwa: In my experience, since the time of my birth, I have had no sense of an issue that couldn't be handled without a deep sense of comfort throughout. From the inception of the issue there was comfort. Being acquainted with the issue, there was comfort in that experience. As I gained more insight into the nature of the issue, there was great comfort in the gaining of that insight as well. As I began to get ideas of what I could do to assist or participate in resolving the issue, I had great comfort in that as well. As there was greater understanding taking place with those parties involved with the issue, I had great comfort as the understandings began to expand. As those involved began voicing their ideas, and opinions, and sharing their experiences that related to the issue, I had great comfort in that experience, in that process of this unveiling, in that experiencing moment to moment of these steps that I was taking along my path in my life.

I know experiencing the issue is a part of my life and how I go through it is also a part of my life. I know with anything that is happening in my life I can experience great comfort and joy. Because I know this is so and I choose to experience and put that idea out, I get back the opportunity to move through it and have all ideas within it be comforting to me. Thus even then in the resolution, as you may perceive it when the issue or those parties involved accomplish some kind of agreement, there is also great comfort in that as well.

There is comfort from the beginning and during the resolving process of developing a communication line for all parties involved. There is comfort there and also in the departing of those involved as they then go about in their own directions, their own path. There is great comfort in that as well.

There is comfort in knowing that those involved were able to receive and grow in the ways that they felt most enriched by. It is a very comforting process, in a sense, for us to have particular issues brought into our realm of awareness. They are opportunities. They are not in any way an obstacle or a problem. We approach such opportunities as a joy in which we get to discover those aspects of ourself and the other parties involved and become more connected and in tune with how they are experiencing life, how they are seeing life, how they are defining life, and for us to share that with them too.

Jefferson: I see.

Ishuwa: So we begin to be on a similar wavelength, as though we are playing music together like musicians coming together in a like way, in a rapport that is comforting for those parties involved. It is a very comforting process. There is no problem, no obstacle, no conflict. The entire experience is very comforting. Do you follow this idea?

Jefferson: Yeah. Let me ask you something else.

Ishuwa: Yes!

Jefferson: Let's go back in your past, perhaps within this particular lifetime of yours. Can you recollect or remember the first time you heard someone speak about Earth?

Ishuwa: One moment.

Jefferson: When was it? Where were you? How old you were?

Ishuwa: I was approximately four years old.

Jefferson: You were four, and where were you?

Ishuwa: I was with my family and there were, you might call elders, but not in any way more wise, they simply were of a focus of, you could say, they were very skilled at guiding and enlightening young ones on our planet, of getting young ones in touch with what it is that they perhaps would like to do in life. Elders can help the young recognize the subtle nudges within the heart so the young can more easily recognize a path that they sense would be of great joy for them, or pathways, or initial paths from which to build future paths upon.

Jefferson: Wonderful!

Ishuwa: It's a bit like a council of Native Americans or native cultures that sometimes still do this on your planet. They come together with the family, with the child, and with some of the elders or wise chiefs as they are sometimes labeled in cultures on your world.

While I was with my family and some elders, they began to assist me in learning how this process works a little more fully. During this experience, I began to see a specific path of life-interaction unfolding that would be great joy.

Jefferson: How lovely!

Ishuwa: And I felt great joy! I felt waves of great joy, and they weren't stopping! They just kept flowing through me! This continued for what you would consider a long time in this meeting, in this council. The Sun would rise over several days, and I kept feeling this flow, this joy! It was very strong, and it had to do with my ability to interact with some on Earth. That then was my beginning, my initial contact with the idea of Earth from the frame of reference of the four-year-old Ishuwa in that incarnation as a Yahyel at that time.

Then I began to make contact with the individual that you are listening to now, (Shaun), who is the channel in this lifetime on your world. I made contact with him in a particular fashion, in a particular way. That contact occurred for him quite some time ago in his present embodiment, and he is only beginning to come into realization of that.

It was great joy flowing through my awareness and through my biology, and through my ethereal, and through my feeling state. It was with great joy that I was coming into awareness that this was something I would have an opportunity to do, to interact and to share in the way that I knew would be a great joy for me!

I already had the understanding that I had a way with languages. I had at that time already communicated with over three-hundred different societies of extraterrestrial races and had a very strong form of translation capacity such that there were many in my family and those within the community and culture of my race that were able to identify that I had strong skills and abilities of this nature. Before I became aware of this ability, my family could sense it very clearly. They felt my great joy from this reckoning in this realization with my connection to Earth. They then also began for the first time to realize that it would be something of an opportunity to interact with Earth humans as a form of translation that would be of great service for their society as well.

So back to the council meeting. Those who were present knew that I was capable of doing translating with extraterrestrial races. They were of the idea that my choosing to be of service in some way as a translator would probably be what would come through from this particular council meeting of mine with them, but they weren't aware that it would be with a place called Earth. At the point in time of that council, Earth was something we knew was a planet, yes, we were aware of. It was a planet we had ideas of and have had interactions with previously, yes. In the library of our interactions, we know of this place Earth.

As a result of connecting with the idea of interacting with Earth, it was then they began to learn a bit more about it, began to focus on it more clearly. This then became exciting for several of them, exciting in many different ways. As a society, as a whole, it became exciting for us as well.

There were two individuals present in the council meeting who understood what was taking place. They were well aware that this was something that would likely occur, the idea of our interaction with your world at sometime in your future, but for the rest of those present at the meeting it was new. During this council, those two elders weren't thinking about ideas related to me interacting with Earth and so they didn't impact what I perceived and what I "linked into" during the council. They were able to remain free from tapping into the possibilities of what I might connect with. They did not alter the discovery for me.

So that would have been the first time Earth came to my aware. It was a wonderful, joyful, playful party! It was a very expansive and uplifting experience for me. In a sense, you could say that it was a wonderful accomplishment.

Jefferson: Okay. So that was...okay...wow...very good! How did you learn more about Earth? Did you start asking around, asking people on other planets? Did you start coming here and observing us or observe us from TV sets?

Ishuwa: I began to put out the idea of, "Let's connect to Earth in ways that will be the most uplifting and the most fulfilling for me, most educational, most important, and certainly most in alignment with my heart." Those ideas and opportunities then came forward and presented themselves to me in a myriad of different ways. Realizing the value of connecting with and tapping into my heart and its gentle nudges of guidance, I paid attention and recognized these opportunities, these nudges. I thus then would follow my heart in that way, take those steps, and thus then those opportunities became clear to me.

There were times when I was talking to others who had actually visited Earth. At other times, I was reading about it in some of our records, in a sense, a history and account that we have gathered over time from our own interactions and from those sharings with other extraterrestrial races as well. I had physical visitations of the planet, and there is also the opportunity to have telepathic communications as well.

There are many other ways as well in which I have come to know this place you call Earth. There are many different types of interactions I have had with many different species and life forms on this planet. I have interacted with it on various timelines in terms of how you perceive time there, different generations, different decades, different centuries, in that sense, different timings in the geological record of planet Earth.

Sometimes there were no people as you would see it today on this planet and I have visited some of those periods as well. I have had some encounters with life forms that aren't anything at all like those that live here today. This has been a great joy to have these opportunities, and again, they always present themselves to me as the result of synchronicities that come forth simply from my following my heart and knowing that doing so always gives me the greatest guidance mechanism for what will be of greatest joy and service for me as a Yahyel in this present journey of great joy and discovery!

Jefferson: Okay. Today you are able to communicate with humans through a channel like Shaun.

Ishuwa: In this form of communication, yes, but it is not the only way I communicate with those here on Earth. There are some telepathic interactions that occur too.

Jefferson: Nice.

Ishuwa: I do not always communicate through a channel like Shaun in this form of spoken word that you are listening to now. This form of communicating provides the opportunity for you to put together the book as you have been working together with Shaun to do. There are still many who enjoy reading books with this kind of information as a form of education, as a form of entertainment, as a form of growth.

Jefferson: And is anyone else on Earth able to channel Ishuwa or just Shaun?

Ishuwa: There are others, yes, but at this time it isn't occurring in this fashion.

Jefferson: Very good. How has your civilization changed or what have you learned about yourself since your first visitation to our solar system and Earth?

Ishuwa: I had the first hand experience of what it's like to live in such limitation.

Jefferson: Oh.

Ishuwa: I was able to see how people can interact in ways that seem to them to be very meaningful, very important, and very serious, and yet be so far removed from their actual nature. They aren't just joking around. There are people there who are very serious in their desire to remain limited. They really don't want anybody to "stir up the pot" and bring about a more expansive awareness. It's a very unusual thing to see someone hold onto a very heavy "ball and chain" and not want to be given a key to be released from that kind of pain and agony. For us to experience people in your world doing that expands our understanding, not only mine, but our society's. We can then more fully appreciate what another person, another life form, is choosing to create even if what they are experiencing is so removed from who they really are.

We learn more fully to accept life forms that have a willingness to create such darkness. We can accept people that go so deeply into despairs that are illusions where they want so strongly to remain and are willing to fight so that no one will take them back into a place of Eden in a garden of heavenly experiencing where they can have a full awareness of their whole true nature. Their choices give us the ability to really accept that and to appreciate and love those life forms that choose to remain so disconnected and live in such an illusion, in such a theater of darkness.

Jefferson: What does being a team player mean to a planet such as yours that is participating in the Association of Worlds?

Ishuwa: We work together to understand more of who we are. We interact with other societies who, in a sense, are us from different points of view. Through cooperation, we are able to learn more about who we are by interacting with and learning about those other societies.

As we come more into a depth of relationship with them, a deeper bond, a deeper sharing of what it is that enlivens them, enriches them, awakens them, has their heart beating so playfully, that then through the team player idea of cooperating and supporting one another helps us to find new ways to share more about one another. We are able to really convey the idea more deeply, more fully, more expansively.

We then begin to step into the shoes of the other and really feel what it is they are feeling, experience what it is they are experiencing, to the degree that we are excited about doing so.

This is one idea then. Cooperating to realize more of our whole nature by experiencing more of what it is like to be these other races, these other beings, these other life forms, to in a sense, live a day in their life, in their shoes, in their home, from their point of view.

Jefferson: A few days ago I asked you what societies of extra-terrestrials are closest to humans on Earth. You said that there are two that at times can be closest to us, and you said there might come a time when we could do a co-blended channeling with them through Shaun. You said if I felt nudged at some point in the future to ask you about them you would check-in to see whether or not it is time to participate in a co-blended channeling through Shaun with one or both of them. So I feel nudged now to ask you, would it be appropriate today to have either of these two races give us a message?

Ishuwa: Well, not at this time. However, we will revisit some of that idea now. We suggested there are seven races that your society and our society are most genetically linked to. One of them being the Annunaki and the other being Zeta. There are five others. You may know of them. We will not refer to them now. Two of those five that we will not speak of today will be then those that would come through in a co-blending. That would occur for another book, in a sense, as though this book is the first of a series of related books!

Jefferson: Yes!

Ishuwa: There is the coming of information through conversations not only with Ishuwa but also with your children that are from your future that are here now, in that sense.

Jefferson: Wow!

Ishuwa: Your ET children have information to share with their parents, in a sense, and with their grandparents, to let them know "how it's going."

Jefferson: Okay!

Ishuwa: Your child and children have learned so much, and most of that is a result of what your society laid the groundwork for us to be able to do. The foundation you built in your society for us to then build upon as we reached out further into the heavens, into the interspatial realms of our infinite universal existence. There is much you can learn from your children and so it is time again for us to share the idea of coming back into your society ever so peacefully to share and to enlighten you how it's been going.

Jefferson: I see. That is exciting!

Ishuwa: Yes! And so that co-blending and the names of those two of the five we have not spoken of yet will be able to begin more sharing from their perspective. It might be in a second book!

Jefferson: Very good!

Ishuwa: But it might not be until a third book. That can happen, but again, when you feel guided or nudged, feel free to speak or to ask about this idea for it lets us know where you are in your frequency around this potential doorway to be open and for that information to then come through more easily, and more readily, and more clearly.

Jefferson: Very good! Are there any beings from your society that are aware of this communication and this book that we're producing or is this book just something that exists for you as a personal experience, a personal interaction between you and I?

Ishuwa: There are some strong possibilities in your time line to see it manifest, that idea of the book, yes. We can see that. We are aware of that, but it isn't then our place to make it happen.

Jefferson: My question was more an attempt to learn if there are people in your society that are aware that we are having this conversation for the purpose of putting it into a book?

Ishuwa: Yes. This dialogue is available to all in our society to tune into in any capacity that they want to, whether it be for one word or for the entire channeling session. There are those who do that because it is something they enjoy, and in doing that, they serve a function for our society in various capacities such as making the information then available, in a sense, keeping a record of it for others who aren't present now so they can come back and tap into it in a timing that is suiting in their day to day interactivities, connect with this in a way and in a timing that would be most exciting for them to do so. There are many present. Some of which have been present in each one of these sessions. Some come and go. Some for the first time. Some come and go regularly in all sessions that you have had thus far. Some have been present for the entirety of one or two of them. Some of those are present for this one. Some are not.

Jefferson: How many have been present in all of the sessions we have had?

Ishuwa: There have been approximately 312,000.

Jefferson: Seriously!?

Ishuwa: That have checked in at some point to this idea.

Jefferson: Okay! It's hard to speak to you in a linear term because when you say 312,000 then I'd have to refer to the idea that at some point they did, therefore since there is no timeline really and the flexibility is big, then it looks almost as if they have really been there all the same time in every session.

Ishuwa: Can you detail what it is you are sharing with us a little bit differently?

Jefferson: Yes. I was just thinking out-loud, but thank you for your curiosity. Let me put it in a question format. For example, I was asking you before how many beings have participated in these interactions that you are having with us since the beginning?

Ishuwa: Yes.

Jefferson: And then you said a big number.

Ishuwa: Over 312,000.

Jefferson: Yes. So basically when you get connected through Shaun to speak to me, do you have all those people there with you while you're talking to us and are they listening to our conversation or learning from that?

Ishuwa: There would be a blending of a group mind, in a sense, that allows for that to take place. So then it really feels more like one mind, in a sense, that I am the one speaking for those numbers.

Jefferson: Ohhhh, I see! I see! Wow! And are they all from your civilization?

Ishuwa: Yes. We were referring only to those from our civilization, but there are others from other civilizations that are present in a similar way as well.

Jefferson: And why are those of these other civilizations present? What is there in it for them?

Ishuwa: The "why" is because it is of joy for them and most joyful for them to be present.

Jefferson: And as they join in, do they do so from their planet by using telepathy or do they come to your planet because it's easier or something?

Ishuwa: We do have a group network, as it were, that they can all tap into, a particular frequency which is like being in the room, but it is a frequency of consciousness they can focus on and then tap into the dialogues taking place through that focused networked channel that is like a central headquarters for this type of communication to take place with you in this way. There are some who are physically present. There are some who will accompany me physically through various sessions. Sometimes I am in various places and they will join me in some of those places.

Jefferson: Very good. So you referred before to a technology similar to a TV where you could see humans or change channels and see another planet. Can you give more details about that technology?

Ishuwa: It allows us to have visualizations that many of us can share at the same time in a similar way, in a sense, we see one image, one screen, and we all are seeing the same screen. We will all experience and translate that image in different ways and then we can explore with other races at the same time what is taking place on that screen, what is being presented, what the images are about.

Several races simultaneously can see the same thing, seemingly see the same thing, and in that way have a shared experience which we all then can if we want, and any number of us will at various times, choose to talk about what it is or simply share what we felt or what we enjoyed about that presentation on the screen. It's not too different from what you would do there in your world. The technology is different, yes. How it is conveyed and the type of screen and materials are different too.

In our society, we do have the capacity to send similar imageries to each other telepathically into our mind's eye, in that sense, and have a similar experience as what you have when you are viewing a television screen or a theater screen in your world. We can share great clarity of image, and light, and colors, and spoken words through images in that way, moving images through the mind's eye, telepathically for a group of us to connect with. But when there are many people from different societies, different races, it can be helpful to have one image, one screen, from which we can all simply look at, for there are many races who have quite different mental, mind, heart patterning frequencies. So it isn't always as easy for them to see the same images within their mind's eye, so to speak, in the same way that we in our world's race are able to see the same image together. Other races don't quite see it the way we do when we work from a mind's eye viewing perspective. Having the television screen makes it easier, in a sense, for the various extraterrestrials participating to have a similar experience, see a similar image.

Jefferson: And who controls what image is going to be going on in a particular channel?

Ishuwa: We all have an idea of what it's to be about, the topic or the central theme, and then there are those who specialize, just as in your world, on bringing forth the images. They have, in a sense, a device to capture the images that are then focused in such a way so as to bring them onto the screen, present them on the screen. It's kind of like how a motion picture camera works in your world.

Jefferson: I see. Who decides what topic is going to be broadcast on a particular day? Is that the elder council?

Ishuwa: It is something that comes about rather organically. There is no director of programs as you may have on your television networks there. It is something that we all tune in to, those who have an interest suddenly for some reason to watch something. We then begin to tune in to what it is we sense we would like, what feels like a topic we'd like to watch with others. As our ideas become more focused, it becomes more apparent what the topic will be about and also what will be the most pleasurable thing to watch as a group. So by having the largest number of people suddenly want to view a particular topic, that then becomes the topic that is conveyed on the screen. It is as though it is the people's choice, so to speak.

Jefferson: When you put on a channel that is showing Earth, do you see humans walking around, or driving in cars, or flying in planes?

Ishuwa: We generally don't have any channels like that. That is something that can be done in a rather focused way by a few individuals. The idea is to learn without interfering in any way with your conscious patternings and goings on in your world. So we don't have a 24-hour cable channel, so to speak, that is always showing "channel Earth."

Jefferson: Okay! I understand. I would like to ask you to tell us what is the most beautiful, conducive, interesting place that you have visited and you can't say they are all beautiful and they are all unique.

I mean, share what you think is a place that is beautiful, conducive, interesting, the best ever to you!

Ishuwa: Are you saying I can or cannot say they are all beautiful?

Jefferson: No, I mean you have to pick one, come-on! Describe one that you think would be interesting to talk about.

Ishuwa: But then if I have to do that and I "put that out," then I begin "getting back" more experiences in which I have to do that!

Jefferson: (Playful laughter). Come-on! So...okay —

Ishuwa: And if I do that, then I begin getting back more experiences that some things might be more beautiful than other things, and I know that isn't how nature actually exists.

Jefferson: Yeah, okay. Let me change the question then. What place do you think we Earth humans would find beautiful if we were to visit in our present state of consciousness?

Ishuwa: Very well.

Jefferson: Thank you.

Ishuwa: You would enjoy a planet in the Helios realm near Sirius. It has a very large form of rain forest in which every being there will come up and greet you with a soft little touch, a little soft electrical vibration, and there is then in that way a welcome feeling that you have in that place. Very colorful! The trees are very orange with some purples, yellows, and greens, and blues. Green is not the predominant color of the foliage of the trees in this rain forest. The raindrops are multi-lingual in the songs that they sing when the rain dances upon the ground in the rain forest. So we sense that would be a very beautiful place in your perception of things. You can invite more of that idea to come through in a dream if you would like.

Jefferson: Where is that again, Sirius?

Ishuwa: Helios, near Sirius. It's a very small planet relative to your Earth. It's rather distant from its Sun, but it is very capable of supporting life as you know it. For the most part, you could be comfortable there for a short visit.

As far as what would be most beautiful from the point of view of others on your world, again, it would be unique for each. For each one of you really can find worlds in any given moment that could be more beautiful then the next, given how you do like to have comparisons, and so there are many levels of beauty and places, in that sense, planets for each of you that you could begin to walk upon. Certainly while in this time of your Earth period, it would generally only occur in your imagination or your day dreaming, so to speak, which as we have said before is every bit as valuable as the world you are presently in physically.

There are some of you that have actually visited these places and perhaps don't remember. Some of you do remember. On your Earth, there are some places you specifically would enjoy. Venturing to some locations in your South America and your Andie mountains. While you perhaps would enjoy the idea of Machu Picchu, there are some communities outside of that at a lower elevation that are more easily accessible but rarely accessed by those from your society. You would find them to be very beautiful as well. You could be guided there if you at some point wanted to journey off into that region.

Jefferson: The planet Helios that you said is near Sirius, what density does this planet exist?

Ishuwa: Approximately a fourth, moving to a fifth consciousness.

Jefferson: Are the beings there humanoid or are they more like light bodies?

Ishuwa: There aren't, in that sense, humanoids actually inhabiting this place. No indigenous people nor indigenous life forms are there in its present cycle of physical life-form expression, but there are many other life forms that will communicate with you if you are there. You would have the ability to have communication in a way that you could have a dialogue of a certain type. It would be like you were communicating with someone here. It wouldn't be like communicating with cats in the way you do where you live, you don't really talk and carry on a two-way conversation with your cats there, generally speaking. There are life forms on Helios with which you could have what would be like a two-way conversation, but you wouldn't be doing it with the spoken word.

Jefferson: Right.

Ishuwa: As I said, there are some life forms there that would, in fact all of them, if they were to touch you it would be a very soft electrical vibration.

Jefferson: Are they the same size as humans?

Ishuwa: There are some, but most of these are going to be much smaller, maybe a foot or two in height. But again, there are trees there and some of those can be hundreds of feet in height. Some are only five to six feet in height, and they are fully grown trees. There is quite a variety of non-indigenous plant life on this planet.

Jefferson: Alright. So Ishuwa, do you have any parting thoughts? Anything you want to share with us as we close this beautiful chapter?

Ishuwa: We are, as we have said before, grateful for the interaction. We acknowledge the time, and the effort, and the riches of your beingness that you share in engaging with our society in this way. We thank you for that! We know there is more that you have to share with others. In the days of your experience, and expressions, and your steps and pathways on Earth, you will become more fulfilled in taking those steps and in sharing in those ways that are presently aware for you and many will be new for you. So allow for the growth to come effortlessly in its own way, in its own time. You will not miss out on any of these experiences. The more you allow yourself to know this, the more you will be in those experiences simply because you are following your heart. You cannot miss anything that comes from the heart as long as you stay tuned in to your heart.

Jefferson: Very good. Wow! Thank you very much!

Ishuwa: We thank you! And you are welcome! We look forward to interacting with you again in this way, and we say good day and great joy with you, and for you, and of you, because of you!

Jefferson: Thank you very much! Bye Ishuwa.

Ishuwa: Yah oohm!

Jefferson: Yes! Indeed!

Ishuwa: Tudo bem!

Jefferson: Where did he learn to speak Portuguese?!

Chapter 12

Making Contact with Your Inner Aliens

"As more people are more at peace with themself and have no more of these alien ideas existing within them, then when we are present, they will feel more comfortable with our presence before them." – Ishuwa

November 5th, 2009

Ishuwa: Always with you in these blending moments together is a wonderful experience and expression of all that we are in these ways that we are choosing to create in this moment of our time together! How are you?

Jefferson: Lovely Ishuwa! It's lovely to speak to you again!

Ishuwa: And for us as well!

Jefferson: How would you like to move forward today?

Ishuwa: This is a channeling between you, Jefferson, and the channel, Shaun. Here you are November 5th of your time, 2009.

Jefferson: Yes!

Ishuwa: The clock time is approximately 1:34 in the afternoon in the Hawaiian time zone. The seconds are ticking by, bit by bit, second by second, as you are creating that idea of seconds and time. It is with great joy that we have this opportunity to interact with you in this way of your timing today!

Jefferson: Sure! And for me too!

Ishuwa: Most wonderful to be here is this way!

Jefferson: Indeed! So, Ishuwa, how would you like to move forward today?

Ishuwa: In whatever way you would like to begin. With suggestions, or perhaps sharings, or questions. As you wish.

Jefferson: In regards to "contact," do you guys intend to appear again as you did in Phoenix, Arizona, in 1997 and 2007?

Ishuwa: We will, yes.

Jefferson: Can you give me the exact day, time, hour, and the meal that's going to be served?

Ishuwa: We haven't decided on the meal yet. It's a tossup between a tossed green salad and a fruit salad.

Jefferson: All right.

Ishuwa: Which do you prefer?

Jefferson: Whatever is done with love goes well.

Ishuwa: We will have love in either dish then. It will be present.

Jefferson: Okay, fantastic!

Ishuwa: In terms of actual dates, generally we don't work in that way. We may set up a time when we are planning to have such a revealing of our presence, and then circumstances might present themselves in which we will then adjust that time and move it to be earlier than the initial time or after the initial scheduled time.

Jefferson: Okay.

Ishuwa: And there are many reasons that can occur.

Jefferson: Sure.

Ishuwa: In your world, you might have a time set up to meet someone somewhere, but then it doesn't work out that way for various reasons. It might occur a little bit earlier, or a little bit later, or not at all.

For us, it's easier not to state a specific meeting time because often in your world, if we don't show up, many people will lose faith in the whole idea of our existence, even though when they set up a meeting with a friend and that friend doesn't show up at the appointed day and time, they don't then lose faith in that person's existence.

Jefferson: (Laughter).

Ishuwa: We understand they don't lose faith in that person in that way because they have had other experiences where meetings are missed and don't take place and they simply re-schedule. Your world hasn't had the experience of re-scheduling with us in that way. It hasn't even had the experience of meeting us physically.

Jefferson: Yeah.

Ishuwa: In time it will occur if your world keeps moving forward along the collective path that it is choosing to take at this timing.

Jefferson: Sure. Can you give a window of years?

Ishuwa: Within the next two months there will be another sighting. The location will generally be in a southern European region of a rather small community.

Jefferson: Oh, nice, all right! So when the actual first contact in public occurs in ten years, or twenty years, or whenever it occurs, how do you feel it's going to happen? Will you buy some airtime on our TV?

Ishuwa: Some would consider it to be just a program or a show from one of the television networks, while other people could become frightened by it and then you could have, in that sense, an experience like what occurred due to a radio program that was broadcast some years ago in your past.

Jefferson: Oh, I see. So, if that's not the way then how do you see it happening?

Ishuwa: One idea is that there will be an understanding that it's going to occur. People will begin to understand that it's going to occur. And then, especially in the regions where it does then occur, there will be arrangements made for people to be present at that interaction and for it to take place in a very precise way, in a format that will be available for several in your public to observe.

There will be individuals from a wide range of backgrounds in your society present. After the public contact meeting takes place, there will be a process in which those who were present will then be able to discuss what they experienced in the meeting, how it occurred, what took place. They will be able to discuss this in such a fashion that the information will then be able to be shared with more people who were not able to be physically present. It will be done in a way so that those people who hear about the contact second-hand will be more willing to accept it. The contact event will seem to be more verified and more confirmed for them as the information begins to come forth. We can't appear at one location and have everybody on the planet see us first-hand.

Jefferson: When you speak to us, or when someone from your society speaks to us, are you going to speak that particular language that you have that allows you to speak to everyone from every country so we will all be able to understand you?

Ishuwa: It will be a combination. It will be in a way that is comforting for those on your world who are present.

Jefferson: Oh, okay.

Ishuwa: They will feel comfortable and understand what it is we are saying. When we are speaking our language, they will recognize that is what we intended to do and they will be comfortable with that.

Jefferson: Oh, okay. Very well. So just before the last question, do you have a word of wisdom to offer those of us who go out in the night longing to connect to and communicate with whichever ET race is out there, taking into consideration we might encounter those who may not have our best interest in mind?

Ishuwa: To follow their heart in that way. To do in each moment the most enjoyable thing that they are able to do. If that is to go out into the night with an intention to have contact with an extraterrestrial, then we suggest those are the steps to take but be open then to whatever does occur.

Jefferson: Very well.

Ishuwa: There is no need to be frightened. If they are, then perhaps it is the thing to explore. Explore the fear. Find out what it is they're frightened of. Burst the bubble, in that sense, of the fear. Burst the bubble. Walk through the fear. Get beyond that obstacle. Understand what was causing them to be frightened. Know thyself.

The fear is masking some idea within themself, a belief or a definition about Existence that isn't an accurate reflection of who they truly are, and so it is, in a sense, like an alien idea that they are frightened of.

When they walk through the fear by finding out how they were defining their self out of alignment with the nature of Existence, then they are making "contact" with that alien idea within them. When they can come through "contact" with this clear understanding and let that "alien" thus then become recognized as just another aspect of their existence that they simply hadn't initially understood, then they will feel at home with it. They will be at peace with it, and thus then they will be more at peace with themself.

As more people are more at peace with themself and have no more of these alien ideas existing within them, then when we are present, they will feel more comfortable with our presence before them. They will not feel the fear, in that sense, from our presence. They will not then run and hide, or worship, or behave in ways of anarchy and destructive manners. They will be more at a civilized capacity to interact with us easily, comfortably and enjoyably!

Jefferson: Good! Very well! So here's where we are going to hear from you your last message for this particular book that you have for us of planet Earth.

Ishuwa: Here?

Jefferson: Yes, right now.

Ishuwa: Last message for the book?

Jefferson: For the book, what's your last message and last ideas that you want to convey for those of us who are right now reading from these pages?

Ishuwa: We'll see you in part two!

Jefferson: (Laughter). That's it? No, Ishuwa, come on!?! See you in part two?

Ishuwa: What is it you would like me to say?

Jefferson: I don't have any expectations. Say whatever you feel most excited about.

Ishuwa: What would you like to see at the end of the book?

Jefferson: I would like to see you teaching us how to follow our highest excitement and then closing up with more about the Four Laws of Creation.

Ishuwa: Yes! Those are ideas for another book!

Jefferson: Right. I thank you very much Ishuwa for all the ideas you brought into this book and for being so spontaneous and teaching us how to more and more step into our own greatness that really lives in that original simplicity that you show and convey in every interaction that I personally have had with you through the channel!

Ishuwa: And most delightful to have that sharing from you in this time! It has been a great joy to have these experiences with you and also to interact with those who are sharing and contributing with us from your world as well. Your world and ours has, and will continue to get, great support for this information in the format of your book, and also in those ideas, and books, and sharings that other people on your world are putting together in their own creative space as well. So we thank you once again for all the time and the effort, in that sense, the application of your energies and focus in the ways that you have, and that of the channel as well, and those who interact in his world with him, for there are those there who also have been sharing in their unique ways.

This is a great joy! We appreciate all of your efforts and their efforts in this construction, this building of a new understanding, this book, in that sense, that others may grow from reading the information contained herein and derive a new energetic understanding of their whole nature in ways they find enjoyable to do!

Jefferson: Great! Let's make this my intention: every time a person finishes reading this book, a rainbow of gratitude appears on your planet!

Ishuwa: Yes! Lovely, and so it is!

Jefferson: Thank you Ishuwa! Yah oohm!

Ishuwa: Yah oohm! Tudo bem for you as well. Bright joys! I look forward to interacting with you again in this way! Go easy on yourself during the process of the assembling of this message of texture, as it were. Thank you. Much love to you dear one! Good day to you!

Jefferson: Yah oohm!

About Ishuwa

Ishuwa

Ishuwa is a human being from the Yahyel civilization. He is an interstellar explorer and a translator for several galactic civilizations. His travels have provided him with a variety of enjoyable experiences interacting with thousands of ET societies that live on planets all over the galaxy.

Ishuwa is thoughtful, fun-loving, and playful. He speaks with clarity, humor, and intelligence. He shares knowledge through the channel Shaun Swanson that can help us build rich and loving relationships with ourselves, each other, our planet, and help us reconnect to our most exciting, fulfilling, and meaningful reality in every moment of every day.

More about Ishuwa at: www.ishuwa.com

About The Yahyel

The Yahyel

The Yahyel may become the first extra-terrestrial civilization to openly meet with us on Earth in person, in peace, in joy, and develop mutually rewarding relationships with our current and future generations. They are part of our galactic family and very similar to us in their physical appearance. They walk, they breathe, they eat, they sleep and they dream together. They value life and one another and they nurture one another in all ways that they can at all times.

The Yahyel live in harmony with their beautiful planet and all forms of life on it. They live in harmony with each other. The Yahyel are helping us remember how to live in harmony with Earth and with one another on all levels of our existence together. In a sense, they are bringing timeless knowledge from outer-space that will help us understand how to fully enjoy our living-space and our heart's inner-space. They help us realize the magnificent and loving beings that we actually are.

As their reconnection with us continues to unfold, they will share more of their history, our history, and more information about where we come from and how we got here.

On March 13, 1997, one of the largest UFO sightings in history took place when the Yahyel flew their spacecrafts over several cities including Phoenix, Arizona, and made visual contact with thousands of people. This event is known as the "Phoenix Lights". The Yahyel continue making new sighting contacts with us in a variety of ways over other cities around the world. Perhaps you have seen them or will see them soon over a city near you!

More about the Yahyel at: www.ishuwa.com and www.yahyel.com.

About the Authors

Shaun Swanson

Shaun began channeling in 1995. He is a channel for members of our galactic soul family including: Ishuwa of the Yahyel, Arvantis of the Arkoreuns, and Onkor of the Sassani. Shaun graduated with a Bachelor of Arts degree from the University of California at Santa Barbara, UCSB.

Shaun does group channeling events and private channeling sessions for people that want to talk with Ishuwa and get answers to questions about their life, life on Earth, ET life, or connect with their galactic family and hybrid children. Shaun also provides private channeling sessions that are a form of consultation and counseling for people interested in spiritual growth, self-empowerment, personal healing and deepening self-realization.

The experience of channeling is wonderfully enriching for Shaun. It connects him to ongoing interactions with a variety of human ETs and hybrid children that have origins in our galaxy and beyond. He experiences our ET soul family as being playful, highly intelligent, compassionate, curious, and delightfully fun. The information they share in group channeling events and in private channeling sessions is just one of many resources available that can awaken us to more of the heartfelt connections that exist with our galactic soul family!

More information about Shaun is available at: www.ishuwa.com.

Jefferson Viscardi

Jefferson Viscardi has a Ph.D. degree, Philosopher of Metaphysical Life Coaching, from the University of Metaphysical Sciences distance learning facility. He is certified by the International Association of Reiki Professionals as a Reiki healer, level III, in the Usui System of natural healing. He teaches on topics related to extraterrestrials, our galactic family, and Christ consciousness.

Jefferson is a co-author of "Feline Humans" and "The Circle of Light and The Philosopher."

More about Jefferson at: facebook.com/dialogocomosespiritos.

Yah oohm!
Being in Joy!

www.ingramcontent.com/pod-product-compliance
Lightning Source LLC
Chambersburg PA
CBHW061632040426
42446CB00010B/1387